A LEGEND IS BORN

It starts out with me signing a $75,000 "bonus baby" contract with the A's.

"Do you have a nickname?" asked Finley, the owner, over the phone.

"No, sir," I said.

"Well, to play baseball you've got to have a nickname," he said. "What do you like to do?"

"Hunt and fish," I told him.

"Fine," said Finley. Barely pausing for breath, he continued, "When you were six years old you ran away from home and went fishing. Your mom and dad had been looking for you all day. When they finally found you, about, ah, four o'clock in the afternoon, you'd caught two big fish . . . ahh . . . catfish . . . and were reeling in the third. And that's how you got your nickname. Okay?"

"Yes, sir, Mr. Finley," I said.

"Good," came the reply. "Now repeat it back to me."

CATFISH

"Uplifting . . . Catfish Hunter in this solid book recalls the best part of baseball as the stories, the joking, the language itself." —*San Jose Mercury News*

"A warm reminiscence of his years on both teams [Oakland Athletics and New York Yankees], his relationships with his teammates, especially the late Thurmon Munson, as well as a sensitive evocation of his life in North Carolina before and after his baseball career." —*Library Journal*

"One of the best pitchers of our time!" —*Kirkus*

CATFISH

MY LIFE IN BASEBALL

JIM "CATFISH" HUNTER
AND ARMEN KETEYIAN

B

BERKLEY BOOKS, NEW YORK

CATFISH: MY LIFE IN BASEBALL

A Berkley Book/published by arrangement with
McGraw-Hill Book Company

PRINTING HISTORY
McGraw-Hill edition published 1988
Berkley edition/May 1989

Contents

ACKNOWLEDGMENTS

A heartfelt thanks from both of us to our editor, Tom Quinn, whose instincts and understanding made this project a pleasure from the start, and to literary agent Basil Kane for bringing us together.

From Jimmy Hunter: I would also like to thank Clyde Kluttz, baseball scout and father figure; Thelma Elliott, a grammar school principal who long ago bent a rule—much to the dismay of the Winfall Grammar School baseball team; Dutch Overton, ex-major-league umpire, scout, and teacher at Perquiman High School; and four other Perquiman High folks I'll never forget— baseball coach Bobby Carter, varsity football coach and baseball assistant Ike Perry, junior varsity football coach Gil Underwood, and principal E.C. Woodard. In addition, I would like to express my appreciation to J. Carlton Cherry, my longtime attorney and friend, and the Oakland A's former pitching coach, Bill Posedel, who taught me more about pitching in the major leagues than anyone else. Finally, much more than thanks to my eight brothers and sisters, my wife and children, and all the fine people of Hertford, North Carolina.

From Armen Keteyian: I would like to acknowledge the assistance and support of *Sports Illustrated* magazine and its managing editor, Mark Mulvoy. I would also like to thank J. Carlton Cherry and his longtime partner, Joe Flythe, for recreating December 1974; New York Yankee Director of Media Relations Harvey Greene; Tom Bannon, editor-in-chief of *Yankees Magazine;* photographer Drew Wilson; John Ware, for advice and counsel; and finally, Tim Pitt, for ensuring that the stories made sense.

FOREWORD

In celebration of his induction into Cooperstown last summer, the Yankees honored Jim "Catfish" Hunter with a special day at Yankee Stadium. With Cat's family and seven other Hall of Famers in attendance—including Joe DiMaggio, Mickey Mantle, and Whitey Ford—we presented Cat with a Cartier tray inscribed with the following words:

JIM "CATFISH" HUNTER
Who taught a new generation
of Yankees how to win.

Nothing new, really. I've said those same words dozens of times since Jim retired in 1979. He was the cornerstone, the rock on which five division championships, four American League pennants, and two World Series rested. Sure, he didn't play in some of the last ones, but he taught us what it took to get there. He was *the* catalyst.

I wanted Cat from the beginning of the free-agent bidding. I'd seen him pitch all those years in Oakland, knowing full well he was the type of pitcher—and person—who could mean a championship for the Yankees. I'm not a creative guy in the sense that I can look at a piece of barren land and visualize a beautiful village or a sprawling, glistening shopping center. But I think I do know how to put a ball club together, and I knew he was one ingredient we desperately needed, part of the missing link between a historic Yankee past and a mediocre present. Cat wasn't a cheerleader, but in his own way he instilled in others the desire for greatness, the will to win, a belief that from hard work comes success. Sure he was an expensive catch. But I knew in order to get the pump running you had to spend the money to prime it.

I'm not surprised he signed with the Yankees, not at all, even though he made his decision on the last day. From studying him I knew he was a man of great pride. Great personal pride. Carolina is strong Yankee territory, and I knew he'd harbored a dream of coming to New York one day. In the end, Cat proved one of this club's biggest bargains, even at $3.5 million. I wish I could make a buy like that every year. Catfish imbued our club with a strong sense of leadership, a Gary Cooper leadership. One that set a new, tougher agenda, inspiring a team desperate for a new sense of direction.

In 1977, when Thurman was fighting with Reggie, and Reggie was fighting with me, and most everyone else was fighting with each other, Cat did his best to keep things cool, to settle us down and focus the club on the task ahead. Whether it meant going out and pitching a shutout or making a statement like I can still remember him making after the "straw that stirs the drink" controversy between Reggie and Munson. "These fellas are both good ballplayers," he said. "We just gotta forget all this crap and go out there and play ball." That was Catfish. Let's play ball. We've got a job to do, so let's get on with it. Together. As a team.

I'll also never forget the final Series game in '78. The damnedest thing happened. A couple of days before I'd watched a grand old movie called *Angels in the Outfield,* starring Paul Douglas and Margaret O'Brien. In that film, the old-time pitcher pitches in the championship game, and of course, he wins it. Two days later they tell me they're going to pitch ol' Catfish in the final game in L. A. We were leading the Series 3–1 at the time, but nervous about a return trip to New York. Anything can happen. I walked into the locker room, and there's Cat, stretched out on the training table, arm being worked on by Gene Monahan.

"Cat," I asked, "you can do this, can't you?"

Looked me straight in the eye. "Yep," he said, and that's all he said. "Yep." I walked out to see him pitch a helluva game and clinch the World Series. He didn't even stay for the party either—too worried about his dad's failing health and the prospect of missing opening day of hunting season with his daddy. Last time I saw Catfish that night was when he and Thurman pulled up to the hotel in a cab. They both jumped out and shook my hand. We hugged each other. "C'mon in," I said.

"Nope," replied Cat. "Goin' home. Goin' hunting tomorrow." And off he went.

Know what impressed me most about Cat? Never once did I ever hear him bitch or complain like so many of my guys today. He just went out and did his job. I think that's why we developed what I'd guess you'd call a quiet camaraderie right from the start. It was a strange kind of relationship in a lot of ways. The only time we hugged was after that '78 Series; we never shouted plastic greetings to one another. But I think, overall, he understood how I felt about him, what I expected. That's why I sought his counsel about naming Thurman and him co-captains of the Yankees. I wanted Cat, but he wanted no part of it, insisting "I'm a pitcher." He recommended I go with Thurman alone, and that's exactly what I did.

And another thing: Cat wasn't afraid of me. No fear. Just a deep, honest respect. In my position, there are guys who are afraid of you that don't respect you. And there are more guys who aren't afraid of you who don't respect you. Either one I don't need. Give me that outspoken athlete unafraid to speak his piece—but one who still respects his boss—anytime. Trouble is, those are few and far between.

Loyalty means a lot to Cat. I see it every spring when he comes down to work with our young pitchers in Ft. Lauderdale. As a Hall of Famer and guest instructor, he could short-time it and nobody would say a word. Not Cat. He's always the first guy at the park and the last one to leave.

At Cooperstown I was even more impressed by the way he addressed Mr. Finley. Nobody was paying much attention to Charlie, but there was Cat, going out of his way to talk to his former owner. That's the kind of guy Cat is—he carries a deep sense of feeling and loyalty for others, from the ball boys on up.

I remember he used to take care of our legendary equipment manager Pete Sheehy during Pete's last years with the Yankees. No other ballplayer took time to do that. He was always waiting around the clubhouse for Pete to finish, making sure Pete got something to eat. I don't know of another ballplayer in the world who would do that for an equipment manager! But he would. That was just Cat. It didn't make any difference if he was earning a million dollars or fifty thousand. Somebody taught him well, his father, or his attorney, Mr. J. Carlton Cherry, somebody. You get the feeling that down there in Hertford he's still Jim Hunter. And that says something for the people of North Carolina.

Would I love to have Jim back full-time with the Yankees? You bet I would. I've tried half a dozen times to hire him as a pitching instructor, but he's not ready to get back into the game. But hell, he's forgotten more about pitching than most of them will ever know. The man was a master. I believe Catfish looks good enough that he could go out and throw—now this is the truth—he could pitch today as well as 50 percent of the guys in the major leagues. In a minute. I almost cried when they left him in that one game in Boston. I got so goddamn mad I climbed all over the manager. I told him, "Don't you ever disgrace that man by letting him take a pounding like that." I raised holy hell about it. Then he comes back and wins a crucial game in the playoffs. You could make a movie out of it.

Finally, some folks claim the Yankees have gone way out of their way to honor Cat—a final farewell in 1979, the retirement of his number, the special Hall of Fame day last August. But that's really nothing. You can't spare any adjectives or superlatives in talking about that man around me. Whatever the Yankees and George Steinbrenner have done for James Augustus Hunter has been well deserved in every aspect.

George Steinbrenner

1

A DAY TO REMEMBER

'Round about 11 A.M., a good hour before the parade was set to start, it seemed like half of Hertford, North Carolina, had showed up at the Harris Shopping Center parkin' lot. Over where a sign said "Shop With the Friendly Folks," the Perquiman High School Band, decked out in black and gold, was filling the air with the sound of tubas and trumpets. Antique cars were polished to a see-yourself shine; Little Leaguers laughed and pawed at each other. Even some of the boys from the Bear Swamp Hunting Club had showed up, their hound dogs barkin' in the back of a pickup.

The Harris Center, in case you were wonderin', is on Grubb Street, 'bout three blocks west of downtown Hertford, right across from Keel's Shoe Repair & Trading Post, spittin' distance from the Hertford Volunteer Fire Department, of which I am an honorary member. At the moment, one of the department's trucks sits idling in the lot. A cardboard sign was taped to the driver's door. It said:

May 9, 1987
Jim "Catfish" Hunter Day

That's me. Both of me, actually. Jim and Catfish. Around Hertford, a farming community of 2200 folks in the northeastern corner of North Carolina, I'm Jim or Jimmy Hunter. Uncomplicated, country born and raised, given to saying "rivah" for river and "dat" for that, and droppin' the "g" from just about everthin' I say (as if you hadn't already noticed). Jimmy's one of those what-you-see-is-what-you-get kind of guys—a man who takes particular pride in being the best damn deer hunter, fisherman, farmer, dog breeder, and family man he can be. Simple as that.

Catfish, well, that's another story. Cat, if you don't mind me stayin' in the third person for a minute, doesn't hang around Hertford. Never has. Never will. He's a bit more slick than Jimmy, kinda country cool, I'd guess you'd say. Cat, you see, did his swimmin' in city waters. His claim to the Hall of Fame was pitchin', pure and simple. Throwin' strikes. Gettin' folks out. Winnin' ball games.

But for all his drive and desire, I believe you're goin' to discover that Cat was never what you'd call a real homebody. A TV-watcher. A letter-writer. A lobby-sitter. No, Cat was actually a pretty playful fella—had to be hanging around with the likes of Lew Krausse, Rene Lachemann, Dick Green, Sal Bando, Thurman Munson, and Sweet Lou Piniella. (I'd like to have been able to change the names to protect the innocent, but in that group, well . . . there was so little innocence.)

The nickname "Catfish" was born—and I bet you already knew this—in the fertile mind of one Charles O. Finley. "O as in Owner," said Mr. Finley. True, but the way that man operated, it could just as well have meant "Obstinate" or "Outspoken" or "Outrageous." Yes, sir, Mr. Finley was as unique an owner as you'll ever want to meet. Unless, of course, you hit baseball's version of the daily double and also had the pleasure of playing for one George M. Steinbrenner III. As baseball commissioner Peter Ueberroth said preceding my induction into the Hall of Fame last summer, just playing for those two men was enough to qualify anyone for a place in the Hall.

And, funny thing is, Charlie and George are still at it. Still playing king of the hill. Still tryin' to prove to each other that one's imprint on the game will be bigger than the other's.

I discovered that fact right after I'd been inducted into the Hall of Fame last July. The Cooperstown committee had cautioned all the inductees about walkin' down Main Street during the day—you'll get mobbed by the crowds, they said. So, naturally, right after the ceremony there's George on one side of the street, signing autographs, followed by a pack of parents and kids a block long. And who's on the other side but Charlie, scribbling away, playing the Pied Piper, just like George. Kim and Paul, my two youngest children, told me they'd finally wiggled their way up next to Mr. Finley. This is what he said to them:

"Is he still over there signing autographs?"

"Yes, sir," came the reply.

"Well," said Charles O. Finley, "I'm gonna sign 'em as long as he does."

Now at this point some of you folks might want to skip ahead a few paragraphs. Chances are you've heard this next story before. Lord knows I've only told it about seven million times in the last twenty-four years. I've told it fast. I've told it slow. I've told it funny. I've told it flat. But very few times have I told it like the first time, the way I explained it to the Associated Press writer who phoned me just after I had signed with the Kansas City A's on June 8, 1964, like how I'm gonna tell it this time.

It starts out with me signing a $75,000 "bonus baby" contract with the A's.

"Do you have a nickname?" asked Finley over the phone.

"No, sir," I said.

"Well, to play baseball you've got to have a nickname," he said. "What do you like to do?"

"Hunt and fish," I told him.

"Fine," said Finley. Barely pausing for breath, he continued, "When you were six years old you ran away from home and went fishing. Your mom and dad had been looking for you all day. When they finally found you, about, ah, four o'clock in the afternoon, you'd caught two big fish . . . ahh . . . catfish . . . and were reeling in the third. And that's how you got your nickname. Okay?"

"Yes, sir, Mr. Finley," I said.

"Good," came the reply. "Now repeat it back to me."

Finley always had a flair for showmanship. He and Bill Veeck, the late Chicago White Sox owner, were truly the P. T. Barnums of baseball—ahead of their times in devising ways to promote and package the national pastime, whether baseball liked it or not. And back in the late '60s and early '70s, it didn't.

Yes sir, it was Finley who was responsible for so many innovations—colorful uniforms, white cleats, night baseball in the World Series, a team mascot, fireworks after home runs, cabdrivers bringing pitchers in from the bull pen, Miss U.S.A. as a batgirl. Of course, some ideas turned out to be *slightly* ahead of their time: the picnic tables and miniature zoo beyond the fence in left; the sheep grazing in right; the mechanical rabbit named Harvey who popped up behind home plate with baseballs for the umpire. They needed some work, but what the heck. At least he tried.

After we won it all for the first time in 1972, though, beating the "Big Red Machine" from Cincinnati in seven stirring games, Charlie Finley stopped caring. He went from the best owner in baseball—one willing to loan the players money, to sign the key player at any price—to the worst. Bar none. Over and out. He had paid the price for a world title once, and frankly, he didn't care to foot the bill again. Fortunately it didn't stop us from winning two more world championships—making the A's of Oakland one of only two teams (the Yankees were the other) to win at least three consecutive World Series.

Not that Charlie didn't try to bullshit us about how much he cared. That was just part of his complex personality. "I'm gonna make that first diamond ring look like it came out of a Cracker Jack box," he told us after we beat the Mets in 1973. That next spring some front office guy got around to handing out mementos of that second World Series win.

I took one look at this glassy green thing and almost threw it away. "You got to be shittin' me," I screamed. "What is this?"

"Your ring."

"Buuulllshit," I said. Finley had promised us another diamond ring, not this dime-store creation. Then I started in on Finley, calling him a cheap son of a bitch and any other low-life thing I could think of.

Well, the writers were eating this up with a silver spoon, and by the time I got back to the locker room, the word was out.

"Hey, Cat," somebody said, "telephone call."

"Riiight. Probably Finley." I ignored it. Just someone messin' with me. Nothing new on this club.

"No, no, really," they said. "It's Finley."

I picked up the phone.

"Jiiimm." He stretched it out, long and low, as always, like he had a mouth full of molasses.

"Yes, sir, Mr. Finley."

"I . . . heard . . . you . . . been . . . talking . . . bad . . . about . . . me."

"Yes, sir, Mr. Finley."

"Whyyy, Jim?"

"'Cause of that horseshit ring you sent down here, Mr. Finley."

"Well . . . there's . . . nothing . . . I can . . . do about it . . . now."

"Yes there is, Mr. Finley," I said. "You can take them all back and put diamonds in them like you promised."

You could almost hear the gulp. "Oh, that would be . . . against my theory. I . . . can't go against . . . my think . . . -ing . . . at the time. I'm not gonna."

"That's horseshit, Mr. Finley." By now I could be heard halfway across Florida.

The air went dead for a second. I could hear Finley turn away and call out to his secretary. A dying man with one last request . . . "Roberta . . . bring . . . me . . . a pill. I think I'm gonna be . . . sick."

I kept on shoutin'. "You're damn right. You should get sick after that horseshit ring you sent us."

Looking Back, Catfish has had himself quite a life so far. I lived Jimmy's boyhood dream for fifteen wonderful years. Control and confidence were the cornerstones of my game and because of them I never played an inning of minor league ball. I was a regular starting pitcher in the big leagues from the time I was nineteen years old; I pitched a perfect game at the tender age of twenty-two, beating the Minnesota Twins 4–0 on May 8, 1968, the only regular-season perfect game in the American League in sixty-five years. Six years later I won the Cy Young Award. Then in December 1974, I made history of sorts by becoming the first true free agent in baseball history, which touched off one of the most outrageous auctions and some of the strangest actions by the clubs doing the bidding. By the time I retired in 1979 after playing my final five seasons with the New York Yankees, I'd won 224 regular-season games (in exactly 500 appearances) and compiled a 3.26 ERA over nearly 3500 innings. Along the way I pitched a one-hitter, five two-hitters, threw forty-two shutouts, and once won thirteen games in a row (1973). I'd also won nine more postseason games, was one of only four pitchers in baseball history to win 200 games by the age of thirty-one (the others were named Cy Young, Christy Mathewson, and Walter Johnson), and just one of three to win twenty or more games five years in a row (1971–1975). And while I'm at it, I guess I should mention the eight All Star selections, the seven division-winning championships with Oakland and New York, and the six World Series, five of them winners.

I was only thirty-three years old when I retired in 1979, a tot compared with Tommy John, the Niekros, and Doyle Alexander. But I'd made a promise to myself back on New Year's Eve 1974 when I then signed that multimillion deal with the Yanks: Five years and home. And that's just what I did—went back home. Back to being just Jimmy. To my 600-acre farm. To a life where there's always something to do, where there's a reward at the end of every day, whether it's plantin' corn, pullin' weeds, or trainin' a dog to track down a deer. Back to my family, to my high school sweetheart, Helen, and to the kids—Todd and Kim, and to Paul (who came along in 1979).

People always ask: How could you do it? Give it all up? Easy. Todd and Kim had grown up with their mom. Now it was time for them to get to know their daddy—the way I got to know mine. I didn't want my children to grow up, get married, and start a family, without ever having really known their father. If I'd played another two, three, or five more years, Todd would have been well into his teens, and that would've meant I'd only have had a few years with him before college. That wasn't enough. Paul would have never really been able to see me. A father's got to be there for his kids. My daddy was always there for me, and I always wanted to be like my daddy—right down to sayin' no to sugar in my coffee or tea.

But my career, my life, hasn't been all sugar and spice. Hardly. From 1976 to mid-1978 my right arm and shoulder were so weak I couldn't comb my hair without cringing, cured only by a miracle manipulation; in 1978—and not too many folks know about this—I was very nearly crushed to death when the top of a huge oil storage tank exploded in Hertford and landed on top of me; two weeks later I discovered I had the most serious form of diabetes; and in 1979 the three most important men in my life—my father; Clyde Kluttz, the scout who signed me out of high school and again with the Yankees; and Thurman Munson—all died within three months of each other.

You want to know how I dealt with all that pain and sorrow? Just one way. By gettin' down on my hands and knees and prayin' more than I ever prayed in my life. By thankin' the

Lord each and every night for lettin' me live today. It may sound corny, but it's true.

I figure that's what this book is for—to open up, to discuss the less publicized periods of my life. Some, certainly, like the summer of '79, will make you want to cry. Others, hopefully, thankfully, like winter ball in Caracas in 1965, the crazy days in Kansas City in the '60s, the fussin' and feudin' in Oakland and New York, will make you laugh out loud. Along the way you'll learn the story behind the success of the great A's teams in Oakland; the importance of the X pattern; why I bought a home in New Jersey at 2:30 in the morning; the mind set of managers from Mel McGaha to Billy Martin; the private, poignant moments shared on the good ship Steinbrenner with Thurm, Reggie, Sparky, Sweet Lou, and so many, many others.

But I'm home now, back to a place where a kid can pedal a bike to town, prop it outside the five-and-dime, leave his mitt hanging from the handlebars, and go inside and drink a cherry soda while flippin' through a comic book. A place where going out in the field takes on a whole new meaning: tending fields of soybeans, corn, and peanuts from dawn to dusk; trainin' and strainin' to keep up with forty of the best huntin' dogs in Perquiman's County. It means taking pride in the fact that I can still pop the top off a Pepsi can with my Remington shotgun at forty paces.

I guess folks back home appreciate the fact that I don't want to be treated any differently. I've always been "just Jimmy," and that's the way I hope it stays. Just for that reason, I tried to put a halt to the "day" they had for me last May. But the mayor got involved; then Paul Smith, a father figure since my daddy died in '79, insisted it was going to happen—with or without me. So there we were, Helen and I, sitting in the back of a white convertible Cadillac in the Harris Shopping Center parking lot, waiting patiently for my day to begin. Todd, seventeen, and Kim, fourteen, sittin' with us. Paul, seven, was perched on the back of a nearby pickup, a catfish dangling from the end of a fishing pole. An American flag, blowing in the breeze, was anchored to the Cadillac's front right fender. The high school band struck up a march as towns-folk passed out pink and yellow balloons; and clowns and jugglers and stilt walkers led the parade down Grubb Street. We proceeded downtown, past Hertford Hardware, White's Dress Shop and the county courthouse, before heading over to the high school.

The football grandstands were jammed with 2000 friends and neighbors. First thing on the agenda was the "Pledge of Allegiance." Then Helen led us in the singing of "America the Beautiful." (We do these things in Hertford.) Master of ceremonies Pat Harrell, who's also the county's superintendent of schools, then asked all the out-of-state people to stand. We gave 'em all a cheer.

"Now, will all those who live in the state please stand."

Louder cheers.

"Now, will all the home folk stand."

Loudest cheers.

Off to my left, where our left fielder used to play, half a dozen rows of folding chairs were filled with living memories: Francis and Freddie Combs, my best baseball buddies since the sixth grade; former Kansas City and Oakland teammate Mike Hershberger, a fine outfielder and friend who had cared enough to fly in from Canton, Ohio, with his wife and kids; my eight brothers and sisters, the loves of my life; and local politicians, state senators, and my personal attorney, J. Carlton Cherry.

It was Mr. Cherry who orchestrated my free-agent auction after I'd been declared free by a baseball arbitration panel on December 16, 1974. I've always said that I didn't know where I was headed until the last day, but what I've never really discussed (but will in much greater detail later on) is how the race to sign me had come down to San Diego and Kansas City, with Pittsburgh, Boston, and the New York Mets closing fast on the outside. I'd already turned down an amazing offer from the Dodgers—$3 million for two years—simply because I didn't want to play for Tommy Lasorda. No hard feelings, Tommy, but I never really liked your camera-happy, hugs-and-kisses kind of managing. Too much show.

Just to make sure, though, I checked with Tommy John, who had pitched against us when we played L. A. in the '74 World Series.

"You like Lasorda?" I asked.

"Noooooo," said Tommy. Just like that.

That's all I needed to hear. If John wasn't very high on Lasorda—and he had played for him—forget it. I passed on the offer. And besides, money wasn't my major concern—not the case with a lot of teams, San Diego, in particular. The Padres put an unbelievable offer on the table: $4.5 million for five years. It included a bundle of cash, stock, even a McDonald's franchise. Only one minor problem: Buzzie Bavasi, the team's general manager, needed owner Ray Kroc's approval to make a formal offer. Kroc was out sailing aboard his yacht, and ship-to-shore communication was rough, particularly around the cocktail hour.

Finally, on December 31, Bavasi made contact with Kroc, who was flying pretty high and was not in any mood to discuss numbers. He wanted an Opening Day pitcher in '75 by the name of Hunter, and damn the torpedoes full speed ahead! "I don't care what it costs," he said. "Just give him any damn thing he wants!"

But the ship-to-shore connection was bad. Bavasi could barely hear the words.

"What?" he screamed into the phone.

"Goddamn it," bellowed Kroc. "I said give him anything he wants!"

Bavasi speed-dialed Mr. Cherry in Ahoskie, North Carolina. Trouble was, at that exact moment, we were sneaking out the back door of Mr. Cherry's office, headed for Suffolk Airport and a plane ride to New York. In a span of six hours the Yankees had come from last to first in the free-agent derby. The price tag: exactly $3,484,626 for five years. Guaranteed.

"I just talked to Mr. Kroc," said a breathless Bavasi, "and he said you can come out here, take his checkbook, and write any damn amount you want."

"Sorry, but we just can't do that, Mr. Bavasi," said Mr. Cherry. "You're five minutes too late. Mr. Hunter has just agreed to become a member of the New York Yankees."

Above all, being a Yankee meant being prepared for one thing: the powerful presence of principal owner George Steinbrenner. I like George, always have, believing that behind all that spit and polish, that bullshit bluster, those "Top Gun" caps, the red phone, is one of the more compassionate, caring, considerate men you'll ever want to meet. In his heart, despite all his money, his power, George gets off on being one of the boys.

Like the time in spring training: The field was soaked,

almost unplayable, but there was George, Yankee jacket on, raking the infield, stopping just long enough to direct the helicopter he'd hired where to dry off next. The writers and minicams were eating it up, as well they should have. "Masterpiece Theatre," starring G. M. Steinbrenner, The Third.

Naturally I couldn't let The Boss get away with this act. No way. So, as he strode into the dugout I got out the needle. "Get enough TV time?" I asked.

"Whatya mean?" replied George.

"You know what I mean," I said. "The TV cameras, the helicopter, raking the field. Shit, it's the first time you ever done any honest work in your whole life. You probably got blisters all over your hands."

"Yeah! Yeah! I love it!" gushed George after looking at the red welts forming on his palms. "I love this kind of work!"

"Oh, really," I said. "Why don't you take time off and join the grounds crew? Really make a life of it."

George the groundskeeper suddenly reverted to George the principal owner. "Ah, no, no, no," he said. "I'm already paying these people. Let them do the work."

That's another thing about George. He's the best-paying owner in the game, but at the same time he demands almost blind loyalty and a religious respect for his dollar. The only judge in these matters is George himself, and when he doesn't think he's getting his money's worth, look out. He tries to intimidate grown men. Stubborn men. Either that, or he fires them and hires Billy Martin.

George tried his tough guy act on me just once. It was back in May 1976, when I shot a Red Man chewing tobacco commercial a day before a scheduled start. I had to do some throwing for the commercial, nothing serious, but then I got hit hard the next day. We lost the game. Now as we all know, George likes losing about as much as he enjoys watching one of his ships sink. He started calling me all sorts of names. Some had four letters. Pretty soon the writers reached me for a response.

"Don't have anything to say," I said.

"What do you mean, nothing to say?"

I said, "I'll talk to George, but not to the press." This was between me and George. Nobody else. When I talk, it's face-to-face, not in the newspapers.

So the next day, in the lobby of a Cleveland hotel, I ran into George. He started right in, threatening, telling me what a no good son of a bitch I was for doing that commercial. I told him he was even more of a no good son of a bitch for screaming about the commercial, which had been scheduled three months earlier. His eyes kinda glazed over; if George had been one of his ships, I think he'd have blown a gasket. Instead, what he said was this:

"You know what, Cat?"

"No," I said, "what?"

"You and I really see eye to eye. We can talk to each other."

Speaking of talk, that's exactly what I had to do at the high school near the end of the Catfish Hunter Day ceremonies. On my personal scale, speech making ranks right below wearing the same pair of underwear for six days straight. But saying thank you is the least you can do after your community renames the road that runs alongside the high school athletic field after you, unveils a six-foot black granite monument to be placed in the town square, and presents you with a new shotgun, some plaques, and about as much love and affection as one could ever imagine.

"Being here is like a dream," I said, standing at the podium. "Twenty-three years ago I played my final game at this high school." Suddenly my voice disappeared. Tears started streaming down my cheeks. I stood there motionless, a human statue, crying, my mind fixed on how much my daddy and momma would have loved to have seen this day. They were so much a part of me, of who I am, of what I've accomplished. I wanted them standing up there. With me. Taking their bows.

"I . . . just wish . . . my mother . . . my father could be here today. My daddy . . . he always had . . . time to . . . to talk to people. To help people. And I want to thank my wife . . . Helen . . . because while I was traveling around for all those fifteen years, she stayed home and raised the kids. . . . I am proud of her . . . and of them too.

"If I tried to thank everyone, I'd be naming everyone in the stands. Participants in the parade, the Hunt Club, Mr. Cherry, my lawyer, who used to drive us to American Legion games.

"You know, when I signed out of high school, I never knew if I would be able to play in the big leagues. But I soon found out the players there were no better than I was. You just had to get out there and do things. It's the same way today. If you want to win, to accomplish anything in life, you can't do it by yourself. You've got to have help. But like my dad used to say, 'You're not going to get anything by doing nothing.'

"We had this little saying above the locker room in Kansas City: 'Winning isn't everything . . . but wanting to win is.' I don't know who put it there, but if you want to be a policeman, a teacher . . . a lot of people talk about giving 110 percent. In my mind there's no such thing. Only 100 percent. And only one person knows if you've given that, and that's you. Do that and you'll become a winner.''

I sat down, holding Helen's hand for a second. I heard the cheers, stared out at the standing ovation. But really, honestly, I should have been the one standing. Cheering. Without the people in those stands, without Hertford, without the lessons learned on a farm and from my family, there would have been no Catfish, no celebration, no Cooperstown.

2

SIMPLE PLEASURES

OTHER VOICES—PAUL SMITH

Dressed in faded jeans, plaid work shirt, and an Albemarle Chemical cap (Farmer's Choice Product), Paul Smith, a big, beefy man with a friendly smile and florid face, stands over a kettle, slowly stirring vinegar and peppers into his famous fixin'—the sauce of choice at the annual Bear Swamp Hunting Club pig pickin'.

The club gets its name from the road that cuts through one corner of Hunter's 600-acre spread six miles west of town. A baseball with the script letter "H" outlined on the seams is painted on the Hunters' barn door. Inside a rambling ten-room red brick colonial home are countless reminders of his career: On one playroom wall hangs a sixteen by twenty inch color picture of Yankee catcher and kindred spirit Munson staring into the dugout. "He'd just fouled a ball off his foot, and he's looking at me because I'm whimpering like a dog," laughs Hunter. Across the room, the glove he wore during the perfect game is right next to his '74 Cy Young Award, the all-state high school baseball plaque, the key to the city of New York, and a Sports Illustrated cover "Red Hot Against the Reds."

In the main den off the kitchen two World Series rings rest loose on antler ears. Eight silver trays from All Star Games are stacked near a toolbox. The bannister leading upstairs is decorated with bats supplied by Munson, Elston Howard, Piniella, Bando, and Green. Seven shotguns fill a glass case below a portrait of his parents.

Outside, not 400 yards away, at the corner of North Bear Swamp and Center Hill roads, stands Hunter's machine shop that doubles as the Bear Swamp hunting lodge. During deer and bird season it's home away from home for some fifty "Swampers," including Smith, fifty-nine, who's been standing over a hot stove the size of a small U-Haul since 6 a.m. The Swampers are roastin' pigs and chickens, bill of fare for the 600 folks expected to stop by for the free meal that begins at 4 p.m.

The NCAA Final Four semifinals are being played today, but there's not a TV or radio in sight. When the talk turns to sports, which it inevitably does, the subject is baseball, not college hoops. Two dozen farmers wearing black rubber gloves chop up cooked pig and chicken on plywood planks, taking long swallows from ice-cold cans of light beer. One Swamper stops by with a camera. Smile guys. The shutter snaps. Presto! Out pops a plastic penis, sending the Swampers into stitches.

"If I live till Monday," says Smith on a Saturday, "I'm goin' to buy me some stock in that film company."

Just then another Swamper appears, a kitchen apron wrapped tight around his waist. He walks around, waiting, watching, for just the right moment. The right object of abuse. Bingo. "Hey, Clyde," he calls to a redhead in his twenties, hair down to the middle of his back. "Take a look at this, will ya." Clyde turns his head. Up comes the kitchen apron. Out pops another plastic organ, twelve inches of stiff salute.

Smith's heavy laughter carries inside the shop, which on this day has been turned into a dining room. The hydraulic lifts and thirty-ton drill press have been stored and replaced by ten long tables covered with white paper, each topped with vases of yellow daffodils. Mounted on the walls are about a dozen animals—deer, fox, and quail—testament to Jimmy Hunter's skill with a shotgun. "Got them all within five miles of here," says Hunter, typically dressed in jeans and a corduroy shirt.

Auto executives would be pleased with the assembly-line efficiency in which three smiling women (Helen, Jimmy's sister Elizabeth, and Helen's sister Nell) dish out heaping helpings of barbecue, mashed potatoes, coleslaw, and rolls. Some folks just stop by and take home carry-out platters. Others ride up on horses, eat, and ride away. The town preacher comes calling. So do two highway patrolmen and the local wildlife officer. By 6:50 p.m., the place is packed. Jimmy Hunter looks at his watch and says, "All right, ten mo' minutes. We eat at seven." By 7:30, 6 pigs, 100 platters of chicken, and 600 rolls are gone. "The hunting club has it every year," explains Hunter. "It's our way *of saying thank you to the people whose land we hunt on all around here." He scratches his head, graying now, hair sprouting from beneath a hunting cap. "You know, more people showed up than I invited."*

Later, Paul Smith sits down at an empty table and talks about Abbott Hunter. "He was a real strong man," says Smith. "He loved the outdoors. Loved to hunt, to fish. But the thing I remember most about Mr. Abbott is he always had time to stop, to offer a word of encouragement. Mr. Abbott was a family-and-friends person. That's the way the boys were raised. He always had time for them boys. They played ball twelve months to the year. Always competitive. Even today they try to outdo each other with their gardens.

"Jimmy? He's just one of us. He doesn't want to be looked up to. He don't want to be pampered. He just wants to be the same ol' Jimmy Hunter he was years ago. Yes, sir. He's just one of us, and that's the way he wants it to be."

Hertford, North Carolina, about sixty miles southeast of Norfolk, Virginia, is a quaint and quiet town tucked away on the edge of Albemarle Sound. To get to Hertford from Norfolk, you just follow highway 64 east to route 17 south past Elizabeth City (our big sister with its shopping malls and movie theaters) and press down a two-lane blacktop past the murky creeks, corn fields, and signs advertising everything from fresh biscuits to faith healers. Take the Hertford exit off route 17 and follow it about a mile or so, over a suspension bridge. That'll bring you over the Perquiman's River and into the center of town, such as it is; a couple of stoplights, hardware stores, a diner, Irene's Dress Shop, the town square.

Hertford's biggest claim to fame is its lasting place in North Carolina history. It's the oldest town in the state, location of the oldest home in North Carolina (The Newbold White House, circa 1685), antique stores, a gingerbread bakery. It's a very pretty place to live, framed by towering pines, blessed with clean air and some truly spectacular sunsets.

I was born in Hertford on April 8, 1946, the youngest of ten children (two died at birth). Elizabeth is the oldest, then come Marie, Marvin, Ray, Edward, Lilly, Pete, and me. My daddy, Abbott, was a tenant farmer, meaning he farmed land owned by other folks (in our case, it was about 100 acres) and a foreman in the log woods. He meant everything to me. I idolized him. He wasn't a big man, five-ten tops, with small ankles and legs. Yet he had amazing strength in his forearms and chest. He loved the outdoors, hunting and fishing, and he possessed an almost inhuman capacity for work. Far as I could tell, he never took a day off from work in his life. Most days he was up at four or five, a hand-rolled cigarette already pressed between his tobacco-stained fingers, ready for fourteen hours of farming or logging pine in the woods. He never complained, never really said much at all, expressing his emotions through a series of smiles and frowns.

But when he did speak, you'd better have listened. He'd only say something once. The next time, wham! He'd communicate in an entirely different language.

Like the time Daddy was painting the brown four-bedroom wood-frame home he'd built for us on thirty acres, two miles west of town. I was barely six, playing tug-of-war on the back porch with Pete. "Watch the paint," said Daddy. Sure enough, Pete let go of the rope, I went flyin', splatterin' paint from here 'til Tuesday. Daddy was right by the back door and saw the whole thing. The first time he slapped me, I spun all the way 'round; and when I stopped spinnin', he slapped me again, twisting me back the other way. Through the tears I told him it was Pete, not me, who had let go of the rope. "Yeah," he said, "but Pete didn't knock the paint over."

Daddy had a similar attitude about money. He refused to buy either land or machinery on credit—"I might not have much," he'd tell us, "but I want to keep it"—paying cash for everything he owned. And though we were far from rich, Daddy always carried $1000 in his pocket. If he saw something he needed, he bought it. The next day he'd go back to the bank and withdraw enough to bring the balance in his pocket back up to $1000.

My mom, on the other hand, was all brightness and light, a warm face inviting talk and friendship. The family historian, she spent hours clipping articles from the newspapers and pasting them in floral-print scrapbooks. Look inside them today and you'll see stories about our success in sports, our awards, poems and the bits of trivia she plucked from the local paper—births, deaths, graduations and other odds and ends.

Most of all, my mom loved to cook. The boys would always take turns cutting wood for her stove, and she'd reward us by filling the air with the sweet smell of cakes, pies, and peanut brittle. But my mom wasn't well; she spent much of her life fighting to catch her breath; she was so tired sometimes that my dad would literally have to carry her off to bed. But Momma never needed much, rarely asked for anything. The only thing she ever really wanted was a special Christmas present one year, but she refused to offer a hint at what it might be.

"No need to tell, because I know I won't get it," was her comment.

Soon enough, however, my dad discovered she had her heart set on a television. Almost nobody in town owned a TV at the time, but one Saturday night, when the rest of us were in town, he went down to Layton's TV and bought one. Cash, of course. Had it in the house and playing when Momma came home. For a long while she couldn't figure out where the new noise was coming from. Then she took a look in the living room. I'll never forget the look and smile on her face.

The house is gone now, nothing more than a field of corn as far as the eye can see. But sometimes in the evening, I'll drive my truck over to the spot and stare out at the sunset. In my mind I can still see the wooden floors, the eight giant elms out front, the two big barns, for corn and peanuts, the aging smokehouse and outhouse and pond out back where mallards and Canadian honkers came to swim, the bannister we loved to slide down. I see the pitching mound in front of the smokehouse door, a shady space out front for fielding practice, the huge, grassy knoll out back where we could hit fly balls and play pitch, hit, and run.

Baseballs were about as rare as summer rain back then, so we made do with potatoes, corncobs, anything round and firm. And when we did get a ball, we cherished it, wrapping and rewrapping its cover when it got worn, slipping a sock over it when all else failed. The only way we got new baseballs was to buy them ourselves. Selling frogs to restaurants was one way to raise the money; loading watermelons and cantaloupes at a neighbor's farm from dawn 'til dusk yet another. We used to load five of those big ten-wheeler trucks a day. Some nights we'd come home at eleven o'clock and be back again at six in the morning, loadin' more melons. We didn't realize we were lifting weights, but those melons weighed anywhere from twenty to forty pounds each. So I got in shape real early in life.

It was, I must confess, a beautiful way of life, one full of
simple pleasures. Work and play. Play and work. Cleveland
Indian games on the radio. My brothers and me piling into our
'59 Ford for trips up north to see my childhood hero, Robin
Roberts, pitch for the Phillies. Singing country tunes along with
Grandpa Jones and Hank Williams Sr. on the way back home.
Sometimes we wouldn't pull in until three or four in the
morning.

"Where you going?" Daddy said the first time we got home
real late.

"Going off to bed," I said.

"Oh no you're not," he said. "It's time to go to work."

My brothers and I musta thrown a zillion pitches to each other
growing up. Every day, Dad would come in from the fields
around noon, eat lunch, and then nap an hour or two on the
porch. We'd gobble down sandwiches and then rush out to play,
learnin' early on to steer clear of the side Daddy was sleeping
on. Every two years the smokehouse door would splinter to
pieces from the pounding it took. Hour after hour. Day after
day. Week after week. Pitch after pitch. It's funny; folks always
wondered where I got such great control. The answer is written
all over those smokehouse doors. The lessons learned in those
backyard games stayed with me the rest of my career. The
biggest one: If you don't throw strikes to your brothers, you
don't play. It was that simple.

About as simple as putting a neighborhood team together.
Fact was, we had nine players within shouting distance of our
home: the four Hunter boys plus the Nixon brothers (Billy, Ed,
and Gene), and Parker and Donald Chessen just down the road.
We'd team up and play any and everybody, riding bikes into
town to beat the city boys and then over to nearby Winfall to
whip the country kids. All the Hunter boys could play. Marvin,
a third baseman/shortstop, would have had a real shot at the pros
if the army hadn't gotten ahold of him; Ray was a slick-fielding
second baseman in high school; Pete, baseball coach at
Perquiman's for the last fifteen years, pitched college ball for
two years. Edward was a catcher in the local semi-pro leagues.

Sunday was always the most special day of the week, a day
when kids from all over the county, it seemed, stopped by for a
game. Sunday was special too 'cause Daddy joined in, a plug of

chew in his cheek, bellowing out balls and strikes from next to the pitcher.

By the time I was eleven, I'd earned a reputation as a pretty fair pitcher and hitter. So it was my elementary school principal, Thelma Elliott, who figured it was time I played in the annual seventh-grade grudge match between the Hertford and Winfall grammar schools even though I was only in the sixth grade. "Went to Winfall today," I later wrote in my mom's scrapbook. "I did all the pitching, and we won 6-2, and I struck out six." Ray asked all these questions: "How many runs did you make?" "How many hits?" "How many errors?" "How many walks?" "How many strike-outs?"

I told him, "I struck out one time and made four runs. Second time at bat I swung and missed the first strike. Next throw was a ball. Then their pitcher threw the next ball and I made a home run and unloaded the bases. I made four runs."

"Sure did," said Ray.

"That's a good bunch of boys over at Winfall," I told my brother Marvin. "Wish I could go to school there sometime. They've got twin brothers, Francis and Freddie Combs. They're really good. I wish I could play baseball with them instead of against them."

"Well," said Marvin, "if you pass your grades and the Combs brothers do the same, you'll join each other in the ninth grade in 1960. You'll be fourteen years old then. I believe before you leave high school you'll win the conference and state championships."

"Listen to Marvin," said my daddy. "Don't let what you do go to your head. If you play good ball, people will certainly brag about it to your face. Just thank them. If you don't play good, they will certainly tell you. Now go to bed and say your prayers."

The next night Daddy, Marvin, and I had a long talk. "Jimmy," said my daddy, "last night I didn't get a chance to tell you all this, but I feel it will help you. I have read about some of the best baseball players that have ever lived getting a swelled head."

"Well, who were some of them?" I asked.

"I can't mention any names," Daddy said, "but it's happened in the major leagues as well as high school. When you win a game, don't get too much confidence in yourself. Remember, it takes nine men to win. A pitcher can't do it by himself. They'll be plenty of times when you lose, but don't let it worry you. You've got to be a good loser as well as a good winner.

"Too much confidence in anyone's self is just as bad as not enough. It's like this: Faith without work is death. And work without faith is death.

"When you grow up to be a pitcher, there'll be times you throw that first ball across home plate and the batter will knock it across the wall for a home run. There'll be times you start a game and have to be taken out. Pay it no mind, and it will make you play harder the next time.

"The reason I'm telling you all this is because you played your first game against another school yesterday, and I hope you will take my advice."

"I will," I said.

"Please do," said Marvin.

OTHER VOICES—FRANCIS COMBS

He retains the confident swagger and unmistakable air of an athlete. Hunter's catcher from ninth grade through high school, Combs eventually signed a pro contract as a catcher with the New York Yankees. Recently he has worked as a volunteer baseball coach, a spotter in football, and as a PA announcer for basketball games at North Carolina State. A successful salesman for a steel company in Raleigh, Francis Combs, according to Jimmy Hunter, "loves baseball more than anything in his life." During Hunter's playing days, Combs regularly traveled to Oakland and New York, to All Star Games, to the World Series, to share in the excitement. One time Combs actually pitched batting practice for the Yankees in New York. Another time, posing as a photographer, he snuck onto the field before an All Star Game.

"I remember the first time I heard about Jimmy," says Combs. "We were in the sixth grade at Winfall Elementary. Every year Winfall played Perquiman's in our annual baseball game. Well, sure enough, Winfall went over to play, and I

*remember the seventh graders coming back and saying, 'We'd
have won if they hadn't put this sixth grader in there, name of
Hunter. We couldn't hit him.'*

*"Jimmy matured early. I think it was all the playin' he did
with his brothers, all the hard work on the farm. He just worked
harder than anyone else coming up. Mechanically he threw hard,
always with pretty good control, and he had a good curveball. I
remember how intimidated, how scared some of those hitters
were. You could actually see kids' knees shakin' when they batted
against him."*

Back in 1960, Perquiman High School could have doubled as
the set for "The Andy Griffith Show"—the girls in bobby
socks, the boys sporting crew cuts and coveralls. By the time I
entered the ninth grade, I was the only kid left at home; the
others were married or in college. High school, like it is for so
many kids, was the most fun I ever had in my life. I'd get up
with the sun, work the fields until eight, and then head off to
school. After school I played whatever sport was in season, and
then I'd head home to help Daddy in the fields. On Sundays I
worked at Bill Fowler's combination country store/gas station,
right across from the high school. On more than one occasion
ol' Bill caught me staring across the street toward the ball field,
a hungry look in my eye. "Aw, go on, Jimmy," he'd say.
"Might as well go on over there and play. Not doing me any
good standin' around the store today."

Marvin, Pete, Ray, and Edward had all played baseball at
Perquiman's, but Daddy had a hard-and-fast rule—no football
for any of the Hunter boys. He was afraid we'd get hurt and
that'd be the end of our promising baseball careers. But I liked
the prospect of putting on a helmet and bashing heads, so I
decided to take matters into my own hands. One day I came
home late from school, and Daddy was sitting on the porch.
Waiting.

"Where you been?" he asked.

"Football practice," I said.

"I thought I told you not to go out for it."

"Yes, sir, but I wanted to play."

"Well, you come home all broke up, then what are you going
to do?"

That's all he said. Walked right off. Yet he never missed one game, watching his son grow into a pretty fair country linebacker and split end. I always wanted to be a quarterback, but the coach, Gil Underwood, wouldn't let me, afraid I'd hurt my arm for baseball.

Ah, yes, baseball. All we ever did was play ball. If we had a twenty-minute break, I guarantee ya' we'd have a game. By the time ninth grade had rolled around, Marvin's prediction had held true: Francis and Freddie Combs had enrolled at Perquiman High School. Francis, tall and skinny, was so skilled behind the plate he eventually became the best defensive catcher in the Yankees' minor league system. His twin brother, Freddie, was quicker, more compact, a pitcher and shortstop with a rocket for an arm. He later earned All-America honors as a defensive back at North Carolina State and started at shortstop for the Wolfpack.

After an 8–5 pitching record my sophomore year, we put it all together and won the state class AA title as juniors in 1963. Our coach, Bobby Carter, had a penchant for discipline and conditioning. (Today, Bobby's coaching at Roanoke Rapids High in North Carolina, winning league titles like he did in the '60s.) As it was, long before we won the state, scouts from a dozen big league teams started showing up at our games, scouting me as a pitcher and shortstop. I didn't disappoint. My season record was 13–1, and in one twelve-inning game I struck out twenty-nine batters. I could hit, too; Houston, in fact, wanted to sign me as a shortstop.

But no matter what I did, good or bad, if Daddy didn't see it, first thing I'd do when I got home was change clothes and charge out into the fields and tell him. Lots of times I'd just hop onto his tractor and replay the game, inning by inning, pitch by pitch, if necessary. Daddy loved it; Marvin used to do the same thing, only in those days Marvin'd be on one set of mules, Daddy on the other, and they'd be hollerin' back and forth across the fields.

"And then what he throw you?" Daddy would yell.

"Fastball. Outside," Marvin would yell back.

"What'd ya do with it?"

"Lined it up the gap in right center."

"Good."

*   *   *

The one subject that my classmates rarely discussed was girls. On a four-item list that included baseball, all other sports, hunting, and family—the subject of girls rarely came up in conversation. I do, however, remember noticing this one girl, younger than me by a couple of years, waving to me as she held open the doors at the grammar school each day.

My junior year I was standing around a school dance, talking sports, when a radiant brunet with a beautiful smile and a twinkle in her eyes walked over. The grammar school girl had grown up. A slow dance played in the air.

"Would you like to dance?" she asked.

As a matter of fact, I did. Her name, as it turned out, was Helen Overton. She was the youngest of eleven children, daughter of the best butcher around. She loved sports. That night she asked me to the Sadie Hawkins dance. Again I said yes. From then on we went steadier and steadier until we were married on October 9, 1966.

3

SELF-MADE MEN

Up with the sun on Thanksgiving Day 1963, I dressed in a rush, eager to explore the woods near our home. My spirits were soaring; it had been a spectacular summer and a glorious fall.

That summer, I had returned for a second season of American Legion ball with Post 102 in Ahoskie. Some of the best ballplayers in the state played for Post 102: right fielder Bobby Harrington and catcher/outfielder Doug Britton from Lewiston; pitcher/left fielder Carl Taylor from Gatesville, and third baseman Charles Riddick and first baseman Frank Rice from Sunbury. Freddie, Francis, and I trucked up from Hertford twice a week. Competition was keen, twice the level of high school ball, and our coach, Al Vaughan, preached all-out hustle.

With Freddie, Francis, and I away at the state playoffs, Post 102 lost its first two games. My first appearance of the summer came in game three with no outs and us trailing 3–0 in the top of the first. I retired all twenty-one batters I faced in the seven-inning game, striking out eleven straight in one stretch as we rallied to win.

My most memorable performance came a month later, on July 10, 1963, our final regular-season game. Nine straight wins had moved us into a tie with Rocky Mount for first place. The winner of our game would be crowned area champ. The stands at Ahoskie Grade School field fairly creaked from the overflow crowd that, I must admit, was adding to my nervousness.

Unable to settle my nerves, I walked the first batter. The next hitter bunted for a base hit. I hit the third. Bases loaded, no outs. Coach Vaughan called time and stepped smartly to the mound.

"Jimmy," he said, "are you aware of the situation? You've got the bases loaded here and there's nobody out and this *is* for

the league championship.'' He took a look around the diamond.
''I want you to strike out the side.''

''Yes, sir,'' I said. What else *could* I say?

Nine pitches—nine *strikes*—later the inning was over. We
won the game 2–1. Before the summer was out, I'd win six
straight games, including two no-hitters, to finish my Legion
career with 138 strikeouts in 87 innings.

The only real constant of that summer—other than the two-,
three-, and four-hour car rides to games—was the presence of
one Clyde Kluttz from nearby Salisbury, North Carolina.
Clyde, a crew-cut farmer with a stern, weathered face, also
happened to be a scout for the Kansas City A's, an ex-big league
catcher (nine teams in five years) whose biggest payday as a
player was $10,000 a year. ''Deserved every penny of it, too,''
he said.

That was Clyde. Honest. Direct. Serious. Not the kind of guy
to shoot ya a curve; always able to tell you the truth. Clyde, I
immediately found out, was different from so many other
scouts. Whereas some liked to buddy up and exchange information, Clyde worked alone. He'd say his hellos and then go off by
himself to watch a prospect. And he rarely relied on just what he
saw on the field; no, with Clyde, a visit to the family preacher or
a school principal told him as much—or more—than what he
saw on the diamond.

Yes, sir, one minute he'd be sitting in the stands talking crops
with my dad, the next he was at the kitchen table passing the
peas to my mother. Clyde was everywhere that summer; I
learned real quick that when the old catcher talked, I listened.

''Hold it with the seams like this,'' he said one day, picking
up a baseball. ''Now throw it and see what it does.'' I threw a
fastball. The ball sunk a good six inches.

''Now hold it cross the seams.''

Another pitch. The ball rose like it had a mind of its own.

''Thanks, Mr. Kluttz,'' I said.

''Don't mention it,'' he said.

That fall, as a six-foot, 175-pound senior, I made all-state in
football (we won the state Class AA title 33–0 after a scoreless
first half) and track (I won the state 440-yard dash). All of which
put me in a pretty good mood as I headed out the door on
Thanksgiving Day 1963 into a countryside I'd hunted for years.

My daddy had been taking me hunting since I was eight years old; later I'd followed my brothers out into the woods. By now I was huntin' all day Saturdays and on holidays. I knew by heart the sound rabbits made running through the brush, could train a dog to scent a deer, and could handle a Remington 1100 shotgun with care. Hunter. What better name could there be? It's who I am, what I do. If it hadn't been for baseball, I always said I'd have become a game warden.

(Of course, some folks'll tell ya I already am. Today in two kennels on my property are forty hunting dogs—Walker hounds, black Lab retrievers, chocolate Labs—dogs for fowl, for birds, for rabbit and deer. Every one's a male—males are preferred for hunting—all named after friends or hunting buddies. There's Eddie, Neal, Mitch, Train, Juggie, Charles, and even one I named Bates. You gotta love Bates. I named him after a guy who used to hunt with us. We've always kept a close eye on Bates. As someone said, "If that dog's ever gonna run off, it's gonna be straight to the liquor store. That's where Bates was always headed.")

So as Buck and Jill, our beagle hounds, worked the woods, Ray and Pete and my cousin Alton kept a sharp eye out for rabbits, squirrels, and ducks in the marshy woods near our home. As usual, we wore our knee-length Davey Crockett hunting coats, the ones with deep pockets, perfect for storing prey, and worked the fields in the same circular pattern, crossing the dirt road in front of our house and moving silently through the fields and along a drainage canal half a mile away. We walked slowly along the canal, near where my house is today.

Thanksgiving Day.

We were halfway home when Pete's shotgun went off.

To this day, I don't know what happened. I was standing next to Pete. I heard a shot. The force of the blast knocked me to the ground, my mind racing. Boy, that was close, I thought. I reached up so Pete could give me a hand.

That's when I saw the blood.

Pouring from the holes in my now shredded boot . . . the blood. . . .

I passed out. So did Pete, who, fortunately, ended up uninjured. Thank goodness, somebody—it must have been Alton—ran for help and got one of my sisters, who rushed me to the hospital. Everything was a blur until the next morning when my dad walked into the room. My foot was a bloodied, bandaged mess. I was afraid to look down.

"Looks like my baseball career is over, Daddy," I said.

My father didn't say it at the time, but he thought so, too. The doctors counted forty-five shotgun pellets in my right foot; they were able to remove only half a dozen or so. The little toe was gone, blown right off by the blast. The one right next to it should have been removed too; there wasn't a lick of feeling left in it.

I hobbled around awhile. Here a hobble, there a hobble. That lasted through the holidays. Finally I got fed up, tired of being babied by family and friends. I ditched the crutches and began walking on my heel. Then the inside of my foot. Then the bottom. Every so often Dr. Polk Williams in Elizabeth City would pull out a few more pellets. By the time my senior year in baseball arrived, thirty remained. So I improvised, inserting a foam-rubber cushion insole in my shoe, cutting holes where the pellets were pressing into my foot.

Not that it mattered to most scouts. News of the accident had scared a lot of them away. All but Clyde Kluttz and a few others. When Clyde heard about the accident, he rushed right over. "You able to play?" he said. I told him I was. From then on he came by every day to talk with me, play catch, encourage and counsel me.

The rest of the so-called experts? Well, they figured I couldn't run real well or pitch. But what they didn't figure on was me. The fact that I don't like to lose at nothin'. Never have. Never will. Baseball, hunting, fishing, pitching horseshoes, growing tomato plants—I want to win. Even today when I pitch to Todd or Paul at home or in an Old Timers or alumni game, I don't try to lose. Helen'd like to kill me for beating the kids all the time. "Let them win once or twice," she'll say.

"When they're good enough, they'll beat me," I'll say. "I'm not gonna ease up on them." That's just the way I am. If somebody beats me, fine. Tomorrow's another day. But don't expect any free lunches. You'll starve first.

Come senior year of baseball season we all played with pretty much that same attitude. After all, we were the defending state champs, and if you wanted to beat us, it was going to take some doing. Especially against the club we had coming back: Francis behind the plate, Freddie and I switching off at short and pitching, Wayne Winslow at first, Ike Stokley at second, Gene

Nixon at third, Jimmy Bryum in center, Alvin Kirby in left, John Stalling in right, and Carter, the taskmaster, in the dugout.

How tough were we? Well, we opened the year with eight straight shutouts. You read it right: eight. Number eight happened to be played on April 15, 1964. I remember the date because that shutout also happened to be a perfect game, a 5–0 win over arch rival Elizabeth City. It was my second no-hitter in a row.

By now the scouts had changed their tune once more. I was a prospect again. A *major league* prospect. Clyde, sensing the shift in thinking, stopped by for a chat. Seeing his face was certainly no surprise; by now he'd almost earned himself a spot in the family portrait, stopping by as he pleased, having dinner, talking to my daddy in the fields and my mom in the kitchen.

Helen and I were sitting together on the porch when he drove up. We were going very steady by now, marriage in the back of our minds, but we were going to wait until Helen, who was only a sophomore at the time, would graduate from high school. Clyde eased up the steps, sat down in a chair, and started talking.

"Now, Jimmy, Helen, I want you to listen real close," he began. "Baseball's a funny business. And that's just what it is—a business. Most ballplayers today, when they get out of the game, within two, three years they're broke. They don't know what to do, so the first thing that happens is they sell everything they've got. You don't want that happenin' to you. Make sure your house, your property, your insurance is all paid for."

He turned to me. "Jimmy, I want you to remember to be nice to everyone. You're going to meet a lot of guys going up and you're going to meet some of those same guys going down." He looked to Helen. "Now, Helen, Jimmy's going to see a lot of girls in the game. They're going to be around everywhere. It's a part of the game. You have to trust him. He's gonna make a lot of money, and it's gonna come quick. He's gonna want to spend it quick. Don't let him do it. Make sure he saves it."

Spoken to us like a true father, which, I guess, by this time Clyde was. He'd been preparing me for this moment for two years. Now he was warning me, teaching me about life in the big leagues. The timing, as it turned out, couldn't have been more perfect. Why? Because, ladies and gentlemen, Charles O. Finley was coming to town.

* * *

The big, booming voice fairly rattled the receiver. It didn't bother to introduce itself, but I had a pretty good idea who it belonged to.

"Ever hear of a man named Clyde Kluttz?" it yelled.

"Yes, sir. Know him real well. Been livin' with me the last two weeks."

"Good," chirped Charlie Finley. "I've been payin' him to be down there, and I just want to make sure I'm getting my money's worth."

Finley informed me that he was planning to come down from Chicago to see me pitch in the state playoffs. At the time, I really didn't know much about Finley or his team, the Kansas City A's. Thankfully, Francis filled in some blanks.

"You don't know that team?" he said. "That's the guy, the owner with all the colorful uniforms. He's out there tryin' to promote baseball. You might like to go with him."

"I don't know," I said. "As long as he gives me some money and half a chance, I'll go."

A short time later, first week of June, Finley arrived for a personal inspection. You'd have thought Elvis Presley, the King himself, had pulled into town for all the commotion it caused. Finley was truly a sight to see: round, robust, hair beginning to gray, and the eyebrows—his most distinctive feature—bushy, growin' like wildflowers in full bloom. Playing the part of goodwill ambassador to the hilt, he passed out green jackets, green bats, and gold-colored baseballs wherever he went—which was just about anywhere he wanted.

"You think they'd let you use these bats and balls during a game?" he asked that day.

Told him we'd try. The balls proved a problem (too slick), but we got as far as home plate with the bats. "Out," said the ump. We argued, mildly, stressing regulation size and weight. Wrong color, said the ump. They're out or you're out—take your pick. We played.

Oh, how we played. By the time the last round of playoffs rolled around, I was 12–0 (a two-year record of 25–1) with five no-hitters. I made it 26–1 in the state class AA quarterfinals, pitching a 1–0 shutout. The next night, playing shortstop, I banged out the four hits that set up our defense of the state title the next night.

Yet somehow, Coach Carter thought my mind was on other matters. A brunet, if I read him right. After we won our semifinal game, he called me aside at the hotel and lectured me for missing a play at shortstop. He told me to, "Stop thinking about that girl and start playing baseball." I wasn't one for back talk, but this made me mad. I told him, in no uncertain terms, that he didn't know what the hell he was talking about. We argued back and forth for a while. Then Carter had his final say. "All right," he said, "go to your hotel room. You're not playing tomorrow. We're sending you home." Since home was about 150 miles away and we were playing for a second state title, I did the only thing any of us would've done. I picked up the nearest piece of pool furniture and sent it for a swim. Then I locked myself in my hotel room.

Thankfully, both Carter and I cooled off, and I played Saturday night—with Finley in the stands, getting a last look-see before getting down to business. Pitching on one day's rest, I lost 5–4—only my second loss in my last two years. Worse, we lost that state title we so much wanted to defend. I felt no joy in the fact that none of the runs against me were earned.

OTHER VOICES—CHARLES O. FINLEY

The calls, one after another, went to Finley's office in Chicago. At the outset the book project was carefully explained. Finley cut right in: "You guys gettin' paid? How much are you gonna pay me?" The second call found a much more reasonable and relaxed voice on the other end. "Love to help you," he said. "But I'm busy right now. Call back tomorrow." Tomorrow turned into fifteen tomorrows. Therefore, the following comes courtesy of a July 1987 Finley interview with the New York Post:

"*I went down to Hertford to visit him and his family in June of '64. He lived in a sharecropper's home with a tin roof. His mother was out in the field with a bonnet on her head and a hoe in her hand, hoeing the weeds in the peanut patch. His father was in the smokehouse turning the bacon and hams. The water for the house came from a pump with a log handle.*

"*I was watching all this and later talked with the family for about an hour. Then Catfish pulled off his boot to show me his foot, and I almost fell over backward. The top of his [right] foot was loaded with buckshot. He proudly told me he and his brother had been duck shooting in the marsh and his brother's shotgun had accidentally gone off.*

"I looked at him and couldn't believe what I was seeing. And yet he was asking for a $75,000 signing bonus. The other scouts were afraid, but I fell in love with him and his parents and his brothers and sisters after seeing what mold they came from. I was impressed with him as a person.

"The next day I watched him pitch in the state championship game and was even more impressed."

As the years went on, I learned more and more about this remarkable man, with relentless drive and a shrewd mind. A man long on memory and short on patience, intimidating from the start. A man capable of the greatest generosities but at the same time a man who welcomed an argument, who detested yes-men. (Maybe that's why the Oakland A's played the way we did—there wasn't a yes-man in the whole lineup.)

Charles O. Finley. A man who made millions upon millions in insurance (at least $40 million, by his count) the old-fashioned way. "I outworked them," he told us time and time again. A man one writer called "the ultimate product of the Horatio Alger work ethic."

Finley grew up the son of a steelworker, peddling rejected eggs in Birmingham, Alabama, office buildings for fifteen cents a dozen. Later, he and a childhood friend picked grapes in the woods and sold homemade wine to neighbors; later still, he became batboy for the Birmingham Barons of the Class AA Southern Association for fifty cents a game and all the baseballs the manager would give him; next he worked as a machinist's apprentice at the U.S. Steel Company's plant in Gary, Indiana, and, after that, supervised a shipyard during World War II. About this time he married Shirley McCarthy and began moonlighting as an insurance salesman. Suddenly his insatiable appetite for work caught up with him; he contracted tuberculosis and spent the next twenty-seven months in a sanitorium. Mrs. Finley fed the family the only way she could—on $40 a week, earned by proofreading stories at a Gary newspaper.

"The confinement tore at me for a long time," Mr. Finley once said. "I had always been so active. Finally I decided to spend my time working. I came up with the perfect plan for providing group disability insurance for the medical profession. Within two years, doctors all over the country were buying it, and I had made my first million—and a whole lot more. My formula is sweat plus sacrifice equals success. Anybody who doesn't believe in it can't work for me.''

Sweat, sacrifice, attention to every last detail. That was the secret of Charlie Finley's success. ''I am,'' he would repeatedly tell reporters, ''a self-made man.'' And come to think of it, so am I.

After Mr. Finley made such a big show in Hertford, everybody figured I was signed, sealed, and delivered. But I couldn't do nothin' until after the playoffs, and that's when Mr. Finley called—right after we lost.

''I'm calling today to sign ya,'' said Finley. ''What do you want?''

I said I had to wait two more days; I'd promised some other clubs, principally the Phillies, Orioles, and Mets, that I'd listen to their offers. I explained all this to Mr. Finley on the phone. Just a day or two more, I said.

''I'm gonna sign ya today, kid, or never talk to you again.'' You don't sell millions in insurance by letting the customer call the shots.

So I sat there a few minutes. I knew Johnny Lee (Blue Moon) Odom had just signed with Kansas City out of Macon, Georgia. I said, ''I'll have the same contract Blue Moon Odom got, plus I'll have a black Thunderbird.''

He asked, ''Well, why do you want that Thunderbird?''

I told him, ''It's a pretty car.''

He said, ''Well, I'm gonna give you enough money to buy that Thunderbird. You buy it from the money I give ya. I'll give ya $75,000. You sign today. Right now. Or that's it.''

I looked at my dad. He looked at me and walked out. I started thinkin'—$75,000? At that time, you know, $75 looked mighty good.

''I'll sign,'' I said.

Finley was so pleased he promised my parents that even if I never pitched again, if my foot failed to respond to treatment, I could still keep my bonus money and he would personally see to it that I got the best medical treatment available.

It was then that he asked about a nickname.

Once I had finished repeating the nickname story to Mr. Finley it was time to explain the sudden addition of "Catfish" to my parents. But the words wouldn't come; too embarrassed, I guess. They would read about it in a wire service report the next day. Momma, fairly shaking, walked over to Daddy, forcing the paper in front of his face. "Look at this," she snapped. "I don't like this one bit."

Slowly the laugh lines opened up all over Daddy's face. Momma wasn't so amused, especially when she discovered the source of the story. I'd never seen her so angry. "I raised eight children, and not a single one ever ran away from home," she told the local paper. "I don't understand why Mr. Finley made up that name and that story. I have never, never, never ever called Jim 'Catfish,' and I never will. I don't like Catfish— Jim's a lot prettier . . . but I guess he could have gotten a worse nickname. If Mr. Finley had known that Jim loves bass fishing, he might have named him 'Big Mouth' instead."

After signing, I went straight to Finley's huge farm in LaPorte, Indiana, for some rest and relaxation and then on to Rochester, Minnesota, and the famed Mayo Clinic. Later on, he gave me a job working in the mailroom of his insurance offices in Chicago and let me travel a bit with the team. At Mayo, the doctors removed a couple more pieces of bone and sixteen pellets from my foot. It began to feel better, helped along, I must say, by the Mayo nurses. I was getting twenty-six-hour-a-day care. Every time I turned around, there'd be another nurse, standing bedside, smiling, asking if I needed anything. They seemed to be trying to draw me into conversation, asking every imaginable question they could. Finally, I caught on. I stopped talking. Which drove one nurse crazy. "C'mon," she said one night in utter frustration. "Talk. We all want to hear your accent."

* * *

My first true taste of professional baseball came that fall in the Bradenton, Florida, Instructional League. What a crew that was in '64: Campy Campaneris, Blue Moon Odom, Chuck Dobson, Dave Duncan, Paul Lindblad, Skip Lockwood, Jim Nash, Joe Rudi, Tony LaRussa, Rene Lachemann, Don Buschhorn. It made no difference that Campy had signed for something like $580 and Lockwood had picked up a cool $125,000. It was all for one and one for all . . . under the watchful eye of camp coordinator Clyde Kluttz, who, as it turned out, was a little like a combination Father Flanagan and Sergeant Schultz guarding Hogan's Heroes at Boys' Town.

By day, Clyde worked our asses off on the field, fine-tuning our strengths, correcting our far-more-obvious weaknesses. By night, we partied together at the Kentucky Colonel Hotel, although Nash and I were so poor we often ended up having dinner with Clyde and his wife, Wayne, eating them out of house and home.

Clyde truly went out of his way for everyone. But there was one guy who hated Clyde's guts. "Rock Head" Harrison was his name. A pitcher, big and strong, a hard thrower, but he wouldn't accept Clyde's advice to save his life. Finally, Rock Head challenged Clyde to a fight.

"You don't want to fight me," Clyde told Rock Head. "You'll probably kill me. But, if you want to fight, let's fight. The fact is I'm telling you the truth, but you don't want to listen." Rock Head, as it turns out, played one year of minor league ball before washing out and joining the army. Later Clyde told me he got a letter from Rock Head thanking Clyde for helping him more than anyone in his life—he just didn't know it at the time. Said the army straightened him out.

Me? I needed some straightening out, too. My foot was throbbing like a bass drum, more than I let on, and I was pitching like a $75 bonus baby instead of $75,000. Club officials were worried about my batting practice velocity, especially with Blue Moon blowing big league heat. So Clyde set me straight. "Folks here saying you got a lazy arm, Jimmy."

So I tried speedin' things up, only to get roughed up. Next thing I know, *The Sporting News* has an article headlined "Should the A's Throw the Catfish Back?" Just what I needed. My chin was mopping the floor as I walked into the clubhouse that day. Moe Drabowsky, one helluva quality relief pitcher and a shoo-in candidate for the Practical Joker Hall of Fame (among other things, Moe once put three goldfish in an opposing club's water cooler), got dead serious all of a sudden.

"Kid," he said, "you read the damn paper, didn't you?"

"Yep."

"Let me tell you something, son. Never read anything about

yourself. You know what you can do. Read about someone else. Sportswriters can build you up, and suddenly you think you *are* up there. Or they can knock you down, and you *think* you're down there. Believe in what *you* can do, kid, nobody else." A short speech, but one that stayed with me my entire career. Nice short-term effects, too. Before camp broke, I pitched a seven-inning no-hitter despite, as my long-time roommate Paul Lindblad recalls, "not being able to break a pane of glass."

Something else that stayed with me was the sight of Joe Rudi. A sidearm-throwing shortstop in high school and junior college in California, Rudi was in the process of learning a new position—left field. Talk about a project. At that time, Rudi looked like anything but the All Star outfielder he would become in Oakland. He couldn't run, could barely hit, and had such a terrible scatter arm that nobody in their right mind would play catch with him. But I'll say this about Joe: He never stopped working. Every day he was out early with a coach named Herzog, as great a coach then as he is a manager now. Over and over Whitey would show Joe how to execute the most basic of outfield movements. "Get down on the ball," Whitey would yell. "Keep the glove in front of you!" "Field the ball out front." Over and over and over again.

While Rudi was putting in overtime, Lindblad, Moon, Nash, and I were working on our fishing. Lindblad, the farm boy from Kansas, loved night fishing. One of his favorite spots was on this railroad trestle that ran across one of the local rivers. "Come with me," he said one afternoon. "Great fishin'."

So the next night Nash and I, fingers crossed, agreed to accompany Lindblad out on the trestle.

I guess we were, oh, about three-quarters of a mile out on this thing when I saw the light approaching from a distance. A single beam drawing nearer and nearer. A shrill whistle. Smoke. Train.

"Now what?" I yelled.

"I'm gonna swim for it," says Nash, looking down into the swirling waters.

"Great," I said. "Not me."

"What's the matter?" asked Lindblad.

"Can't swim."

By the time Lindblad had stopped laughing, the train had

gained another quarter of a mile. (Little did I know that he'd anticipated the entire episode and had come prepared with an escape plan.)

And here it was. "Just lay down your poles along the side of the track," said Lindblad. "Then get down underneath, where the beams are, lay on your side, and the train will run right over you."

Riiiight. No problem. Just lay right down here and the train will run right over you. First, I lose my toe; now my whole body is going to be crushed. But what else could I do? I certainly wasn't jumping; I'd never see shore. So down I crawled, holding on for dear life. Waiting. Listening. Praying. Nash kept lifting his head, looking around. I could see the headlines: "Promising Pitcher Decapitated in Bizarre Train Accident."

"Never again," I shouted at Lindblad when the track had cleared—and my teeth had stopped chattering. And I meant it. Never again. Until the next night, that is. In those days, "never" had a much broader meaning. Especially when the fishin' was good.

4

KANSAS CITY, HERE I COME

A handy-dandy little history lesson on the late, not-so-great (downright dismal, actually) Kansas City A's.

After going fishin' for the Phillies, the White Sox, and the Tigers without so much as a nibble, Charles O. Finley landed the Athletics for $4 million cash on December 19, 1960. "I'm a baseball nut," he said at the time of the purchase. "I may be outsmarted, but I'll never be outhustled." Unfortunately, you couldn't say the same for a club doing its best (worst?) to live up (down?) to the history of its predecessors from Philadelphia. In the previous twenty-seven years, the record states that Connie Mack's club had finished in the first division only twice and dead last thirteen times. Ancient history as far as Mr. Finley was concerned.

"What this team needs," he said, "is a little color."

So one of the true pioneers of modern-day sport went about his business. He had the ballpark painted yellow, turquoise, and orange; he installed the first "Fan-O-Gram," an electronic board on which messages were spelled; he installed "Little Blowhard," a small tube that rose from the ground and blew the dust off home plate; and he introduced Harvey, a mechanical white rabbit with buck teeth and a green and gold jacket that rose from the ground and brought fresh baseballs to the umpires in its paws. He outfitted his team in crazy (at the time) two-tone kelly green and "Finley" gold uniforms. He installed picnic tables and built a zoo for monkeys behind left field and grazed sheep behind the fence in right. He allowed Old Drum, a fourteen-week-old, sad-eyed German shorthair pointer, to frolic in the outfield before games. He passed out Stetsons and balloons with free tickets attached.

There were rumors, however, right from the start, that Charlie had bought the club in hopes of shifting it to another city—like Chicago, perhaps even switching franchises with the White Sox. He denied any deception. "This team is not going to move out of Kansas City," he said during a January '61 testimonial dinner on his behalf. "I'm not in baseball to make a fast buck. I'm in baseball to build a team for Kansas City and then keep it for my family."

But by midyear, on his way to losing (so he said) $800,000, speculation grew that the team was headed for Dallas, or San Diego, or Atlanta, or Louisville . . . Pick a city, any city. Again, Finley denied it. In a dramatic (what else) show of his good intentions, he publicly burned a piece of paper he said was an escape agreement that had given the previous owner the right to cancel his lease any time season attendance fell below 850,000. The team, Finley insisted, would remain in Kansas City "regardless of attendance." (It wasn't until the end of the year that folks learned the paper ol' Charlie had burned was blank.)

After the team lost a cool $1.7 million in 1962, Oakland and other cities, such as Dallas—willing to spend $9 million to build a ballpark—became inviting alternatives to an impatient owner.

Finley then got into a major squabble with the city's esteemed sports editor, Ernest Mehl, over support for his team. Commissioner Ford Frick forced Finley to apologize to Mehl, but it didn't matter anyway. Finley wanted no part of Kansas City. He signed a two-year contract with the state of Kentucky to play in Louisville beginning in 1965.

Now wait just a cotton pickin' minute, said the other American League owners. Nobody asked us about moving anywhere. In a 9–1 vote (give you one guess on the one), they forced Finley to return to Kansas City or face expulsion and forfeiture of his franchise. He returned, kicking and screaming all the way.

"The American League isn't home free yet," Finley said at the time. "Nor are they rid of me. I may have lost the first round, but I don't think I'll lose the next one." But he did. In 1964 he signed a four-year lease with Kansas City, not subject to cancellation.

"I believe we have a good team capable of great things," he said upon signing. "With a break or two we should definitely be in the first division. Certainly our spirit and dedication will continue to be high. I sincerely hope the fans of Kansas City will support their team. I know they will have good reasons to be

*proud of it. So I'm eagerly awaiting the familiar cry of 'Play
ball.' "*

So was I. That's all I wanted to do upon arrival in Kansas City.
Play ball. My foot had finally recovered. At least now I could
push off the rubber without wincing. I knew I couldn't have
picked a better club—or city—to start my career. Kansas City,
with its midwestern charm, cowboy boots, and western hats,
made me feel right at home (I always said that if I ever left North
Carolina, I'd live in Kansas City). The A's, unfortunately,
didn't go anywhere. At least, not in the standings. They lost 105
games in the 1964 season to finish in last (tenth) place—plus
ninth in team batting and tenth in pitching and fielding. The
front office was in uncontrolled chaos: three general managers
the first five years; five managers since '60. But unlike stable
franchises in Baltimore, Detroit, or Boston, opportunities
existed for players in Kansas City. No job was secure. If you
performed, you played.

We opened the 1965 season with five "bonus babies" on the
roster—pitchers Lockwood, Odom, Buschhorn, and myself and
catcher Duncan. It's nice to say we earned it, but really, the club
had no other choice. Had we been demoted to the minor
leagues, another club could have signed us for just $25,000.
That was the rule. (Naturally, Finley tried to find a way around
it.) He did with Joe Rudi, peddling him to another club for some
seasoning, only to bring him back a few years later in a trade.
He tried to play games with me, too, requesting I sign another
contract, one that would be dated 1965 instead of '64; it would
allow me to be sent to the minors without penalty. I asked Clyde
Kluttz what to do.

"Don't sign nothin' else," said Clyde. "You already signed
it. That's my advice." And I took it.

Our skipper that year was Mel McGaha, a name not destined,
I'm afraid, to make any managers' Hall of Fame. Mel was what
you'd call a button-down guy, hard-nosed, a southerner from
Bastrop, Louisiana, who'd spent twenty-one years kicking
around the minor leagues in places like Winston-Salem, North
Carolina, Columbus, Georgia, Mobile, Alabama, and Shreve-
port, Louisiana. Finley had hired Mel to replace Eddie Lopat
midway through the '64 season.

It didn't take us long in spring training to come up with a moniker for Mel: the "Drill Sergeant." I mean, this man's idea of a good time was eighty-yard wind sprints. His method of managing? Put the nine best-conditioned players on the field and see what happens. So we exercised—boy did we exercise—running our asses off in Bradenton. The routine rarely varied: Trainer Billy Jones would torture us as Mel paced briskly between lines of panting players. "Keep working, keep working," he'd shout. "Don't die on us now."

Wouldn't think of it. At least not until Mel took ten or fifteen specially selected victims for another thirty minutes of basic training. Mel just didn't know when to call it quits. And we lost one of our best pitchers, Chuck Dobson, because of it.

Mel had this office near the right field line from where he could look out and watch practice. One day he noticed Dobson and me dutifully doing our "pickups," an age-old pitching drill where your partner rolls a ball just in front of you and you bend down, pick it up, and toss it back. In small doses it's good for the legs, but tough on the back. In this particular case, Dobson's back.

"Why isn't the sissy doing them?" asked Mel, pointing at my partner.

"Because the sissy will be in the hospital if he does," said Chuck.

"Well then," said Mel, "let's see how long it's gonna take you to get to the hospital." By my count, it was, oh, fifteen minutes before the ambulance arrived. Off went Chuck to the emergency room.

After "Camp McGaha" ended, we opened the season against Detroit. Not that too many folks cared. The 18,000 who did show up—the smallest opening-day crowd in A's history—saw Moe Drabowsky lose 6–2 to Detroit. Our lineup:

> Campy Campaneris, SS
> Mike Hershberger, RF
> Ed Charles, 3B
> Ken Harrelson, 1B
> Tommy Reynolds, LF
> Bill Bryan, C
> Jim Landis, CF
> Dick Green, 2B

* * *

The next evening all of 2028 were on hand to see us lose 11–4. It never got much better. We were short on just about everything you need to win—starting pitching, defense, and clutch hitting —consequently, we didn't. By May we were once again in last place. Drabowsky, John Wyatt, Wes Stock, and Orlando Peña were already worn out and needed relief. Me? I pitched batting practice and tried to stay out of the way. After a while, I guess McGaha figured, "What the hell, he can't do any worse. Let the kid pitch." So on May 13, 1965, a Thursday night in Chicago, I got my shot. History will reflect that on the mound for the White Sox was Gary Peters, a twenty-game winner in '64, who was looking for his ninth straight win. Diego Segui, a fine right-handed pitcher with a nasty forkball, was on the mound for us. Unfortunately, Diego survived only 1⅔ innings, allowing four runs. Drabowsky pitched the next 3⅓ innings, allowing three runs.

My turn. One month past my nineteenth birthday I made my first appearance in the big leagues. I pitched the sixth and seventh innings like I'd been doing it all my life: no hits, one walk, two strikeouts. Of course, the 2028 fans scattered about Comiskey Park barely blinked. Too busy, I'm sure, checking out the stabbing in the stands. Honest. Talk about a tough crowd. Dick Green's wife was there, and she ended up watching the game in the dugout with us.

Three days later McGaha was fired. Charlie didn't give him much notice; when approached by reporters after a game, McGaha was heard to utter, "I just heard about this three minutes ago." McGaha's replacement was our Triple A manager, Haywood Sullivan, now co-owner of the Boston Red Sox. Haywood was the Bobby Valentine of his time, the youngest manager in the big leagues, barely thirty-four, a former reserve catcher for six years in the majors, and one very *big* man. We were all petrified of Sully at first, but we quickly found him to be a gentle giant. What can I say? The guys took advantage of him.

Before reading on, understand this: It's not easy staying sharp and committed on a club that's losing 100-plus games a year, that's out of the pennant race by *cinco de Mayo,* that celebrates two-game winning streaks. The mind wanders. Pranks are pulled.

And yes, I was one of the "pullers." I love instigating things, harmless pranks that break the monotony of road trips and the day-to-day routine. One of my better early ones involved our center fielder Nelson Mathews, a big, tall, skinny kid from the midwest somewhere who went on to become a schoolteacher. If Nelson ever played regularly, I'm sure he'd have broken Reggie's record for strikeouts. A marginal player, Nelson nonetheless was fun to be around. So on one road trip Nelson and I crowded into one of those photo booths you've seen at bus and train stations. Well, no sooner do we get the pictures than Nelson and I head over to the lunch counter at the train station. I turned up my collar, put on a hat, and pulled out my deputy sheriff badge from my wallet. (I'm an honorary deputy sheriff in Hertford.)

Behind the counter is an older woman taking orders. I flip out my badge and, at the same time, present a black-and-white of Mr. Matthews.

"'Scuse me, ma'am," I begin. "Have you ever seen this man before?"

A look at the picture. Then, slowly, a turn to the right. Then back again, catching a quick glance of the hardened criminal? escaped convict? sitting right in front of her face.

Another quick look at my badge. Another look at Nelson.

"Oooh!" she gasped. "He's . . . ah . . . no I've never . . . ah." She gave a little moan and ran to the back.

Well, naturally, Nelson and I laughed ourselves silly. Until, that is, I turned around. Now somebody was following *me*. I dumped the hat, turned the collar down, and ditched the badge in my back pocket. Enough 007 stuff for one day.

"The only zoo in the major leagues."

I was never quite sure what the writer who wrote that meant. It's certainly possible that it had something to do with Mr. Finley's management style. More than likely, though, it was those monkey cages in left, the rabbits roaming the outfield before the game, the pigeons, pheasants, and sheep penned up in right.

The main attraction in this early version of *Animal House*, however, had to be the mule. Not any mule. Charlie O., the mule. As handsome and impressive an animal, pound-for-pound (of which there were 1200), as you'll ever hope to see. Charlie O. (the owner) knew the value of Charlie O. (the mule) and treated him like royalty. Four-star hotels, air-conditioned travel trailers (with piped in stereo), a huge silver bucket for food.

Of course, I've got to admit it: The mule *did* draw bigger crowds.

Before home games, Charlie O. would stand proudly along the third base line, fans lining up to pet or ride him. During the games, the rule was we had to ride Charlie O. in from the bull pen. Fifty bucks a ride. (As many times as guys like Drabowsky and Segui pitched, they should have retired millionaires.) I rode Charlie O. just once, looking over my shoulder the whole time, waiting for one of my bull pen buddies to shoot that mule in the ass with a slingshot.

Charlie O. (the owner) had this Rule about the mule. Actually, he had a lot of rules, but the golden one stipulated that whenever we came into a town for the first time, the mule would hold something similar to a press conference, like he was Mr. Ed or something. Charlie O. (the owner) would hold the press conference on a platform specially built so Charlie O. (the mule) could satisfy curiosity-seekers. Usually this bit of blarney took place right outside our hotel. We all stood there like good soldiers, smiling away, wondering what the hell we'd gotten ourselves into. This was not a voluntary act, either. One time John (Doc) Blanchard, a veteran catcher just traded from the classy Yankees, balked at standing around passing out Charlie O. paraphernalia like he was some campaign volunteer: Charlie O. bats, Charlie O. hats, Charlie O. pins, Charlie O. pencils. Talk about feeling like an ass.

Charlie O. (the owner) didn't want to hear any lip. Not from Doc. Not from *anyone*. "Tell Blanchard if he doesn't want to do it, he can not do it down in Des Moines."

Another time I was standing on the platform outside the fabulous Plaza Hotel in New York with Lachemann and Lockwood when a kid comes up and says, "I'd like five bats." The rules, according to Mr. Finley, were one bat per customer. "Fuck it," said Lachemann, lapsing into his all time favorite four-letter word. "Let's get rid of these fucking things and check into the hotel."

Suddenly, Charlie O. (the owner) appeared, barely missing the five-for-one deal Lachemann had just completed. He stared a hole through Lockwood. "Son," says Charlie, "you're gonna have to come down off that platform and get the bats from the players like everyone else."

Lachemann about died. "Holy shit," he said, "Charlie signed that guy for $125,000 last year, and he doesn't even know who he is."

I'd wager one pitcher most of you don't know much about is Buschhorn. Too bad. Don was so skinny we started calling him "Chicken Breast," but believe me, there was nothing funny about the way he pitched. Live fastball. Best curve on the ball club. At the beginning of the year, to the envy of all us bonus babies, he was penciled in as the fifth starter. He held his own for about his first ten games, until one rainy day in Minnesota. For some reason, just before his scheduled start, Don got a bad case of cold feet. Maybe it was the weather, dreary and dark; more than likely it had something to do with the prospect of pitching against a Twins lineup that included Harmon Killebrew, Bob Allison, Rod Carew, and Tony Oliva. Whatever, Don just didn't want to pitch. "My arm's hurt," he told me.

"What happened?" I said.

"I hurt it toting my suitcase."

Pretty lame, I thought, but what the heck. The weather was so terrible, chances were one in a million we'd play. "But if you tell them you're hurt, you won't pitch again for another three, four days."

"I'm gonna tell 'em," said Don. And he did. Shortly thereafter he injured his hamstring something terrible and never pitched again. His career was over at the age of twenty-one.

So a couple of days later, with Buschhorn on the back burner, I got the nod; my first start. It came against Detroit, the nucleus of the team that would win a World Series in 1968 already in place and playing together.

What Finley did for me that night I'll never forget. Charlie could be so thoughtful, so gracious when the mood struck him. In this case, he knew my parents would be sitting on pins and needles waiting to know how I'd pitched. So what did Finley do? He called them on the phone and held the receiver next to the radio. He told them they could listen to the game as long as they liked. He was picking up the bill.

Can't say I made "Ma Bell" much money that night. Not that I didn't get support. The A's scored six runs in the first inning—a one-inning season record for the club—and two more in the second to stake me to a cozy 8–0 spread. Victory number 1 was mine. Unfortunately, I lasted only two innings and two batters into the third as the Tigers rallied for six runs of their own. We won the game, but I ended up with a no-decision.

Five days later I got another chance. This time it was against Sudden Sam McDowell, just twenty-two years old, already leading the league in strikeouts. I fell behind 2–0 after four innings (no) thanks to homers off the bats of Rocky Colavito and Fred Whitfield. That's how it ended: 2–0. I pitched well, but not well enough. My first decision would be recorded on the losing side of the ledger.

Back to the bull pen.

I didn't start again until early July, losing another game and having no-decisions in two others. Then I won my first game. It was part of a historic (or so it seemed at the time) doubleheader sweep of the Red Sox in Boston. My teammates, unbelievably, staked me to an 8–1 lead after three innings in Fenway. I withstood a Tony Conigliaro grand slam homer (the only grand slam I allowed in fifteen seasons) to finally break into the win column.

By this time I had been around the league a couple of times and felt like I belonged. But my apprenticeship, my dues paying, was far from over. One of the biggest lessons I learned came courtesy of senior umpire Ed Runge. "You'll like this guy, Cat," my teammates told me the first time Runge was behind the plate. "He gives you everything."

Great. A friend in high places. I fired my first pitch, a fastball, right down the middle.

"Ball," screamed Runge, yanking off his mask like someone had just yelled "Fire!" He stared out at the mound, begging me to argue. I didn't say a word.

Another pitch. Another fastball right down Main Street.

"Ball two!"

Same yank. Same look. Still I don't say boo.

We play the same game a couple of more times—me throwing strikes, Runge playing hard to please—and still I don't let out a peep. A few weeks later Runge is set to go behind the plate again. Before the game, we happened to meet.

He gives me a quick once over. "I see you don't argue with umpires, kid."

"No, sir," I said.

A smile. "It's a good thing."

From then on I was a card-carrying member of the Ed Runge Club. Anything close was a strike. I'd passed the test.

You might want to circle August 15 on your sports calendar. That was the day in 1965 that Lew Krausse returned to Kansas City. You may remember Lew: tall, brown hair, as fine a pitcher as there was in the league when he put his mind to it. And, oh yes, may I also add one of the wildest, craziest guys ever to grace the game. Not life-threatening crazy. More like a party-till-you-drop kind of guy.

A bit of background: Lew, I discovered, was one of the biggest bonus babies of us all. He had signed for $125,000 out of high school in Media, Pennsylvania, making it to the majors at the age of eighteen. Then, in his first start, he pitched a masterpiece, a three-hit shutout. Later Lew had a hard time and was shipped back to the minors for "seasoning" most of the next four years. So when Lew arrived in '65, he was twenty-two, three years my senior, and much wiser in the ways of the world than me—quiet, shy, speak-only-when-spoken-to me.

So Lew took it upon himself to—how shall I say it?—broaden my horizons. We ended up rooming together in Kansas City at the Bellrive Hotel, which I guess is best described as part boarding house and part rest home with room service. The best part about the Bellrive, other than its location (five minutes from the ballpark) and the bartender who knew the importance of a cold beer or a stiff scotch and water, was the rent: C-H-E-A-P.

Occasionally, as can happen when you've just turned nineteen and have Krausse as a companion, you come into conflict with various rules and regulations. Like the one on a sign posted outside the back door of the Bellrive, the one that read DOOR WILL BE LOCKED AT 11 O'CLOCK. First time we noticed it, the hour was closer to two and neither Krausse nor I wanted any part of the front door. Not in our condition.

"Cat," he said, "we just have to set a precedent around here. We're not going to walk around front."

So we just tore the door, an old metal thing, right off its hinges.

Next night, the door's been replaced. The sign now read: THE DOOR WILL BE CLOSED AT MIDNIGHT. Aha, an extra hour. Still not enough time. We were forced to employ the same removal procedure.

Next morning, a tap-tap-tap on our door. It's the hotel manager, a wry smile on his face.

"Here, you may need this," he says, handing us each a set of keys. "Thought you might want to know someone kicked the back door in last night. Here's a couple of spare keys in case you need them."

Another one of the truly redeeming qualities about the Bellrive had to be bellhop Tommy Shine. "Shine," we'd mumble into the phone after a long night on the town, "get your ass up here and get all the ice water you can get your hands on. And aspirin. Right now." Got so we had Shine so well trained we stopped having to call him. Which took a lot of pressure off our throbbing heads. Around noon, we'd open our door and, sure enough, there'd be a pitcher of ice water, a newspaper, and some aspirin. Now *that's* what I call room service.

Of course, Krausse wasn't alone in his efforts to show me a good time. Other members of that social society included Green and Lindblad. Lindblad, I quickly learned, had never sat still for more than a minute in his life. He was *always* up to something. And Green? The ultimate instigator. Think of a track starter and you begin to develop a sense of Green. He'd bring everybody together, get us into position to play, and then, as soon as the pistol was fired and we were off and running, Dick would slip away. He never missed a curfew in his life. Two minutes before the witching hour he'd be laughing, joking around, right in the middle of whatever we were doing. A minute later he was gone. To this day Green, now the president of a thriving moving and storage company in Rapid City, South Dakota, denies any knowledge of our missions. "I wasn't the source of anything," he says, laughing. "It's a bum rap. Krausse was the crazy one. Catfish, ah, he'd go along with it. I'd watch on the sidelines." Riiiight, Greenie.

We pulled so many silly stunts—Krausse never met a fire extinguisher he didn't like—that the four of us got something of a reputation among our teammates. It's probably important to note here that we never did anything truly destructive or dishonest. We were just nineteen-, twenty-, and twenty-one-year-old kids having some good clean college-type fun, and no matter how silly we got the night before, we never neglected our conditioning.

I guess you'd have to say our best local hangout had to be The Apartment Lounge. The Apartment was one of those classic bars made comfortable with soft couches and good music. I'd been introduced to "Apartment living," so to speak, by Hawk Harrelson and Luke Appling early in the season. "It's a great place to grab a burger and a beer, soak up some atmosphere," said Hawk.

Hawk immediately took me over to meet the owner Jack Haley, a gregarious ex-ballplayer. No sooner had I shaken Haley's hand when he whispers, "Have a beer if you want, kid, but keep an eye out for the ABC [Alcoholic Beverage Control] guy and stay near the back steps." So there I am, crew cut, underage, fresh off the farm, listening in as Haley tells Harrelson, "Hey, Hawk, there's the guy who said he was going to kill me."

Sure enough, Haley points across the room and says, "Yeah, the guy was in this afternoon and said he was going to put a cigarette out on his girlfriend's face. I told him not to do it. He said he'd be back tonight to kill me. Well, there he is."

Right, and the A's were about to print World Series tickets.

So Hawk, making macho, goes over to this huge man and what you might call intervenes. The guy picks up the six-two Hawk like he's a helium balloon and sets him outside an open window. Now he turns and starts coming toward Jack. Greaaat. I'm the only thing between this giant, Haley, and a chorus of angels. "Hey, Jack," growls the giant, "I'm gonna keel ya."

Well that's all I needed to hear. I reckon there were about ten to twelve steps down those back stairs. I never hit a one of them going down. At the bottom I moved into my Olympic sprint and continued running until my lungs were about to burst. Behind me all I could hear was the sound of heavy breathing. Damn, I thought, the maniac's after *me* now. I tossed a fast glance over my shoulder. It was Jack.

"Jack," I screamed, still at full throttle, "what the hell you come this way for?"

"Hell," he said between strides, "I ain't no damn hero either."

A bedtime story.

Once upon a time there was this pitcher named Krausse. Every night before bed he had this little, oh, ritual. Some folks fluff up their pillows. Others say their prayers. Lew, well, he was a little different. Every night upon his return to the Bellrive he would open our bedroom window, pull out a pistol, and fire two warning shots into the night. That's right, shots. As in, "Hi honey, I'm home," but with a lot more noise. I don't remember where Lew got the gun, just that it was an old .38 special and he loved to take pot shots into the air. I always felt safe, however; Lew was no novice around guns. He knew how to handle them and always made sure he was firing off into thin air. Which was fairly easy, because we lived on the twelfth floor of the hotel, high enough to ensure that nobody would get hurt by a stray bullet. Or so we thought.

Our story picks up with Lew and I struggling home one night around 2 a.m. As we stroll past the front desk, feeling no pain (yes, this time we took the more conventional route), the night manager informs us of a minor change in room assignments.

"There is a big convention in the hotel, guys," he says, "so we had to move your stuff down to the third floor."

"No problem," I say.

Sure enough, Lew gets inside our new room, throws open the window, does his thing, and hits the sack. About 6 a.m. the phone rings. It's Finley. He's so mad he's breathing fire. He wants to speak with Lew. *Now.*

"Do you have a gun?" Finley asks.

I could almost see the wheels in Lew's head grinding through the fog, a scotch and soda mist if memory serves me right.

"Yes, yes I do, Mr. Finley," Lew says.

"Did you shoot it off last night?"

"Yes, sir, I did."

Lew said Finley never hesitated. "You get that gun, and you get your ass out of that hotel," he ordered. "You get down to the train station and put it in one of those storage lockers. When you get back home, call me."

Lew flew out the door—the first time he'd seen daybreak since high school, I think. By the time Lew got back, our room was crawling with cops. Detectives, lab technicians, forensics guys dusting the windows for fingerprints, checking trajectories.

"What happened?" said Lew. "What're you guys looking for?"

One of the officers spoke up. "Well," he said, "last night there were two shots fired into the Phillips Petroleum Building next door. Seems two cleaning ladies were up there and . . . well, they had to dive for cover when these bullets . . . bing . . . bing . . . bing . . . began ricocheting all over the place.''

"Oh," said Lew.

Oh. Lew evidently had forgotten to factor in our nine-floor drop; it also didn't help matters much that Phillips was having labor problems and the cops had to spend time checking out the disgruntled union angle. Lew could have been in big trouble, but as it was, after they discovered Lew was at fault, the cops let him off with a stern warning.

But Finley wasn't finished with either of us. He decided then and there that he had better keep a closer eye on his two young pitchers. A private investigator, unbeknownst to us, was hired to shadow our off-field activities. It wasn't until the end of the season, when Finley called us both into his office, that we knew we'd been tailed.

"Boys, I don't know if you know this, but I've had a private detective following you for a while now," said Finley. "Thought you might like to know his findings. He says in his report here you two didn't do anything he felt was out of the ordinary for nineteen- and twenty-two-year-old single males who are professional athletes." A short pause. "But he did say he hated to see his assignment end. Said he was having the time of his life!"

OTHER VOICES—LEW KRAUSSE

Lew Krausse, forty-four, is now the president and co-owner of Professional Metals, an aluminum, steel, and brass distributor in Holt, Missouri. He says he learned his lessons from his crazy days in Kansas City, that with a little more discipline he'd have gotten a lot more out of his talent. He respects the moves Finley made. With all that said, he leaps wholeheartedly into the life and times of Krausse and Hunter.

"I had been around a lot longer than Cat had. He was really naive in the beginning on what to do and what not to do. The first time I saw him I thought, 'My god, this is the biggest hick I've ever seen.' But everyone protected him. As I recall when he came to the big leagues, he had one J.C. Penney sport coat. Before the

year was over, I had him in sharkskin suits and alligator loafers.
I know if he went back to North Carolina looking like that they
would have thought he was a big hood from Chicago.

"If we were sitting in the bull pen and the manager wasn't
around, we would have our game plan—what we were going to
do that night, where we were going to go—and nine times out of
ten it was The Apartment Lounge. Scotch and water was all Cat
ever drank. He was as dedicated to scotch and water as Cutty
Sark ever was. The Apartment was truly a great place; every
athlete who ever came into Kansas City hung out there.

Aside from The Apartment Lounge, Charlie O., and the games
themselves, the biggest source of entertainment had to be the
animals. Nothing was sacred. One time Greenie brought a goat
into the locker room and left poor little Billy in Luke Appling's
office. Goat shit everywhere. Another time at the Washington,
D.C. Zoo, our bull pen catcher Phil Roof took a direct spit in
the eye, a counterattack from a pissed-off baboon at whom Roof
had been tossing cherry pits.

We had the most fun with the monkeys. Every day they got
fed by their trainers and then again by us. Our feedings
consisted of a steady diet of pills—vitamin A, vitamin C,
greenies, any pill we could beg, borrow, or steal from trainer
Billy Jones. Of course, not even Roof was dumb enough to stick
his hand into the monkey cage, so we improvised, combing the
outfield grass before the game for grasshoppers. From there it
was easy: Stuff a pill or two down the hopper's throat and toss it
in the monkey cage. See the monkey catch the grasshopper. See
him snap off its head. See him eat the body and throw the rest
away. Wait five minutes. See the monkey go ape shit, running
and screaming all over his cage. (Talk about hopped up.)

Despite all this monkey business, I proved to management
and myself that I could pitch in the major leagues. By winning
three of my last five decisions, I ended the year 8–8, encourag-
ing for a nineteen-year-old kid on a team that lost so many
games.

The highlight of the final month of the season had to be
watching the immortal Satchel Paige in action. In mid-
September, Mr. Finley coaxed the fifty-nine-year-old Negro
League star out of retirement, ostensibly to qualify for his
pension, but also to put some fannies in the seats. So it was, on

September 25, 1965 that we had Satchel Paige Night in Kansas City. In honor of the occasion, Finley—who never missed a trick—had a rocking chair and a nurse waiting for Satch when he walked down to the bull pen to warm up.

I still have a picture of me sitting on Satch's lap, the youngest and oldest pitchers in the major leagues that season. It was truly an experience to be around a master like Satch; Lache, who warmed up Satch, and I sat in the pen and talked about the old days, how Satch never got a rubdown in his life, how he just sat right down under a boiling hot shower and let the water wash away all his aches and pains. And what a night it was! Satch and his signature ''hesitation'' pitch stood the Red Sox on their ears. He allowed just one hit in three innings, a harmless opposite-field single by Carl Yastrzemski. We should all grow old so gracefully.

5

CATTIN' AROUND

I don't remember now whose bright idea it was to send the four of us to the winter ball in Caracas, Venezuela, but it's safe to say that South America will never be the same.

Shortly after the '65 season, Krausse, Lindblad, Lachemann, and I arrived in that capital city just in time to find ourselves smack-dab in the middle of an election campaign. Free or otherwise we weren't quite sure. All we knew was that the local government seemed to have cornered the market on machine guns. Everywhere we looked—the supermarket, street corners —soldiers stood stiff-backed, machine guns at their sides. They even had guards standing at both ends of our dugout. For safety, they said. Ours or theirs? Who knew?

I guess that in a lot of ways Caracas represented my sophomore year in college, having just completed my freshman, that is, rookie, year in Kansas City. Like fraternity brothers, we all lived together in a two-story apartment complex, subsisting on cold beer and warm takeout, ignoring the local sights in favor of spending every spare moment at the *Valle Ariba,* an exclusive country club nestled at the foot of the local mountains. Golf and swimming in the morning. A return to the city for ball games and for beer drinking at night. Not a bad life, actually.

There were a couple of problems, however. As I said, the political climate was pretty hot; the actual climate was even hotter. I thought the sun shined in Hertford, but as I quickly found out, there's sun, and then there's *sun.*

On my first off day I ventured over to the *Valle Ariba* to catch some rays. I figured I'd spent my whole life outside, baking in a southern sun, how much different could this be? *Very* different, as it turned out. By the time I got back from the club, my skin felt like it was a five-alarm fire, broiled and blistered beyond belief.

"Here, try this," said Lindblad, tossing me a jar of Noxema. I slabbed the whole jar of white cream on my lobster-red burns. I looked like a mummy. Unfortunately, I didn't sleep like one, I tossed and turned all night.

Naturally, I was scheduled to pitch the next day. I barely survived the cab ride—three hours of bumps and shakes—to Valencia only to discover greater torture in trying to pitch. I felt paralyzed. Valencia hitters were ripping balls into everywhere but orbit. Between innings Lachemann cornered me in the dugout. "Why don't you just stay in here," he said. "You're throwing all of about seventy-eight miles an hour."

"Am I gettin' 'em out?"

"Yeah. By the grace of some fuckin' Venezuelan god."

"Then leave me alone."

Of course, that was too much to ask of Lachemann. He kept coming to the mound reminding me to start throwing the ball harder.

"Lache," I said, in absolutely no mood for conversation. "Just get your ass back behind the plate and catch. I'm doing the best I can."

OTHER VOICES—RENE LACHEMANN

Rene Lachemann, the barrel-chested first base coach for the Oakland A's, sits in the visitor's dugout at Tiger Stadium, chewing a cigar stub. Ten minutes earlier Lachemann had been the butt of a well-played clubhouse prank involving the disappearance of a turkey sandwich. Lachemann, it seems, had been dreaming of the sandwich the entire time he was shagging batting practice only to discover, upon his arrival in the locker room, that said sandwich had disappeared.

"Now I'm pissed," muttered Lachemann at the discovery of the theft. Then louder, for all to hear, "Someone stole my mother-fuckin' turkey sandwich." He turned instantly to face a snickering circle of A's—potential suspects each and every one. "Okay," roared Lachemann. "Who was it?"

A small smile came to the face of A's reserve outfielder and designated hitter Steve Henderson. Lachemann caught it. "Henderson, you mother fucker," he screamed. "How can you do this to me? I picked you up last year, took you to Venezuela, took you through fuckin' rehab, and you steal my fuckin' turkey sandwich."

Henderson was pleading innocent just as Oakland manager Tony LaRussa was strolling past. "Hey, Lache," said LaRussa, clearly in on the ruse, "why don't you check their breath? We'll hold them down if you open them up." Seconds later LaRussa returned, red hat in hand. The white lettering read, "Rene Lachemann Fan Club." LaRussa pulled the cap off his palm to reveal—voilà!—one missing sandwich.

"This yours?" asked LaRussa.

Lachemann's mood mellowed. "Sorry, Hindu," he said, employing Henderson's nickname. "You weren't really trying to fuck with me were you?"

After devouring the sandwich, Lachemann smoked his cigar and talked about Caracas in 1965.

"I don't know how we got back alive," he laughs. "God, we did some crazy things down there. Every fuckin' Saturday morning some guy would come down the street selling something. We'd have gotten home about three or four in the morning, and by nine he'd be out there selling drinks or something. We lived on the second story of this apartment complex. Every time he came by one of us would yell, 'Here he comes again. Who's going to get him this time?' And we'd bomb away with a beer bottle. He'd look up at the balcony, start screaming in Spanish. We'd go after him again. Bang. He hated us.

"Since I speak Spanish, I had to do a lot of the talking. Lindblad had his nose pressed in the Spanish-American dictionary the whole time, but by the time he had figured out what to say, it was too late. One time we had to take a cab somewhere. Big fuckin' cabdriver. I was in the front; Cat, Lindblad, and Krausse were in the back. We got in some traffic jam on the way somewhere. Now Lindblad, the original Ugly American, loved to call the locals pot lickers. So he yells up to me, 'Hey, Lache, tell this fuckin' pot licker to get his fuckin' ass in gear.' The big guy turns around and says, 'I'd watch your mouth.' Lindblad about crawled under the seat. He didn't say another fuckin' word the rest of the fuckin' trip."

*   *   *

After three weeks in Caracas I'd have paid the club to send me home. I was homesick, tired of all the South American "customs" and itching to start hunting some deer. But contracts are contracts. I couldn't very well just up and leave. So I did what any able-bodied ballplayer would do. I faked an injury and headed straight to the doctor's office.

Now when I say doctor, I mean a local guy who spoke no English and probably got his medical degree by mail. I just figured my only chance to communicate was to scream bloody murder every time he touched my arm. It worked. Sort of. Two hours later I had my passport home—my right arm in a cast from elbow to wrist.

"What the fuck happened to you?" yelled Krausse when I walked in the door. Lindblad and Lache couldn't even talk, they were laughing so hard.

"Go ahead and laugh," I said, "but I'll be outta here and you won't."

"Forget that," said Krausse. "Finley'll kill us if he sees you in that sling. Let's go to the ballpark, tell the manager you have a sore arm, and get you sent home."

Well, it wasn't so easy. For two weeks the owner—who had no interest in losing one of his best pitchers—never called the A's. Meanwhile, I walked around wearing a cast in 100 degree weather. Finally, I called one of our scouts, Felix Delgado, and told him that my arm was killing me, that it'd been placed in a cast. "Don't worry," said Delgado. "By the time the playoffs come around, your arm will be fine."

Playoffs? I told Felix to screw the playoffs. He'd better get on the horn to Kansas City. I wanted to speak with the A's general manager, Eddie Lopat.

"What's wrong?" asked Eddie.

"My arm's in a cast."

"A *what?*"

"A cast." I didn't tell him it was hurtin'. Only that it was in a cast. No harm, no foul.

"Well then," said Eddie, "get yourself to the airport and come on home."

I left the next morning. Or so I thought. The airport was on the other side of the mountains, and to make sure the cabbie knew what I wanted, I'd said, "airport" in Spanish and began flapping my arms like I was Orville Wright or something. The cabbie nodded. No problem. Home free.

Three hours later the cab was back in front of our apartment complex.

"What are you doing?" Lindblad asked as I walked in.

I was hotter than the day I'd needed all that Noxema. "Will you please come downstairs and tell this sumbitch where the hell the airport is!"

Paul did exactly that, and the next day I was winging my way home, whispering a grateful *hasta la vista* to Caracas.

6

THE DARK AGES

In 1966, in our annual rite of spring, Finley fired his manager. This time Haywood Sullivan got the ax; Finley replaced him with former San Francisco skipper Alvin Dark. Winner of the Rookie of the Year Award in the National League in 1948, Dark had gone on to play thirteen very productive years with the New York Giants and four other clubs at shortstop, serving as captain of two pennant-winning Giants teams. As a manager he'd led San Francisco to the National League pennant in '62 before getting fired two years later in something of a mild sex scandal.

You see, Alvin had become a born-again Baptist, spreading the word of God in and out of the clubhouse, a practice that, frankly, rubbed a lot of guys the wrong way. Then one day Alvin fell in love with an airline stewardess. She was married; so was Alvin. When that love—and their divorces—became public, Alvin was called everything from a hypocrite to a fake. He lost his job in the process.

In spring training he proved to be just as devout, working up to a real fervor at times. He wanted to get "close" to his players, be their friends. Alvin's idea of managing was to be ten different places doing twenty different things all at the same time. Playing cards with the coaches. Teaching the pitchers. Coaching the infielders. As we later found out, he tried to do too much, and it hurt us. But now, in the first blush of spring, you couldn't help but like his enthusiasm. Especially in contrast to the likes of McGaha.

I certainly had no complaints. I threw so well that spring that Alvin—"from his heart"—praised me to high heaven. "Another Robin Roberts," he called me, rewarding my performance with an Opening Day assignment against the defending American League Champion Minnesota Twins. Four hits and eight innings later, however, I was 0–1, on the short end of a 2–1 ball game. It would be just the first of fourteen losses in our first seventeen games.

The problem was this: We may have switched managers, but our lineup hadn't changed. All we could hope for was improvement, a gradual bettering of the ball club. Campy probably epitomized our problems better than any other player. By now, it was easy to see, he was developing into a dynamic offensive player. Playing shortstop was another matter. Campy was so tight at times, so heavy-handed, so stiff in his fielding movements, that we took to calling him Iron Hands. I remember one game a year earlier when I'd come in to relieve Wes Stock. The first pitch I throw is a ground ball right at Campy. Olé—right through his legs. Next batter, another pitch, another ground ball to short, another olé. Now here comes the manager to take *me* out. "What the hell you doing?" I yelled, pointing behind me. "Why don't you take *him* out?"

Still, you had to laugh. Campy was one funny fella—whether he knew it or not. He loved to call me "Fish"—it came out Fiissssh—which I heard for the first time after Big Frank Howard hit a shot to short that took one bounce and almost burned a hole through Campy's chest. I think the ball was gloved by our left fielder on one bounce.

The next time Howard lumbered up to the plate, Campy was at the mound in a flash. "Hey, Fiissssh," he said. "I want you to pitch this guy away. Waay, waaay, awaaay."

I should have listened more closely because by mid-June I was suffering from symptoms (chronic sore neck, complete loss of control) of the "Dreaded Dinger Disease." Never heard of the DDD? Pity. It's the number one killer of pitchers of all ages. It can strike at any time, especially—and here's the twist—when you're throwing them.

Pitching to Howard could be particularly dangerous. One night he hit a shot off me that I swear landed in some third world country. We're talking time travel here. Then, in June, the Twins tagged me for three homers in one inning (they hit five overall in that inning, tying a major league record).

But you know what? The best way to combat DDD is to face it head-on. I knew my success from high school on up had always been based on one factor—throwing strikes. Everything flowed from there. Throw a strike, get in front of the hitter, and make him hit your pitch. Simple as one, two, three. Problems started when I got behind in the count. Or, as happens, when I missed on the edge by an inch or six. Now what was supposed to be *my* pitch was suddenly becoming *their* pitch. One swing later my neck'd snap back and I'd end up watching fireworks fill the evening sky.

Take it from someone who knows (after all, don't I own the American League record for most home runs allowed, career, with 374), home runs are part of the game. The only way to beat DDD is to avoid walks and pitch according to circumstance. Above all, never let it get to you. Look at it this way: So the guy hit a home run. He's off the bases. Now work on the next guy. Some members of the media never fully grasped that concept, much as I tried to explain it. Consequently, the home run became the catch-all question of my career. "What about all the home runs, Cat?" they'd ask.

The most stinging example of this kind of mind set popped up one day after I pitched a two-hitter in Oakland. I thought I'd done a helluva job, giving up a single run on a home run. After the game our announcer Monte Moore had me on his postgame show. His first question? "Jim, what about that home run?"

My blood roared to a quick boil. I don't know, I guess after pitching a two-hitter Monte might have at least waited until the *second* question to talk home runs. "Well, Monte," I said, biting off the words, "he didn't get a cherry now did he."

Monte's mind went blank for a minute. His mouth stopped working. The only thing coming out was "aba aba abaa . . ."

"What I meant Monte," I said, saving his ass, "is that's not the first one I ever gave up."

Bingo. Monte was breathing again. "Oh yeah, Jim, that's right, that's right." I'm sure his audience could hear the sigh of relief.

So here's my final answer: What about 'em? The two guys in front of me on the all-time home runs allowed list are Warren Spahn and Robin Roberts, and, as far as I can tell, they're resting right comfortably in baseball's Hall of Fame.

Although we continued to lose in '66 (another eighty-six defeats), the one thing we never lost was, thankfully, our sense of humor. Hard to believe, I know, but it gets pretty boring in the bull pen at times. Staring at the same faces. Listening to the same old lies. Even monkey tricks get stale after awhile.

So we—and by that I mean Drabowsky, Krausse, Lachemann, and me—started reaching out and touching others. Our families. Our friends. Girls back home. Long-lost relatives. Take-out restaurants. All courtesy of the bull pen phone. You name it, we dialed it. Most times, I'd call home. My mom would answer. "Jimmy," she'd say, "where are you?"

"In the bull pen, Momma. How's Daddy and my dogs?"

One time, a couple of seasons later, I was working on a shutout against the Orioles in the sixth or seventh when the phone rang. The voice was muffled, but I'm told the words rang clear: "Get Krausse up." So Lew starts loosening up, Alvin figuring Lew's just getting some extra work between starts. But then Lew keeps throwing. The phone rings again. It's Dark.

"What the hell's Krausse doing? Sit him down."

Down he goes. A couple of minutes later, I'm still cruising, another call. "I thought I told you to get Krausse up. Hurry up, git him up!"

No sooner does Krausse begin throwing than the phone rings again. It's Dark again.

"What the hell is going on out there?" he says. "I told you to sit him *down!*"

We found out later that the calls were coming not from Dark, obviously, but from right field and the Orioles' bull pen. Some Polish prankster by the name of Drabowsky.

You can call this story Cat and Dogs. I've always loved animals, dogs in particular. I say that because in 1966 some fan sent me a beautiful Irish setter puppy, AKC, papers, the whole bit. They gave it to me right before a flight to Washington, the closest point to Hertford, and since we had a charter, the dog had the run of the plane. Right after we landed in D.C., half the team headed for this famous barbecue place right across from the airport. We got about fifteen orders of ribs, french fries, chicken. Cases of beer. Then we all sat down on the floor of our room at the Shoreham Hotel. The dog digging right in with the rest of us—french fries, ribs, and chicken.

"Cat," said Krausse, "that dog is gonna have to take a shit real soon, and I don't want him to shit in our room. It'll smell for three days."

Well, no sooner had Lew spoken than the puppy shit a

pyramid about six inches high and four inches in diameter, right in the middle of the room. Now what?

The light went on in both our heads at about the same time. Wasn't Harrelson staying right next door? I took a piece of that cardboard dry cleaners use in shirts and scooped up the puppy shit. Fueled by more than a couple of beers, I calmly walked out our door, faced Harrelson's door, and fired away. Bull's-eye. A perfect strike. Puppy shit went everywhere.

I went back and dialed room service. "Hi, this is Hawk Harrelson," I said. "Could I get a bucket of ice sent to my room immediately."

"Certainly, Mr. Harrelson."

Certainly, Mr. Harrelson. So down the hallway comes this unsuspecting busboy, whistling away, carrying a bucket of ice. He gets right up to Hawk's door . . . he starts to knock . . . the next thing we see, the busboy's down, ice everywhere, shit all over the place.

It took Harrelson about five seconds to figure out who did what.

The last story is semisymbolic, because up until the middle of the year we played like shit. Then all of a sudden the A's got it together. Jack Aker had developed into a solid stopper and Campy and the newly acquired (a common phrase under Finley) Danny Cater moved up among the league leaders in hitting, as we returned home to—what's this?—big crowds and sixth place.

Me? I was still struggling, a .500 pitcher (8–8) hurt by the home run. But Krausse and the others were picking up the slack. One of the hottest pitchers was Odom, just now returning to Kansas City after a two-year absence. Moon had signed just before me in '64, a high school superstar in Georgia, where he had a 42–2 record with eight no-hitters, leading his team to back-to-back titles. (Finley signed him personally.) So when I was recovering from my shotgun accident, Moon was already firing blanks in the big leagues.

Fact is, he almost pitched a no-hitter in his second start. Would have had one if the official scorer had had any guts. I know. I charted the game. Moon threw an unbelievable 209 pitches, allowing just two cheap infield "hits," one that our third baseman threw about 6000 feet above the first baseman's head, the runner still three feet from the bag. "Base hit," said the official scorer. "Bull-shit," said the ballplayers.

Moon started five times that year before being sent down for experience. By '66, he was really ready, and he proved it out the chute, going eight innings in a 2–1 decision over Detroit. I've always felt that Moon had the best stuff of any pitcher I've ever seen. Anyone. His ball moved all over the lot; catchers cringed when it came time to catch him. Moon would win sixteen games in '68, fifteen a year later, and in thirteen seasons was 84–85 with two All Star appearances. I've always felt that he was something of a "half-Moon." If only he could have controlled his pitches more. Hit the spots. He would have won dozens more games. But, in the end, he couldn't control the movement of his pitches, and it cost him.

Last summer I read where Moon was having trouble. Something about putting a gun to his wife's head during a domestic argument. So I called him.

"What the heck's going on, Moon?" I asked.

"Got into a little bit of trouble, you know," he allowed, pausing before he added, "I thought everybody had forgotten about me."

I told him nobody had forgotten anyone, which made him feel good. Then I talked to his wife, so things must be looking up because Moon and his wife were back together.

But no matter how good Moon looked the summer of 1966, he too was overshadowed, blown away by one of those certifiable phenoms who arrives every summer. You know what I mean. One year it's a Valenzuela. The next year a Gooden. The next, a kid named Clemens. But I'll tell ya, back in the summer of '66, the name was Nash. Jim Nash.

A big, strappin' country kid with fire in his eyes and a fastball to match, Jim (Jumbo) Nash arrived from Mobile in July, so poor we had to take a collection in the clubhouse to pay his cab fare. But he quickly made others pay. His calling card: that fabulous fastball and, at the time, pinpoint control. When the dust had settled, the twenty-one-year-old Nash had won twelve of his first thirteen decisions and compiled an ERA near 2.00—good enough to win the American League Rookie Pitcher of the Year Award.

I wasn't surprised. I knew from watching Jim back in the Instructional League that he was special, one of those do-it-all kind of guys, the type who can cartwheel across the kitchen, do backflips, and pluck out a tune on a dime-store ukulele. Where did Finley find all these guys?

So it was Nash, Krausse (fourteen wins), and Blue Moon (sixteen wins) making the news. Me? I was treading water, recovering from an appendectomy that kept me out of the lineup until mid-September. I returned just in time to have a hand in our seventh of seven straight wins, a 1–0 shutout of Cleveland. It was all part of my scoreless streak that stretched to 45⅓ innings, just 1⅔ off the American League record. Yes sir, our pitching was coming along just fine. Hitting, too, thanks to Cater, Campy, and Hawk. We ended the year winning fifteen of our last twenty-four games, pushing up into seventh place (ahead of Washington, Boston, and New York). Our seventy-four wins were the most by a Kansas City ball club since 1956.

Want to know truly the most amazing thing about the entire season? Certainly not my 9–11 record and 4.02 ERA in twenty-five starts. No, it was Finley. He hardly said a word the last half of the year. It seemed the more we won, the less he said. Talk about incentives.

The following spring, in 1967, Dark was at it again, praising all of us to high heaven. "I'm just tickled to death, just plain tickled to death," he said. "I've got the greatest bunch of guys I've ever had. I didn't realize there were this many good kids left in the whole world."

Just how good we were, both on and off the field, would be an open question by year's end. *Serious* question. But not now. Now we were *Boy Wonders*. At least that's what the papers called us. A pitching staff averaging just 21.8 years of age and stocked with some of the most impressive arms in the game: *Sports Illustrated*'s preseason cover boy Nash, twenty-two, Odom, twenty-one, Hunter, twenty, Krausse, twenty-three, and Chuck Dobson, twenty-three, on the mend from arm trouble the year before. And in the bull pen, relief ace Aker, twenty-six, who set a league record for saves (thirty-two) in '66.

Yes, for the first time since Finley had shelled out those four million bucks to buy the club, fans in Kansas City had some certifiable hope. And heroes. We even wore white. (So what if it was only on our shoes.) Nash set the tone for all of us in the season opener by stopping the defending World Champion Baltimore Orioles 11–3. Meanwhile, Dark tried to toughen up his "good kids" to show us he was in charge. So it was that Alvin pinch-hit for me in a tie game (2–2) with the bases loaded and nobody out. Not a bad move, except that it was the *second* inning. I was so mad I didn't know what to do. *Should I strangle Alvin and spend the next twenty years of my life in Leavenworth?* Nah. Instead, I just walked over to the stands and handed my helmet, my jacket, and my bat to the nearest fan. "Take them," I said. "I don't need 'em."

I stormed into the dugout, thought better than to fight with the manager, and instead picked up the water cooler and started pounding up the steps leading to the clubhouse. Bam. Bam. Bam. Right up to the top of the stairs before throwing the cooler back down.

The next day I'm running pregame laps and Alvin trots up next to me and just keeps staring at me. He doesn't say a word. Inside the clubhouse Dark tore into me in front of the whole team. "And you, Jim Hunter," he said. "For the way you ran laps today and for the water cooler, that will cost you $250."

"Oh yeah," I answered, "do I get to keep the water cooler?"

Alvin didn't know what to say to that. Just dropped his head for a second, thinking.

Finally, he said, "Yeah, you can have it. For another $250."

Five hundred dollars to a guy making $13,000 was a bit too steep. I told Alvin he could keep the cooler.

By early May, I was 3–1, four-hitting the Orioles and shutting out the Senators 1–0; by mid-June, not long after a new kid named Reggie Jackson had joined our club, I'd already thrown four shutouts and run my personal scoreless innings streak to nearly twenty-six innings. For the second time in three seasons I made the All Star team. When it was over I think folks around baseball got a taste of just what kind of pitcher Catfish Hunter was turning out to be.

I remember the All Star Game like it was yesterday: The standing ovations for Mantle and Mays, bypassed in fan voting but selected to the squad by the managers; fellow All Star pitchers Joel Horlen, Gary Peters, Dean Chance, and Jim

Lonborg; sharing the excitement of the first prime-time TV All Star Game; and finally, fifteen of the best All Star innings—the longest All Star Game to date—ever played.

I made some history, too. Called on to relieve in the bottom of the eleventh, I ended up pitching five full innings, the most by any All Star pitcher since 1956. I'd breezed through the eleventh and twelfth; no small feat against a lineup with the likes of Lou Brock, Willie Mays, Roberto Clemente, Henry Aaron, Orlando Cepeda, Richie Allen, Pete Rose, Willie McCovey, and Bill Mazeroski. In the top of the thirteenth, McCovey doubled to open the inning before being bunted to third. But I buckled down, striking out Allen and coaxing pinch hitter Rose to fly out to center.

Two innings later Boston outfielder Tony Conigliaro robbed Cepeda of a home run to open the inning. I was tiring. My first pitch to the next hitter, Cincinnati Reds' slugger Tony Perez, was a strike. The second one landed 375 feet over the fence in left center for the eventual game-winning homer. Tough luck, everyone said. You did a great job. And I had. In five innings I'd allowed just four hits and struck out four, showing the rest of the country that Catfish was a name they might want to remember, a kid who could compete against the very best.

Speaking of which, it's no deep, dark secret that not every deserving ballplayer makes the All Star team. So it was with a certain "star" out of the midwest, a veteran, who, it turns out, had as much of a cult following as any Cub or White Sox.

Her name was Chicago Shirley.

Shirley was a groupie. Not *any* groupie. A perennial all star, a legend at meeting—and mating—pro athletes of every race, creed, and color. And since Chicago was—and still is—home to American and National League baseball teams as well as the NFL, the NHL, and the NBA, that's a lot of athletes. But Shirley only went for pros. She wouldn't touch a sportswriter or announcer if you paid her. She just loved jocks.

With this in mind, our mission, as Krausse and I accepted it, was to find a way to get a snoopy sportswriter shacked up with Shirley. Naturally, it didn't take long to come up with just the right ruse: We found Shirley and told her a new guy had just come up, a rookie, and, in the immortal words of Krausse, "He's hung like a wild ape."

"You've got to try him out," I said.

"I'll be by," said Chicago Shirley.

We told the unsuspecting writer Shirley had spotted him across a crowded room (actually it was in the hotel bar), and lo and behold, she was just *dying* to meet him.

Well, you can imagine what happened the next day. The reporter started raising hell, cussing us out for setting him up. Then Shirley started up, swearing away, telling us how she never did media guys. Plus, "The guy was like fifty years old," said Shirley. "What are you guys tryin' to pull?"

"Well," said Krausse, "did you kick him out?"

Chicago Shirley let a thin smile cross her lips. "Nah," she said sweetly, "I figured as long as he was here, I might as well take care of him."

One of the things that helped take care of me that year was—I know you're going to find this hard to believe—was . . . bowling. *Bowling?* That's right. I'd bowled a fair amount as a kid. Not well, mind you, but I loved throwin' the ball. In Kansas City I stayed at it, making the discovery that a little pin action the night before I pitched helped stretch out the muscles in my arm. It was a relaxing, refreshing exercise. So for a while there, every night before a home game start I'd slide over to a local alley and roll a game or two. The first time I did it I won the next day. The second time, too. And the third. And the fourth. I think if I'd kept at it, I probably would be carrying a 220 average by now and would've won five or six more Cy Young Awards. Unfortunately, finding bowling alleys near hotels in big cities is about as tough as making the 7–10 split. You miss a lot more than you make. Such is life. My streak ended, on the road, when I couldn't get a game. I certainly hope Dick Weber understands.

At 6:45 on the evening of August 3, TWA commercial flight 85 took off from Boston's Logan Airport on its way to Kansas City. It was an off day for the Kansas City A's, the end of a long, grueling road trip. Before the five-hour flight was over, what happened (or didn't happen) on that plane would become the center of one of the most bizarre baseball stories of the year.

First, some background: Most major league managers permit

the consumption of a certain amount of beer and alcohol on planes. We're supposedly mature, and we deserve to drink a beer or two on occasion. On this occasion, Dark was not one of those managers. I don't remember why—his religious convictions, our poor play—but we flew dry from Boston to Baltimore, the first stop on our flight home.

Fortunately, the stewardesses on the flight, who were based in Kansas City and knew us, had no problem with slipping us a couple of minibottles. By the time we hit pit stop number two in St. Louis, some of the guys were hitting the bottle a bit better than they'd hit the baseball the last few weeks. Nothing outrageous, but by the time we landed in Kansas City, around 10:30, we were all feeling pretty good.

We never heard one word about our actions on the flight until a week later when we were in California to play the Angels. Krausse and I were in our room at the Jolly Roger Hotel in Anaheim when the phone rang. It was you-know-who. Nothing jolly about his disposition.

"Yes, Mr. Finley," said Lew.

"I'm fining you $500 for raisin' hell on the airplane flight."

Lew's mind raced back to our flight from Kansas City to Washington. Then out to L.A. He'd been a choir boy both times. "Hell," he said. "I fell asleep on those plane flights. What are you talking about?"

"Not those flights," said Finley. "The one from Boston to Kansas City a couple of weeks back."

OTHER VOICES—LEW KRAUSSE

"I was single. A couple of the other guys were married. One of the guys, who was in the bathroom with a stewardess, he was married. I was having a bad year, and the way I look at it, Finley needed someone to put the blame on. And, ah, he pinned it on me. We thought the club's broadcaster was involved. He was the guy who opened his mouth and told the whole story—who was drinking, who wasn't. He had the story all screwed up. But he was afraid for his job, and he would have done anything Finley would have asked him to."

* * *

After talking to Lew, Finley immediately issued a statement banning alcohol on all remaining flights, adding, "The Kansas City Athletics will no longer tolerate the shenanigans of a few individuals who obviously do not appreciate the privilege of being treated like gentlemen." A lead balloon if ever there was one. Jack Aker, our player rep, responded by criticizing Finley for his use of "unauthorized go-between spies," who were "undermining the morale of the club." A pretty fair pissin' match.

Dark got drawn into the whole mess when Aker showed him our letter, a response to Finley's crackdown. Dark agreed with our stand but told us exactly what would happen if the letter ever became public. "You're going to get me fired," he said. "But if that's what you guys want to do, go right ahead."

Meantime, Finley was on his way to Washington. He eventually confronted Dark at the Shoreham Hotel and demanded that his manager back the suspension of Krausse. Dark declined, and Finley fired him on the spot. Two hours later, however, Finley had second thoughts and rehired Dark for two more years—with a substantial raise in pay. Charlie then called up a slew of administrators and coaches to celebrate. At that exact moment a beat writer from the *Kansas City Star* asked Finley his reaction to the players' statement.

"What statement?" asked Finley.

The beat writer handed Charlie a copy of our letter.

"Well," said Alvin, looking on, "I'm fired again."

Finley, a very ornery man when he wanted to be, blew a fuse. He started screaming for Aker, who just happened to be out on the town and, in the process of missing curfew by, oh, 2½ hours. When Aker finally wandered in at about 2:30 a.m., Finley roared his demand for a retraction. Aker not-so-politely told Finley to buzz off. By 6 a.m. Dark was fired again, replaced by Luke Appling—the price Dark paid for backing his players. Finley countered with another statement, the one contending that Dark had "lost control of his ballplayers."

So there was Alvin, a good and decent man, a damn good field manager, one of the best, standing in our clubhouse at D.C. Stadium, tears in his eyes, tongue-tied. He loved our team, the guys, truly believing we would win a pennant by 1971. "You're only about two years away," he said. "I really wish I could have stuck around to see you guys win."

Harrelson jumped into the frying pan next. Hawk was so upset at how Finley had handled the Dark matter that he went so far as to call Finley "a menace to baseball." That tore it. When Finley heard that comment, he called up Harrelson in his hotel room and gave him his outright release. A stupid thing to do, really, since he could have traded Hawk—hitting .273 at the time and leading the team in home runs—instead of just giving him his freedom. Within hours Harrelson had agreed to a big bonus deal with the Red Sox. Us? We were shit out of luck. No manager. No first baseman.

A couple of months later, in a decision he now says he'll always regret, Charlie finally made good on all his "move" threats, informing the city that he was not going to renew his stadium lease. That little bit of news touched off a full-scale civic and player revolt. Aker and others vowed to quit if they weren't traded; our fans, such as they were, just stopped caring. It showed. We died in September and ended up 62–99, thirteen games worse than our record the season before. So much for our season of promise.

Me? I'd had a pretty good season. Or so I thought. I won thirteen games and lost seventeen, but my ERA was a sparkling 2.80, fourth best in the league. I started thirty-five times and worked 260 innings. I figured I deserved a raise. A big raise.

After things quieted down a bit, I asked Mr. Finley for more money. I'd made $7000, $9000, and now $13,000 my first three years in the major leagues. It was time to up the ante.

"Your record's not good enough," Finley said.

"Well," I argued, "I agree thirteen and seventeen isn't that great, but Mr. Finley, if you check around, I think you'll find a 2.80 is a pretty good earned run average."

"ERA don't mean shit," said Finley. "You gotta win."

Now what? Just then a thought popped into my head. I hit about .350 that year. Hmmm.

"What about my hitting?" I asked.

"Well, let's take a look at that," Finley said. He pulled out season stats and saw the figure.

"Well, lookey here. You hit way over .300. I'll give you $5000 for that!"

In October the American League owners approved an expansion to twelve teams. Kansas City and Seattle were awarded new franchises. The former Kansas City A's were now headed west to a new city, with a new manager. Out went Appling. In came ex-Chicago Cub coach Bob Kennedy, a rugged ex-Air Force pilot. Ready or not, California, here we come.

7

PERFECTION

Oakland

What I knew about this city, our new home, would fit on the tip of my nose. Oakland was in northern California. It was warm. It was somewhere near San Francisco. So much for AAA travel tips.

I could have cared less about Oakland's ongoing cultural debate with San Francisco, its inferiority complex, its Cinderella–Ugly Stepsister comparisons to the city by the bay. Somebody else's problem. Mine was getting hitters out. And for that, Oakland and the Oakland-Alameda County Coliseum proved the perfect place to play.

Granted, it wasn't the prettiest place in the whole wide world. Not even the whole wide city. A gloomy, gray circle, the Coliseum seemed to swallow up small crowds. And, yep, the park was small—330 feet down the lines, 385 feet in the alleys, and 410 feet to dead center—but so what? I always loved pitching there. The foul ball areas were the biggest in baseball, eating up one would-be souvenir after another. Plus, the ball never carried at night. (Actually, the best time was early afternoon, as Lindblad, Green, reserve catcher Jim Pagliaroni, and I discovered, especially when the ball was smacked with a three-wood and a Titleist at the local driving range, otherwise known as home plate.) We'd blast away day after day, whenever we could beg, borrow, or steal equipment. An ace meant hitting a booming drive straight over second base, clearing a six-foot fence in dead center and up a canyon to the scoreboard. We're talking maybe 440 feet straight up the gut.

Also, accommodations in Oakland provided some peace of mind. Unlike Kansas City, there was an apartment complex close to the park, which brought our wives and team closer together. When we hit the road, Helen, Kathy Lindblad, Nancy Hegan, and Cater Rudi banded together. Shopping, babysitting, even regular Wednesday night bowling. Happy households and a sense of security put our minds at ease, contributing to the togetherness of the team.

Remember where I mentioned small crowds? That's the one thing that wasn't perfect about Oakland. For the first three to four years we played pretty much by ourselves. Heck, we got outdrawn by a World Team Tennis match one night. It got so quiet at times that Bando nicknamed the place the Oakland-Alameda County Mausoleum. And it wasn't like Finley was just sitting on his hands. Hell, he spent more than $1 million to create and install two computer scoreboards. He held every promotional day known to man. Auto Industry Day. Farmer's Day (I did hog calling). Bald-Headed Man's Day. You get the picture.

Problem was, Finley did too much, taking on duties of the general manager, farm director, business manager, and ticket manager. His insistence on running the entire front office hurt our credibility with the fans, whose attitude seemed to be, Hey, win about six straight and we'll catch you on the flip side.

As players, we'd been together long enough now, farm bred and raised, to know it was only a matter of time before we made our move. And time, as our new skipper, Kennedy, said, is "something you can't create." Kennedy was an interesting fella'. For recreation, he spent hours, head tilted skyward, watching jets streak across the sky. I swear Bob knew the make and model (and, at times it seemed, the serial number) of every plane overhead. You'd hear an engine roar, and he'd look up and say, "Oh that's an F-7 Tiger Shark" or something like that.

As a manager, however, we thought sometimes that all the neck-tilting affected his thinking. He was constantly shuffling the lineup (we had seventy-five different lineups in our first eighty regular-season games). And time and time again he'd make wacky moves—bringing in left-handed relievers to face right-handed pinch hitters. But somehow they worked. At least enough to keep Finley off his back.

Kennedy's best asset was his attitude. He loved the game, and that helped bring us together. All we needed was time. You could see that just by watching us beat both the American

League Champion Boston Red Sox and the World Champion Cardinals the last week of spring training.

Yes, sir, Oakland was perfect, all right. Just how perfect remained to be seen. And shown.

I started our 1968 season opener in Oakland, a fact quickly lost in the glamour and glitz of a California celebration. In Hertford we dedicate a stadium with a little paint and a preacher. In Oakland, Governor Ronald Reagan threw out the first pitch. Charlie O. (the mule) arrived via police escort. Rick Monday and Bando, no fools, escorted Miss California to home plate. Baseball Commissioner William Eckert spoke. And Charlie O. (the owner) paraded around, proud as a peacock. All 50,000 of us felt a chill as the lights were killed and a lone spotlight in centerfield focused in on the flag. Suddenly, like an encore at those rock concerts, matches were lit all around the park. As we all sang ". . . bombs bursting in air," fireworks exploded into the night sky.

Unfortunately, Baltimore Oriole first baseman Boog Powell set off a few fireworks of his own that night, including a ten-megaton home run. We lost 4–1.

A month later I was right at my familiar .500 figure at 2–2. In my third start, against Cleveland, I'd pitched 6⅔ innings of no-hit baseball before tiring. So my start on May 8, 1968, held promise. I'd face the Minnesota Twins in only the twelfth home game ever played in the Coliseum/Mausoleum. My career record? An iffy thirty-three and thirty-eight. I was twenty-two years old.

It started out like any other game day. I got up at eight, had some breakfast, and lounged around until ten. Then I hit the sack again 'til noon before heading over to the clubhouse for cards and company. I walked into the cage for pregame batting practice around 4:30. Kennedy, however, had other ideas.

"Get outta there," he growled as I stepped into the cage. "Let some real hitters hit."

"Whatya mean?" I asked. "I'm gettin' loose. I'm hitting tonight, right?"

"You can't hit," said Kennedy. "Get out of there. *Now*."

Horseshit, I'm thinking. I've proved I can hit; I'd always taken great pride in my hitting. Hell, in high school I was one of the best hitters on the team. (In the pros, I would actually bang out 149 hits and 6 home runs and knock in 51 runs in fifteen seasons.) So I just grabbed my bat, whipped it up against the cage, and walked out.

Pissed off, I left in a huff and headed for a rubdown. Mentally I went over the Twins' lineup—Carew, Killebrew, Allison, et al. How, if you missed, they could pound the crap out of you.

Lachemann warmed me up. Game time was 6 p.m. Twilight time. The night air was seasonably cool for the 6289 fans in the stands. Out in left was the rookie Rudi, just called up from Vancouver. Early in the season Rudi had been the pet project of Joe DiMaggio, who, in a brilliant move, had been hired back into baseball by you-know-who. DiMaggio was now a full-time coach as well as executive vice president. Except for a brief stint as a spring training instructor for the Yankees, Joltin' Joe hadn't been in baseball in seventeen years. He fell in love with what he saw in the A's—especially the relentless Rudi. "I have become attached to these kids," he said. "I've never seen a group so eager to learn."

OTHER VOICES—JOE RUDI

Two hours before a night game, Joe Rudi, outfield coach for the Oakland A's, sits in the visitor's locker room biting into a Dove Bar. The silver-haired coach is tanned and trim. Carefully, he pulls up his stirrups and slips on uniform number twenty-six. Then he speaks. "Joe D. taught me to go back on the ball," he says. "He would hit fly ball after fly ball directly over my head. He was trying to teach us how to turn, to the outside, and then follow the flight of the ball. A very difficult thing to do. When I first started doing it, the ball would end up twenty feet the other way. I had no idea how to stay in line, how to keep my bearings. Joe was real patient. He taught me how to concentrate on picking the ball off the bat, being ready, like a baserunner, to go in any direction, the importance of being on your toes, getting down, getting the glove out, and fielding the ball in front of you.

"Sure I remember May 8. It was my first day back in the big leagues. I stood out in left, nervous as hell. Cat pitched a

brilliant game. I had to make a tough catch, a sinking, slicing line drive. Got it about knee high.''

My opponent that night was right-hander Dave Boswell—who proved tough, matching zeroes through the sixth. I took a walk to the water cooler in the bottom of that inning. Over my shoulder I could hear Hershberger's voice.

"Didn't someone get on in the early innings?"

"Nope," somebody said.

I scooted on back to my seat at the other end of the bench as quickly as possible. I didn't want to hear any of that conversation. I knew I was pitching a no-hitter. Beyond that, I wasn't sure. I thought maybe I'd walked somebody somewhere. I sat alone as Monday doubled and then took third on a wild pitch. Now it was my turn to hit. In the third inning, still pissed at Kennedy, I'd doubled to right center. This time I scored Monday the best way I could—by beating out a bunt to third.

Sixth inning. No runs. No hits. No runners.

Seventh and eighth. Same empty line. Hard stuff now— fastballs and sliders—on almost every pitch (I would throw only three change ups and one curve all night). Working fast. Painting the black. In the bottom of the eighth I hit again. And hit again. Singling home two more runs to make it 4–0. I was three outs away from history.

OTHER VOICES—HELEN HUNTER

Helen Hunter was sitting in the twenty-seventh row that night. Long before her husband, she realized the significance of his efforts. "I knew all about it," says Helen. "I was sitting with some of the other wives, who were trying to console me. I started to cry at the end of the seventh. I was crying in the eighth, and I was crying at the end of the ninth. I was really excited. They knew what I was going through."

In Hertford, Abbott and Lillie Hunter sat huddled together in their bedroom, ears pressed to the radio.

In the front room, brother Ray, a radio inches away from his ear, couldn't stand the suspense anymore. He ran into his parents' room.

"Mommy, Daddy, Jimmy's pitching a perfect game!"

"Hope it continues," said Abbott Hunter.

Ninth inning.

John Roseboro at the plate. Ground out.

Pinch hitter Bruce Look is next. He goes down on strikes, my tenth strikeout of the evening.

Pinch hitter Rich Reese is announced in place of relief pitcher Ron Perranoski.

In Raleigh, North Carolina, on the campus of North Carolina State, Francis Combs raced out to his car to listen to the final batter.

At six-three, 200 pounds, Reese was one of the best utility players in the game, perhaps the premier left-handed pinch hitter in the American League; he was eight for thirteen off the bench in September the season before.

Fastball.

Reese fouled it off. Strike one.

Fastball. Low and inside. Ball one.

Fastball. Same spot. Ball two.

Fastball. Swing and miss. Strike two.

One pitch away.

Slider. It knifed through the strike zone, cutting the plate in two.

"Ball three," said umpire Jerry Neudecker.

I was going to have to earn this no-hitter the hard way.

Nothing but heaters now; I knew I could get them over. Reese wouldn't budge.

Three and two.

Fastball. Fouled back.

Fastball. Fouled back again.

Another fastball. Another foul.

One more time. Another fastball—another foul ball.

I stared straight past Reese, looking for the sign from my catcher, Pagliaroni. He flashed for another fastball. Taking no chances now. The windup . . . the pitch . . .

Foul ball. The fifth in a row.

In Hertford and Raleigh, North Carolina, the volume knobs on the radios were turned up.

One more pitch. One more fastball. Reese swung—and missed! Strike three! On my one hundred seventh and last pitch of the night, I'd earned my no-hitter.

But wait. Suddenly here's Bando sprinting over from third. Screaming, "Perfect game! Perfect game!" I honestly didn't know until that moment that I'd become only the tenth man in major league history to pitch a perfect game and the first American League pitcher to throw one in regular season since 1922. In fact, I was so dumbfounded by the whole experience, I wrote "no-hitter" on the ball instead of perfect game.

"Call your dad," said Mr. Finley as the champagne flowed and he told me I was goin' to get a bonus of $5000. I called. It was 2 a.m. back home.

"The hound started barking as soon as the game ended," Daddy said. "Kept at it all night." A pause. Then: "Congratulations, Jimmy. I'm real happy for ya."

One more score to settle. I stepped smartly into Kennedy's office. My head was swimming in a sea of champagne. "Well, Mr. Kennedy," I said. "Can I hit now?"

Kennedy's smile said it all.

"Kid," he said, "you can do anything you want."

While we're passing out perfect game praise, a healthy chunk of credit goes to pitching coach Bill Posedel. "Chief"—so called because of his Navy background and, as he so tactfully put it, the fact that "I've pissed more saltwater than you guys have ever seen"—had been around the Kansas City organization since '62. He'd made the grade as a pitcher (five years in the bigs with the Brooklyn Dodgers and Boston Braves), later scouting and working as a roving pitching coach for the A's. On the big club he handled the young staff perfectly—running us to death but at the same time giving us the freedom to make mistakes and learn from them, to develop our own style. Rare was the day he second-guessed; instead, he offered suggestions on mechanics, not lectures. Best of all, he believed in us, he knew the odds were against us, especially with our popgun offense and leaky defense. "Well, boys," he used to tell us all the time, "if you shut them out and hit one out, you got a good chance to win."

After the perfect game I needed some advice to help settle me down. Overnight I'd become a semicelebrity, so "famous" that letters addressed just to "Catfish, Oakland, Calif." got deliv-

ered straight to my locker. Naturally, it was Chief who did the
settling, telling me to stay within myself, not try to duplicate any
historic moments, to use my strength—control—to win ball
games. Still, I was nowhere near consistent, swinging a game or
two on either side of .500 for most of the year.

As a team, however, we were moving up, inching our way
into the first division. Our young staff was finally strong enough
to finish what they had started. By July we'd completed as many
games (twenty-six) as we had in all of '67. Nash had found his
Rookie of the Year form, learned the hard way that no matter
how hard you throw, if you don't spot the fastball, speed don't
make a damn bit of difference. Odom, Krausse, and Dobson
backed Nash up nicely with better-than-average stuff (and stats),
while Campy, leading the league in stolen bases, the versatile
Cater, and the slugging Jackson carried the load offensively.

By the end of June we'd rattled off seven wins in nine games
and were only half a game out of second place, 29–15 against
the top six teams in the league.

Then we promptly lost seven in a row.

Despite the slump, we eventually finished the season 82–80,
by far the best club record in sixteen years. The only reason we
missed the first division was that Minnesota rallied for three
runs in the eighth inning to edge us 4–3 on the last game of the
year. I managed to break even at 13–13. Campy had a
spectacular offensive year, leading the majors in stolen bases
with sixty-two and hitting .275, while rookie Jackson clubbed
twenty-nine home runs. Blue Moon won sixteen times and made
the All Star team. On the other hand, Rudi hit just .177 and
Duncan hit under .200. For us to improve, those numbers were
going to have to. And once again, we'd be doing it under new
management. In a move I'll never quite understand, Finley had
fired Kennedy.

Kennedy's replacement in 1969 turned out to be another
Finley ''retread,'' former New York Yankee outfielder Hank
Bauer, who managed Kansas City to rousing ninth-place fin-
ishes in 1961 and 1962. Bauer managed from the same training
manual as Mel McGaha. A hard-nosed ex-Marine who'd been
awarded two Purple Hearts and a Bronze Star for action in
World War II, Bauer, or ol' Burr Head, as we liked to call him,
lived and breathed discipline. A belief that became crystal clear
after Burr Head caught us checking out halter tops with

binoculars from the bull pen one day in spring training. As soon as the last out was made, Bauer ordered us to "huddle up."

"Gentlemen," he said, "we are going to do a little running."

We did a little running like marathoners do a little running. Over and over, foul line to foul line, Bauer tossing balls over our heads, and forcing us to sprint after them to make the catch. After about the tenth sprint, a stray dog joined in. Running and yapping, he nipped at our heels. Soon as Krausse sat down to catch his breath, the dog started humpin' on him real good. That kept us laughing through the thirty-seventh line-to-line sprint (better believe we were countin'). After that, we started singing "I . . . Want . . . To . . . Be . . . A . . . Marine . . . I . . . Want . . . To . . ." Next day Bauer came out in the local paper and said: "We may not win games, but my pitchers will sure be in shape." An enlightened approach. Especially, if you're playing in the fifteenth century.

When the '69 season started, I wasn't the Opening Day pitcher for the first time in three years. All that running in Florida had given me shin splints and kept me off my feet for nearly three weeks. When I did recover, it wasn't long before another case of the Dreaded Dinger Disease put me back in the bull pen. I went winless from May 11 until June 25 before I beat the Kansas City Royals 3–1. Reggie, meanwhile, was on a rampage.

I've always said that for my money Reggie Jackson was the strongest, most dynamic personality I ever saw play the game. Of course, Reggie would be the first to tell you just that—all part of his appealing charm. To me, Reggie was another Ali—cocky, confident, and like the three time heavyweight champ, born with the God-given ability to back up his boasts. It seemed to me that what Reggie—a black kid of Spanish, Indian, and Irish blood, the product of a broken home who grew up in a white Jewish Philadelphia suburb as the son of a dry cleaner and tailor—wanted more than anything else was acceptance. By the media. By the fans. By his teammates. So he courted them all, especially the press. Reggie always dressed right next to the clubhouse door, so he could grab the reporters as they walked in.

Reggie needed that attention. Not so much for the ego strokes, although those were sure nice, but as a source of his strength. He fed on publicity and the limelight like a drug, using it to fuel his latest need and deed. The difference between Reggie and a lot of other loudmouthed players was this: Reggie produced. And the bigger the game, the higher the stakes, the better he played. I swear there were spells when Reggie literally took our whole team on his shoulders and carried us for a week, two weeks at a time. Glove, bat, arm, legs, he did whatever it took to win. So when he talked big, we just chuckled. That's Reggie, we'd say. Hell, we just wanted to play baseball. Reggie wanted to be loved. We let it go at that.

Rollie Fingers turned out to be another jewel. A diamond in the rough our manager could call on to dazzle the opposing team whenever the score got close. But what a lot of people don't know about Rollie is that he spent his entire minor league career and several of his first seasons in Kansas City as a starter. Talk about a basket case. Rollie got so jittery between starts he couldn't eat or sleep for three days. He was what you'd call one of those spur-of-the-moment pitchers; if he thought about the situation ahead of time, he invariably messed up. He also didn't have a whole lot of stamina. He'd start, throw three innings of zeroes, and then bam, balls started flyin' all over the park. Posedel didn't need a crystal ball to see that Rollie was more suited for short relief, his fastball, slider, and fearless attitude perfect for the job. All Dark or Dick Williams or any other manager had to tell Rollie was "Get these next two, three guys out, and everything will be fine," and that's just what Rollie did—341 different times in his seventeen-year career, a major league record for saves that may never be equaled.

Of course, Rollie did have his weak points. He wasn't the guy you came looking for to complete the *New York Times* crossword. Witty? Absolutely. But definitely not Phi Beta Kappa. I mean Rollie's favorite pastime was watching Saturday morning cartoons. I remember one time Bando slipped Rollie a ball with about six stiches busted, cover hanging off. "Just get one quick strike before the umpire tosses the ball out of the game," whispered Bando. Sure enough, no sooner was Bando back at third than Rollie calls time and steps off the rubber.

"Ump, ump," he yells, "I need a new ball. Cover's coming off this one."

Bando just shook his head and laughed. "Look at this guy," he said over and over in the locker room afterward, "ever see a dumber guy in your life?"

Another thing about Rollie. He has also been the all time leader in another category: most bitches, career. I swear when the sun rose in the east, Rollie bitched, asking, "What's wrong with the west once in a while?" He just loved to rag.

Well, bitch or no bitch, whatever the '69 A's were doing, it was working. We moved into first place near the end of the All Star break as Reggie hit home run number thirty-three and we won—don't faint now—sixteen of twenty. Rollie chipped in with nine saves and five wins.

In August, however, our pennant drive burst like a soap bubble. Reggie, worn down by the media pressure, went into a coma; he didn't hit a home run for about three weeks. (He still finished with 47 home runs, 118 RBI, and a .275 average.) Sal fell asleep at the plate (1–16), as did our unsung hero Cater (0–16). Monday was out of it for good—a broken bone—and Blue Moon, troubled by arm problems, pitched in a funk.

Me? I couldn't buy a win. I lost eight straight decisions during one stretch (more on why later) and crash landed at 9–15. We got close once more, in early September, but we promptly dropped something like fifteen of our next eighteen. Charlie axed Bauer and signed easygoin' John McNamara, who later became the manager of the Boston Red Sox, to finish out the year.

Mac's laid-back style proved to be a breath of fresh air. I won my last three starts—closing with a three-hit shutout, my first complete game since late July—to finish 12–15 with a 3.35 ERA. Home runs were still hurting me—I'd allowed thirty-four dingers during the season. If I was planning to pitch to my potential, it was time to make my move.

Speaking of moves, one man almost single-handedly kept the transportation industry in business in 1970. I'll say this about Charlie: When he wanted something, he went out and got it. A relief pitcher, an outfielder with some pop in his bat, a strong-armed catcher, a power-hitting first baseman. One, two, three, four, Charlie got them all. Before the '70 season, he traded away my partner-in-crime, Krausse, Hershberger, and catcher Phil Roof to Milwaukee for Don Mincher, a slugging first baseman. Mincher would replace Cater, shipped east to the Yanks for left-handed starter Al Downing. Nash, who never really found a second "out" pitch to complement his fastball, was exchanged for outfielder Felipe Alou. Diego Segui and Mudcat Grant also returned to our club to bolster our pitching staff.

Finley also tried picking up the pace promotionally. It didn't work near as well as his trades did. One time he told our announcer, Harry Caray, famous for his "Holy Cow" expression, to change his catchphrase to "Holy Mule." That went over like a lead balloon. Then Finley commissioned two team *songs*. Can you believe it? One, naturally, was titled "Charlie O. The Mule." A country and western number, if I'm not mistaken. A chartbuster it wasn't.

But Charlie did some lovable things, too. He cherished kids, so as a Valentine's Day surprise, he mailed 300,000 Valentine cards to local high school students, good for free admission to a game. "I want the teenagers of the Bay Area to come out and get acquainted with our young and outstanding baseball stars," he said. However, the neighbors around the park complained the game was getting a little too close to their homes—they were upset over the exploding fireworks that were set off each time an A's player hit a home run. They got a court order to stop the noise. But Charlie had the last laugh in this controversy. He passed out sparklers and made us parade around in front of our dugout after every four-bagger. Honest.

I started strong for a change, 5–2 out of the gate, keeping us on the heels of the defending Western Division Champion Twins. I upped my mark to 9–5 in early June with help from Mudcat Grant. Soon afterward, I celebrated the Fourth of July in Anaheim by winning my thirteenth game (against five losses) before 43,000 or so, the biggest crowd since the club moved to Orange County. Reggie exploded out of his season slump (one that threatened to see him shipped back to the minors by Finley) with a tape-measure homer and single. Mudcat collected his thirteenth save on his way to pitching forty innings of one-run relief.

I've always respected Mudcat. I still see him occasionally during spring training in Florida. Back in '70, Mudcat was one cool dude, lead singer in an off-season nightclub act in which he worked with a backup group called The Kittens. One time Mud got booked up in Tahoe, figurin', I guess, that this was his big break. He lasted one set. The manager of the club paid him off in full and left 'Cat with these parting words: "Don't bring that weak shit back in here no mo'.'' Well, whatever Mudcat wasn't on stage, he was in full voice on the mound. A good curve, a sneaky fastball, he was smart, and he knew how to pitch. Together we kept purring along. I was 15–8 by early August; Mudcat had nineteen saves and five wins.

The biggest excitement of the year, however, had to be the overpowering presence of Vida Blue.

You couldn't help but notice the loose, flowing grace, the compact motion, all the marks of a terrific athlete. In high school in Mansfield, Louisiana, Vida, the oldest son of an iron worker, had thrown thirty-five touchdown passes his senior year. He could have been the first black quarterback at Houston. Despite twenty-five college football offers—including those from Notre Dame and Purdue—he signed for $50,000 with the A's the same year he struck out all twenty-one batters in a seven-inning high school game. In the minors it was more of the same. He broke Nash's strikeout record in Double A; he threw a no-hitter in Triple A.

In the majors Vida made good copy right off the bat. Stories ran daily on how he always pitched with two dimes in his pocket—''a little superstition of mine''—chewed a toothpick, and popped his gum. He popped his fastball too, an overpowering pitch that in the beginning Vida could sink, sail, hop, drop, or dart. Mostly it smoked. "I don't just try to finesse a batter," he would say, "I just try to hit the corners, jam a guy, and break his bat. I enjoy breaking people's bats.''

In his first start of the season, Vida hit a three-run homer and won 7–4. Next time out he threw a one-hitter and beat Kansas City. In his fourth start he no-hit the Twins 6–0. Unfortunately, not even everything Vida did (which was just about *everything*) was enough. Minnesota clinched its second straight American League West pennant on September 22, the same day the Twins won it all in '69. By the same number of games—nine. Omens? As it was, I won eighteen games, the most of my six-year career, lost fourteen, and led the league with forty starts. Campy hit twenty-one home runs. Rudi, responding to the teachings of Chairman Charlie Lau, hit .309. (In spring training, Lau and Rudi had been inseparable, spending hours in the batting cage, Charlie's voice carrying all over the park: "Stay off the plate now, Joe. Take it the other way . . . that's it, that's it, don't uppercut . . . You're dipping your head . . . That's better . . . that's better.'')

We still weren't drawing, playing third fiddle to the Giants and Raiders. It seemed as though most fans felt that we were somehow held captive by Finley and deserved a better fate. One by one the bumper stickers started appearing all over the Bay Area.

The message: FREE THE A'S.

8

CAT CALLS

Now, I'm not one to quibble about publicity, but somehow the megaphone story never got the credit it deserved.

It all started with us sitting in a bus on the tarmac at Milwaukee's Mitchell Field while waiting to be driven downtown to the Pfister Hotel. We'd been screwing around as usual on the plane, drinking, joking, and cutting up, all of which had darkened the black mood of our new manager, Dick Williams, who in those days was doing a pretty good impression of Darth Vader.

A scrappy major league outfielder with average skills, Williams had worked his way into the starting lineup of the 1956 Orioles before a shoulder injury cut short his career. I think Dick resented that a bit, carrying a small chip on his shoulder as he moved on to manage the Boston Red Sox to the pennant in '67. Like McGaha and Bauer, Williams carried a crisp military presence, a my-way-or-the-highway attitude. But Dick Williams was different. Very, very different.

Until the time Dick was hired, the A's were a talented team sadly lacking in *baseball* discipline. Oh, we knew about curfews, running laps, the dos and don'ts pounded into our heads by the likes of McGaha and Bauer. But consistently execute the hit and run? Score a runner from third with less than two outs? Consistently hit a cutoff man? For-get it. I think that's the reason Charlie hired Dick after he was fired by the Red Sox. He knew Williams's reputation for molding young men into winners. Big winners. Williams laid down the law from day one in spring training. Before he let us pick up a bat, he ran us through drill after drill after drill until we got it right. And I do mean *right*. "You guys keep screwing around," he yelled one day, "and we won't hit for four weeks. Think I'm kidding? This [fundamentals] is an area we're going to do right, and I don't care if we don't do anything else all spring."

Believe me, he caught our attention. Then, as the season wore on, Dick made sure we never forgot his message. On airplanes he'd prowl the aisles, getting right into the face of a player who wasn't playing up to his personal standards. Dick didn't invite debate. He didn't mince many words. His motivational method was simple: Humiliate, intimidate, make you want to show him up. Prove to the world that Dick Williams was wrong.

Because of that attitude, a lot of guys on the club had trouble dealing with Dick. Campy was always in the doghouse. Reggie, too. "Don't get on me," Reggie would shout. "I'm the bread and butter of this ball club." Dick didn't hear a word; he told Reggie to start playing better defensively or his ass would be riding the pine.

Despite his abrasive personality, Dick was a helluva skipper. For one thing, he had great instincts. He knew when to play a certain guy against a certain pitcher, and he possessed a sixth sense for knowing exactly when to pull a pitcher. Like Earl Weaver in Baltimore, Dick kept detailed charts and notes involving one player's success—or failure—in a variety of situations, and he used those charts as the basis for his decisions.

Second, Dick was blessed with a talent commonly found only in mothers and grade school teachers—he had eyes in the back of his head. We couldn't get away with anything. Well, almost anything. One time Lindblad and I were playing "flip," a pregame ritual where the ball and bodies fly around pretty good. Sure enough, I dove for a ball and broke the thumb and a finger on my glove hand. I didn't tell the doctor. (That would have been suicidal.) About a week later Williams walks by and asks, "How's your thumb, Cat?"

"What thumb?" I asked.

"The one you broke playing flip," says Williams. "Don't try and fool me," he added. "I know everything."

Another time he threatened to fine me for not wearing the right glove. I had gone on a road trip without mine and was making do with a new one. Naturally, on a close play at first I dropped the ball. "Forget that glove again," said Williams, "and it will cost you $1000."

"Yes, sir," I said. How he found out I was wearing a different one I'll never know.

One of the best can't-put-anything-past-me stories happened one night while we were in the midst of a losing streak. We had lost again, and that night we left the hotel to loosen up and forget about the streak. Turns out we also forgot about curfew. Dick didn't. At the witching hour he went into the lobby and handed two brand new baseballs to the elevator operator.

"Do me a favor, will ya?" he asked. "When the rest of the A's come in, have them sign these for you. Keep one and put the other in my box, okay?"

"Sure, Mr. Williams."

The next day Williams calls a team meeting and says, "You, you, you, and you, you're all fined $200 for missing curfew."

"Curfew?" asked Gene Tenace, one of the offenders. "What do you mean curfew?"

That's when Dick pulled out the baseball.

"Sign this ball last night, did you?" he asked. You could almost hear six of us say "Ah, shit" in unison.

"Well, I know one thing," Tenace said afterward.

"What?"

"I'll never sign another autograph after curfew."

Of course, the way we played early in 1971—the failed hitting, the fumbled ground balls, the stupid baserunning mistakes—nobody was asking for too many 'graphs. Going into the "megaphone" Milwaukee series, we'd bumbled our way to about eight losses in a row. Dick was fit to be tied.

The whole megaphone incident started when I was getting off the plane. I'd had a couple of drinks, so when I noticed the megaphone in the overhead compartment above my seat, I figured, ah, what the hell, nobody's going to miss it.

I must have been sending out smoke signals or somethin' because Lindblad piped right up with "Just leave it right there, Fish. That belongs to the FCC."

"But I can use this back home," I said. Maybe it was the scotch doin' the talking.

"You'll probably end up in jail."

Well, just as I was slippin' the megaphone into my bag, a stewardess caught a glimpse and notified ground personnel. I knew I was in trouble when a United Airlines employee started whispering in Dick's ear as we sat down in the bus.

"All right, you fuckers," he began. "I don't know which one

of you did it, but some lousy motherfucker stole a megaphone from that damn plane, and we're not leaving this spot until that somebody comes clean.''

Dick definitely had a way with words. Four-letter ones in particular. During that first few minutes of waiting he used just about every one he knew. Some two and three times. Still nobody fessed up. ''I'm getting goddamn tired of standing up here,'' he fumed and he stormed off the bus.

I looked at Lindblad. ''Here,'' I said, ''you take it.''

''Thanks.''

Like a good roomie, Lindy bailed me out. He tossed the item in question out the window without even looking. It landed right in Dick's arms. To his credit, Dick never missed a beat—he just handed it over to the United rep and walked away.

It was three weeks before Dick said another word about it. Then one day he just sorta sidled up next to me. He was feeling much better, in part, I'm sure, because we'd won twelve of our next thirteen after his upbraiding on the bus. I figured he wanted to talk about how we'd moved into first place. Fooled me. ''Hey, Cat,'' he said, ''you reckon that megaphone would have worked good on your dogs?''

''I'd have loved to find out,'' I said.

One of Finley's best calls came early in the season when he decided to trade Mincher, catcher Frank Fernandez, and my roomie, Lindblad, for burly first baseman Mike Epstein and superb left-handed reliever Darold Knowles, a definite stopper. Mincher had hit twenty-seven home runs the season before but was under .240 with just two home runs now. Charlie was never one to wait around. The hardest part was saying goodbye to Paul. He'd been brilliant for us in 1970 (8–2) and was 1–0 when the trade hit.

Epstein and Knowles, however, proved to be key pieces of the pennant puzzle. Epstein had played fullback at the University of California, Berkeley, during the Craig Morton era, majoring in social psychology, and was one of the deepest thinkers on the club, a solemn and moody man at times—especially if he wasn't hitting. Still, Epstein had great talent, as evidenced by the Rookie of the Year and MVP awards his first year in pro ball in the California League and repeat honors the next year in Triple A (when he hit something like 30 homers and had 100 RBIs). In the big leagues Epstein had developed a reputation as something of a clubhouse lawyer. He threatened to quit after being farmed out by the Orioles one year. Instead, he got traded to Washington. Two years later, after hitting thirty home runs for a team going nowhere fast, Epstein sulked until he was traded to the A's. At the time he shifted over from the Senators, Mike had one homer and one double in twenty-four games. His average was a measly .247. But during the next thirty-seven games he hit over .300 and stroked ten homers.

Knowles, on the other hand, proved the perfect left-handed complement to Rollie Fingers. Now our staff was set: Fingers and Knowles backing up Odom, Hunter, Dobson, Segui, and the hottest, most magnificent player the game had seen in a long, long time: Vida Blue.

By late June we had stretched our lead to eleven games over Kansas City, and Vida was already 17–3 and leading the league in wins, complete games, shutouts, strikeouts, and ERA. No other pitcher in the majors had more than twelve wins. His fairy tale come true continued when he started the All Star Game in Detroit and became the second-youngest pitcher in history to pick up the win. When he won number nineteen in Tiger Stadium a few days later, *Tiger* fans began chanting "We want Vida! We want Vida!"

Everywhere we went it was Vida this and Vida that. In New York, the largest crowd to see a night game in three years turned out for "Blue Tuesday." (The scorecards were even printed in blue.) One night, anyone named Blue was admitted for free and about 125 people qualified.

Getting into the act, Finley offered Vida $2000 if he would change his name to Vida (True) Blue. (Never a dull moment.) "We'll have them take the name Blue off your uniform and have them use True," said Charlie. "I'll tell the broadcast boys to call you True Blue. How's that?"

Vida didn't much like all the attention. "It's a weird scene," he said. "You win a few baseball games and all of a sudden you're surrounded by reporters and TV men with cameras asking things about Vietnam and race relations and stuff about yourself. Man, I'm only a kid. I don't know exactly who I am. I don't have a whole philosophy of life set down."

Not long ago Vida had a well-publicized problem with cocaine. It really surprised me. But then again, after all the accolades, the buildup, the pressure to produce, to equal the greatness he'd achieved in '71 and later years, maybe it wasn't such a surprise. I read in *USA Today* that Vida's now ranching in northern California and looking to get back into baseball. I wish him the best.

With our growing success, the emergence of Jackson, Rudi, Fingers, Blue, Campy, myself and Bando as legitimate big-league stars, our aggressive attitude on and off the diamond, the fact we'd go on to win the pennant by seventeen games, you'd have thought the fans would be breaking down the doors to see us play. Wrong. We drew less than a million in 1971, and once again, Charlie pulled out all the promotional stops. We had Shriners Day, Helmet Day, Hot Pants Day (which drew 11,000 lovelies and not so lovelies), greased-pig chases, Farmers' Day. Nothing really helped.

So, down the stretch, other than practicing my hog calls, the only real drama was whether I would win twenty games for the first time. That'd always been a dream of mine, winning twenty. The day before I was due to get my first crack at it, we roll into our Kansas City hotel from the airport at about 2 a.m. Soon as I set foot inside my room I start throwing my suitcase around, hustling to get out the door.

"Where ya goin'?" asked Sal.

"Goin' huntin'."

"Now?"

I told him that's exactly where I was headed. Soon as I'd changed clothes, I figured I was a ninety-minute drive from a farmer friend who let me hunt his land. I'd be there before dawn.

Sal just shook his head. "You're crazy," he said. "You got a chance to win twenty games tomorrow and you're going huntin'. You're nuts."

"No, I'm not," I said. "It's the most relaxing thing I can do. That way I won't be sittin' around this hotel bored to death."

So off we went—me, Greenie, and Knowles. We stayed in the fields 'til noon, had a fine lunch prepared by the farmer's wife, and then headed back to Kansas City. I was back at the hotel by two.

"What you gonna do now," asked Sal, "get some sleep?"

"Nope," I said. "I'm gonna take a quick shower, go to the ballpark. You goin'?"

A quick chorus of nooooos.

"Oh, yes, you are. C'mon. To the park, all of you."

Sure enough, when all was said and done, I had my twentieth win, 2–1 over the Royals, and to top it off, I knocked in the winning run. All Bando could do after the game was mumble "You've got to be kidding me" over and over again.

Two days later we won the division. It had only been about forty years since the last one. I finished up the regular season 21–11 with a 2.96 ERA in thirty-seven starts. Eighteen last year, twenty-one this year. I was on a roll now, one that wouldn't end until the 1976 season.

Playoff time. The hard-hitting Orioles from Baltimore complete with their prime-time pitching staff of Dave McNally, Mike Cuellar, and Jim Palmer. A big mountain to climb for any club, and frankly, we didn't quite have the right equipment. Not yet. Sure there was Vida and his twenty-four wins, but everywhere he went a band of reporters and photographers was sure to follow. In the opener Vida threw six strong innings of three-hit, one-run ball before Baltimore rallied for four runs in the seventh to win the game 5–3. Afterward Vida just sat in his underwear for the longest time—the classic picture of a tired, drained young man.

I got the call in game two. And I made only four mistakes. Naturally, all four ended up in the seats. Two home runs by Boog Powell, one each by Brooks Robinson and Elrod Hendricks. Funny thing, Powell's right hand was supposedly so messed up he tried to bunt off me in the eighth. Unfortunately, he fouled the pitch off. His next swing was a two-run homer, the final runs in a 5–1 loss. "With a hurt arm, a broken leg, anything, he's still tough," I said after the game.

On the verge of a Baltimore sweep, we tried to shake things up the next day. The strangest sight had to be Charlie, ditching his trademark green jacket in favor of what he called his "Vida Blue" blazer. Williams benched Duncan, Rudi, and Tommy Davis in favor of Tenace, Angel Mangual, and Monday. Mudcat sang the national anthem. Nothing worked. Baltimore beat Segui 5–3 to complete a rather humiliating three-game sweep. Even worse was the fact that we played the game at home in front of 17,000 empty seats. But what the heck. The Birds beat us with three twenty-game winners. There was always next season. *Our* season.

Parading down Grubb Street during Jim "Catfish" Hunter Day ceremonies in my hometown of Hertford, North Carolina.

Me thanking all the folks.

Ahoskie American Legion Post 102—the roughest, toughest team in North Carolina during the summer of 1962. That's me, smilin' away, bottom row, third from the left.

The loves of my life, my mom, my dad, and Helen, gathered 'round as I signed a $75,000 "bonus baby" contract with Kansas City in 1964.

The ubiquitous Mr. Charles O. Finley—as unique an owner as you'll ever want to meet.

Kansas City scout Clyde Kluttz takes a close look at my injured foot during Instructional League in Bradenton, Florida.

A perfect night. May 8, 1968: Oakland 4, Minnesota 0. As in no runs, no hits, no walks, no errors.

Perfect

DOWN

Hunter $5,000 Richer

Hunter's 20th Win Earns New Cadillac

Oakland Tribune *Sports*

Unnoticed Superstar

Suffers a Hairline Fracture

No, this isn't some peace-lovin' rock music group. Just some of the Boys on the Bus—clockwise, Sal Bando, lower left, Dave Duncan, Joe Rudi, Rollie Fingers, Mike Epstein, Gene Tenace, and me.

A future Oakland A, Paul Hunter, working on his control.

Until my arm popped like that bubblegum, letters poured in with cures for my shoulder problem.

Some of the home folk who came up from Hertford to see Jimmy Hunter pitch.

A man of mystery—but my first choice in any pickup game— ex-Yankee great, Thurman Munson.

Lou Piniella poking one out during his playing days, while probably thinking about that homer he hit off me in Kansas City.

George "Top Gun" Steinbrenner III often swings first and asks questions later when it comes to running the Yankees.

A rare, radiant athlete who could back up his boasts, Reggie Jackson had an insecure side, too.

Jimmy Hunter in pinstripes.

One of my few happy moments back in 1979—a year marked by the death of the three most important men in my life.

That's me giving Ryan Combs, Francis's little boy, a lesson in nature.

Three beautiful chips off the old block—
Todd, 17, Kim, 14, and Paul, 7.

Little Leaguer Tony Hughes showing
me where it hurts after getting
plunked by a pitch back in the summer
of 1980.

Dog days down in Hertford—me with three of my forty hunting hounds.

It felt good to be back in Oakland and wearing the green and gold again while pitching in the Equitable Old-Timers All Star Game last summer.

It was smiles all around as Helen and Paul watch my induction into Baseball's Hall of Fame in July 1987.

Jimmy Hunter in his farming hat.

The Equitable game in Oakland brought twenty-four Hall of Famers together, including this happy quartet of Hunter, Joe DiMaggio, Willie Mays, and Billy Williams.

That's Helen, Kim, and Paul posing in front of some of my baseball trophies.

9

THE BOYS ON THE BUS

You don't have to be a National Merit finalist to figure out why we won three straight World Series. Execution and excellence in every part of the game—pitching, hitting, speed, and defense. Plus, we had an ace in the hole: Fingers, emerging as the best reliever in the game. When Rollie rolled out of the pen, we turned it up a notch or two. What else does a team need? The intangibles: chemistry, cohesion, a competitive fire. An attitude that says, Come game time, no matter how pissed off we were at each other, when we crossed those white lines, we were playing as a team. The Oakland A's. You had to beat us. All of us.

And I'll tell you something else, folks. That attitude's not found in any how-to instructional manuals. It wasn't, like on so many clubs, bred in our clubhouse. No, our group therapy classes were conducted someplace else. On a bus.

Not on any bus. On the *team* bus.

To us, the bus became a rolling "players only" lounge, a refuge from reporters, wives, kids, owners, and umpires, a psychiatrist's couch on wheels. When the Oakland A's boarded their team bus, before or after games, it was open season. If you had something to say, you said it. A bitch, you bitched it. It turned out to be just what the doctor ordered, especially in a sport where men with king-sized egos walk in each other's shadow eighteen hours a day, 250 days a year.

What was slightly different in our case was that therapy worked both ways. You gave *and* you received. Most of the time Gino Tenace and I and Kenny Holtzman and George Hendrick, a very funny man, took our spots in the very back of the bus. Sal sat a seat or two in front of us. The guys who couldn't take the razzing stayed up front. Not that it mattered. Nobody got away with anything. Especially rookies. If you couldn't take the heat, we buried you. You could run, but you couldn't hide. Especially if you happened to "ass up"—our expression for screwing up, not running out ground balls, missing signs or cutoff men, playing for "me" instead of "we."

The two most prominent ass kickers? Why Drs. Bando and Hunter, of course.

Understand that when Captain Sal spoke, even E. F. Hutton listened. Sal always played in such a controlled fury, with so much heart, he just naturally evolved into the team leader. He loved to talk to me on the mound, remind me of the little things: what guy liked what pitch, what he did two weeks ago late in the game. Sal had a remarkable mind for the game, situations, remembering what hitter hit what pitch. That's why I always believed he would have made the best manager of all the A's. I heard that the Milwaukee Brewers, Sal's last team, asked him three times to take over the club, but Sal turned them down every time. He'd had enough of packing suitcases and wanted to spend more time with his family. So he's in the banking business now in Brookfield, Wisconsin, and doing special assistant work for Brewer General Manager Bud Selig.

Back in '72, Sal and I were both on a what you'd call a special assignment. When necessary (usually during losing streaks and times of lackadaisical play), he and I would huddle together in the locker room after a game. We'd whisper back and forth, picking our prime candidate for abuse. Once on the bus, we went immediately into our act.

"Hunter," Sal would start, "I'm gettin' sick and tired of all the bullshit home runs you're giving up. I feel like they're taking target practice at me. Don't be afraid to pitch a guy *outside* once in a while." Sal loved the home run theme. I guess he felt the material was always fresh. "You know," he'd add, "if this shit doesn't stop, I ain't goin' out on that field anymore. I'm gonna get killed down there, all the shots guys are hitting."

My turn. "C'mon, Fat Boy," I'd say. "A guy with your body, all the protection you got in that stomach. Nothin' could happen. Besides, when's the last time you got a hit with anybody on base? Spring training?"

Off we'd go. Back and forth. Back and forth. Mostly it was just some cell block screaming. Sometimes, though, when the situation merited it, we'd go nose-to-nose, like we were itchin' to fight. About this time Campy, our resident Cub Scout, would run up the aisle screaming, "You'd better git back there quick! Fish and Bando, they gonna fight! Hurry! Hurry!"

Williams, an old hand at our act, stayed glued to his seat. So Sal and I stayed at it until, boom, our target for the night made the slightest peep. It didn't have to be much. A simple "Shut up and sit down, will ya?" or "Lay off" would suffice. Anything.

Bam. The conversation suddenly shifted. We jumped all over the guy; it didn't matter who. Rollie, Reggie, reserve second baseman Ted Kubiak, Epstein, Knowles. One time we got all over Greenie, whose wife was wearing him out at home.

"Hey, Greenie," somebody'd say, "you know if you spent a little less time taking care of business at home, maybe you wouldn't be too tired to run out those ground balls."

The next time it was Reggie, who loved to show off his arm, daring runners to take an extra base on him. Reggie would stand out there in right and fake, fake, fake the throw, begging the runner to test his arm. Trouble was, every runner passed the test, with Reggie throwing the ball somewhere in the cheap seats.

"Hey, Reg," Sal would say. "Helluva arm you've got there buddy, helluva arm. But how about throwing the damn ball into the infield so somebody can catch it."

Nobody was safe. Knowles got ripped for his mismatched outfits. Holtzman for wearing the same clothes all the time. And Moon. Boy, Rollie loved gettin' on Moon. Especially the year Moon kept talking about how he was going to win the comeback player of the year award. Comeback this. Comeback that.

"But, Moon," said Rollie. "You gotta be someplace first to come back from."

The cuts were quick and pointed. In and out. Then all of a sudden someone, say, Blue Moon, would take only so much shit before lashing out at, oh, Duncan. Pretty soon, bing, bing, bing, words were ricocheting all over the bus, setting off a chain reaction. After that, all bets were off.

Didn't some guys get pissed off? You bet. That's the whole point. Let 'em know we weren't gonna stand for goldbrickers or prima donnas. Meanwhile, the bus just kept on rolling . . .

It didn't take long in '72 to establish ourselves as the team to beat in the American League. In June we won seven straight, and by July 4th we had the best record in baseball—45–24— and I was 9–4. Everyone else was contributing too. Rudi was hitting .330, second in the league. Reggie, Epstein, and Duncan were among the league leaders in home runs, Sal was in the top five in RBIs, and the worst ERA on the staff was 2.61. And that belonged to Vida, struggling to regain his brilliant form of a season before.

In 1971, Vida Blue had won the Cy Young Award (the youngest recipient ever) and added the MVP award for good measure. He'd won twenty-four games, lost eight, pitched 312 innings, struck out 301, and had an ERA of 1.82. In spring training 1972 he demanded a raise from $14,500 to $92,000; Charlie countered with $50,000. (Charlie didn't have a pet mule for nothing; he could be the most pigheaded of men when he wanted to be, which was often. One time the White Sox refused to let the mule into Comiskey Park. So Charlie rented a parking lot across the street and put the mule on display with a bunch of models and a band that blared "Muletrain" as a serenade.)

But Vida had some mule in him, too. He threatened to retire at the ripe old age of twenty-two and take a job as vice president of public relations for some steel products company in southern California. He almost said it with a straight face. As I recall, the company's big sale item at the time was something called an Over-John, a storage cabinet that sat over a toilet.

No kidding.

But thankfully, with more than a little help from Commissioner Bowie Kuhn, both men worked out their problems and Vida signed in May after a five-week holdout. Unfortunately, he wasn't the same pitcher he had been in '71. He was throwing just as hard, but like Jim Nash, Vida wasn't hitting spots. Hitters were sitting on the fastball. And hitting it. Vida would win just six games for us in '72.

But even without Vida we had the look of champions. And it was *some* look. The radicalization of the Oakland A's had officially started back in spring training with Reggie telling Finley he was keeping the mustache he'd grown in the off-season. You could almost hear the wheels turning in ol' Mr. Finley's head.

"Great idea, Reg," he said. "Great idea."

Well, that's all the bull pen had to hear. Knowles, Fingers, and I started growing mustaches, too. Finley loved that. "I'll pay anyone $300 if they grow a mustache." Nineteen players and coaches took him up on it. As Holtzman said, "For $300, I would grow hair on my feet."

Nobody went *that* far, but it didn't stop us from letting hair grow, waxing our mustaches, letting it all hang out, wearing paisley shirts and other "mod" fashions of the time. Columnists started comparing us to the cast of *Hair*.

Finley, for good measure, was wheeling and dealing like Monty Hall—trades, sales, releases, minor league promotions and demotions, some forty different deals in all before the season was over. Almost every one helped the club in some way. Off the field Finley showed something of a Midas touch, as Greenie and I can attest. Early in the year I'd given Mr. Finley $50,000 to invest. About six months later I walked in and said I'd like to cash in my chips.

"All right," said Charlie, "let me look at some papers and see what you've got. Come back tomorrow."

I did. Finley had a check waiting for $100,000—double my money. I almost kissed him.

"But what about the taxes?" I asked.

"Don't worry about it," said Finley. "You're building a new home, right? I already paid the damn taxes."

Of course, when Bando and the other guys heard about this, they made a beeline for Finley's office. A year later Sal was back, asking for his money and probably thinking of ways to spend the 100 percent return on his investment.

"How much money did you give me last year?" Finley asked. Sal told him.

Finley got out his checkbook and filled in the blanks. The check was for $50,000.

"But that's what I gave you," said Sal.

"Well," said Finley, "I guaranteed you wouldn't lose any money, didn't I?"

"Yeah, but I didn't make any money," said Sal.

"Well, neither did I," said Mr. Finley.

Meantime, players were coming and going like crazy. The most bizarre deal had to be the acquisition of former thirty-one-game-winner and all-around bad boy Denny McLain from Texas. McLain had been banned from baseball for associating with bookmakers, and he never really amounted to much for us. (He won exactly one game.) Too many Sunday nights and

Mondays gambling and partying in nearby Lake Tahoe and Vegas with Fingers and reserve outfielder Brant Alyea.

Ken Holtzman had come over from the Cubs in exchange for Monday, who never quite lived up to his potential in the eyes of the organization. At just twenty-six, a refugee from the Chicago Cubs, Holtzman was just the established frontline left-handed starter we needed—particularly with Blue on the blink. Holtzman had won seventeen games two years running for Chicago and had two no-hitters to his credit. It was easy to see why. All he ever threw for strikes was the heater and a change-up. Fastball, fastball, fastball. Change-up. Fastball. Fastball. He'd only show you the curve in the dirt. Never up. But he moved that fastball up and down, in and out, showing it, taking it away. Plus, he was a battler. He could beat you with his arm, his glove, *and* his bat.

Dave Hamilton and Bob Locker, two lesser-known but crucial parts of our pitching staff, made major contributions. Hammy was our left-handed long man and fifth starter. What's funny about Hammy is that he was so scared of Williams that his knees wobbled every time Dick spoke to him. Lock was often in a world of his own. He was very quiet and a physical fitness nut; his idea of a great time was putting on a ten-pound vest and doing forty laps around the park. He probably had the best stuff of anybody on the staff. In the bull pen his hard sinker dropped a foot and was practically untouchable. But, as happens, Lock seemed to lock up a bit in a game; consequently, his ball stayed straight. Still, he provided some solid middle relief and some huge laughs in the clubhouse. I remember one time Lock went up to San Francisco and found a street entertainer who made his living impersonating W. C. Fields.

Lock brought ol' W. C. into the locker room one day. The guy was hilarious. He stopped at my locker and went into his spiel: "Ah, yes, my young man. I was married once to a little chickadee from North Carolina." And forget it with Rollie. He thought he'd died and gone to heaven.

By August that's where we figured to be headed. The pennant was ours. Or so we thought. In one symbolic stretch Holtzman pitched a three-hitter, Vida added a two-hitter, and I allowed just five hits over nine innings. All shutouts. Rudi was leading the league with a .330 average. And for good measure, Sal took a poke at Kansas City catcher Ed Kirkpatrick after Dick Drago had the misfortune of hitting Sal on the leg with a pitch.

Suddenly, the wheels came off. We lost seven of eight to fall just one game ahead of Chicago and its newly acquired slugger, Dick Allen. Allen, the former "bad boy" of Philadelphia, St. Louis, and L.A., was so popular the team actually revised its media guide in *midseason,* taking the manager and other players off the cover and putting Allen on instead. That's what thirty-two home runs will do for you.

We played the White Sox in August, clinging to the league lead. The first game was one of the longest of my life; seventeen innings before being called by darkness. We'd scored in the eighth and twelfth to tie. The next day I was scheduled to start, so I was on the mound for the eighteenth and nineteenth innings of the suspended game. I had no stuff at all, but I got the win when Rudi socked a two-run homer ending the five-hour and thirty-one-minute marathon. And, sure enough, I started the second game and went eight innings—some of the best stuff of my career—allowing one earned run. Unfortunately, that run was all the White Sox needed to beat us 1–0. Tit for tat.

The next day we lost again and fell out of first place for the first time since May 20. But thanks to Matty Alou, who came over from St. Louis and did nothing but hit line drives for the rest of the season, we recovered. I won number twenty on September 17, beating Texas on three hits and pushing our lead to five with fifteen games left. I would end up winning twenty-one games, lose only seven, and compile a mouth-watering ERA of just 2.04 in 295 innings. Some pitching, if I say so myself. We held on to win the division by 5½ games and the right to meet the Tigers in the playoffs.

Our American League championship series against Detroit had to be one of the most draining, emotionally exhausting experiences of my life. We beat the Tigers—and their manager Billy Martin—in five gut-wrenching games, but it took every ounce of energy and more than a little luck. The series offered a little of everything—bat throwing, errors by catchers/first basemen who were filling in at second, game-winning pinch hits by prophetic Puerto Ricans.

Oh, and a fight. I almost forgot about the fight.

It was Reggie and Epstein who went at it this time. Over tickets. Playoff tickets. *Free* playoff tickets. I don't know who started it, but one thing led to another, and they lit into each other in the locker room like a couple of bulls. Somebody broke it up. Afterward I was walking past the whirlpool where Hendrick was soaking away his aches and pains.

"Hey, Cat," said George. "I want to know one thing."

"What?"

"Who in the hell grabbed Epstein and broke up the fight?" I told him I didn't know who was handling peacekeeping that day.

"Well, whoever it was," said George with a sly smile, "I'm going to kick *their* ass. I wanted to see Epstein kick the shit out of Reggie." Reggie, as one might guess, had his detractors.

We won game one, 3–2, on a pinch hit from the most unlikely of heroes, Gonzalo Marquez. At twenty-eight, Marquez didn't play the year before because his mother was sick in Puerto Rico. The only reason he made our playoff roster was because Knowles had fractured his thumb taking batting practice the week before. But Dick, ever the hunch player, took one look at Gonzalo's seven hits in fifteen at bats in September (including three game winners) and put him on our bench. I found out later that Gonzalo had told Campy that if he got a chance to pinch hit he'd win the game. And that's just what he did.

Game two was all Blue Moon, who fired a three-hit shutout. Somehow, though, Moon's brilliance got lost in the Bat Throwin' Incident. You may remember it. Campy gets hit on the kneecap by Tiger pitcher Lerrin LaGrow. Campy's quick temper explodes. Campy starts rushing to the mound. Campy stops. Campy takes a real good look at LaGrow, who's staring back. Campy throws his bat instead. Campy gets ejected and, sadly, suspended for the remainder of the playoffs.

Now it was back to Detroit. All we had to do was win one of three, and we'd be playing in our first World Series. It certainly didn't happen in game three, as Joe Coleman shut us down 3–0 on six hits, three each from Alou and Rudi. Game four found me on the mound, and we got about as close as any team can get before blowing a three-run lead in the bottom of the ninth. The black and silver American League championship trophy was in our locker room after we scored two runs on an RBI double by Alou and a Kubiak single in the top of the ninth to take a 3–1 lead. (I'd thrown 7⅓ innings of one-run ball.)

That's when second base came back to haunt us. During the year, with Greenie injured and then not hitting, Williams had rotated eleven different guys into that spot. Now Tenace was out there for only the third time in his four-year career.

OTHER VOICES—GENE TENACE

Standing next to the batting cage in the Astrodome, Gene Tenace, bull pen coach for the Houston Astros, oversees his pitcher taking pregame batting practice. Outgoing, outspoken, Tenace laughs at early memories of his days on the bus—and of catching Hunter for the first time.

"Catfish is the only pitcher in my fifteen-year career who never shook me off," says Tenace, shaking his head. "I remember getting called up to the big leagues and having one of those meetings where you go over the hitters. I asked Cat what he wanted to throw. 'Whaddya mean?' he asked. 'Whatever you put down.' Sure enough, I put down a sign, he throws the pitch. He never shook me off. Not once. Hell, I coulda caught the game in a rocking chair. Afterward I thought I was the greatest catcher in the world. Until my next start. Then I had to catch Blue Moon Odom, and all he did was shake me off."

Tenace is asked about the '72 playoffs, how he felt playing second base. "I felt pretty confident with a two-run lead and our pitching staff," he laughs. "Next thing I know, a base hit here, a base hit there, and the bases are loaded. Then Bill Freehan hit one to Sal, a possible double-play ball. Sal threw it to me—a little high and wide—and just as I was going to catch it, I got blasted. I went one way, the ball another. Everybody was safe. They scored two runs and won the game without us ever getting an out. Talk about embarrassment.

"Now we figured we had a long night ahead of us. Moon started the next day, and he was unbelievable. In total control. Then Reggie and Epstein pull off a beautiful double steal. Reggie makes a terrific slide to score from third, except he rips his hamstring from the tip of his butt down to his calf. We had to carry him off. But, hell, the way Blue Moon was pitching, we figured we weren't going to need many runs. All of a sudden in the sixth he can't go back out. He just broke down. The pressure *got to him. Vida took over. He was upset at not starting a playoff game, but he held on to beat Dee-troit, throwing four shutout innings of relief.*

"Talk about a wild ending. The fans in Dee-troit knocked over the fence around the outfield. Now I've got to hit, and I don't have a hit in five games. It's my last at bat. Woody Fryman's pitching; Hendrick is on second base. I got a base hit to left, George ran home, and after it was all over, we were all so scared of the crowd, we didn't even hardly celebrate. We just ran right into the clubhouse."

Believe me, after beating Detroit in the playoffs, playing Cincinnati, the "Big Red Machine," couldn't be any tougher. Sure they had Rose, Tolan, Morgan, Perez, and Bench. But we were loose, confident. The night before the first game, Bando, Tenace, myself, and a couple of other guys went out to dinner. Whom do we see but Bench, the great Reds catcher, surrounded by one of those—what do you call them?—entourages. He musta thought he was a god. Talking real loud at his table about how they better not throw me this way, that way.

I walked right over to him. "I'll throw it right under your nose if I want to," I said. Bench just stared at me, like you're not supposed to talk to a superstar like that. Horseshit. We had some pretty big superstars on our club.

OTHER VOICES—GENE TENACE

"Dick gave me a vote of confidence before the Series. After the experience in Dee-troit, playing the Reds was a breeze. Almost like spring training. I was so relaxed.

"I remember going to the park on the bus right before the first game. Cat, Knowles, Hendrick, and I were in the back as usual. Knowles spoke up. 'I got a prediction,' he said. 'I had a dream last night. I'm predicting either Gene Tenace or George Hendrick is going to be the MVP of the Series.' Now remember, this is before the first pitch has been thrown. We all just looked at each other. I said, 'I hope you're right, because if one of us wins the MVP, it means we won the Series.' ."

* * *

What a series. Seven games. Six decided by one run. No complete games on either side. In so many ways it belonged to Gene Tenace. He hit home runs his first two times up—the only player in history to do it—and drove in all three runs as we edged the Reds in game one at Riverfront Stadium.

Gene was so much like Sal; he didn't take any grief from anybody. When he first started catching, there was no pattern to his pitch calling, but as time went on, he improved. And as he proved in the Series, he was a great fastball hitter. His swing reminded me a lot of Killebrew's—short, compact, with a lot of pop. He'd eat fastballs for lunch; the way to get Gino out was to use the curve. Thankfully, the Reds never quite figured that out.

In game two I scattered six hits through six, and by the time I tired in the ninth, we were leading 2–0. Perez opened the inning with a single over Campy's glove. The next batter up was third baseman Dennis Menke. Just one more hitter, I thought. Then Rollie. Always Rollie.

My first pitch was a mistake, a fastball down the middle; I had hoped to pitch Menke inside. He turned on it and hammered the ball deep to left. It rose up, up toward the twelve-foot wall. I figured it was gone. Lord knows I'd had enough experience judging home runs. But this time I was wrong. Rudi raced back to the wall, turned his back to the field, and twisted his left hand, his glove hand, across his body just before crashing spread-eagled into the wall. When he turned around, the ball was lodged in the webbing of his glove. It had to be one of the greatest catches—maybe *the* greatest—in the sixty-nine year history of the Series. A couple minutes later Dick sent for Rollie, who shut the door for our second straight win.

OTHER VOICES—JOE RUDI

"I was playing Menke straightaway at the time. He was a line-drive hitter, not known as a big power hitter. Not like Bench and those other guys. When he first hit the ball, I thought it was out. But, as it turns out, it was exactly the type of hit they'd worked with me on for two years: a ball straight over my head and, on this one, a little to my left. I broke on the ball, ran like hell until I got to the wall, flipping my glasses down. Then I

turned back in. I put my hand out, concentrating on the ball and just feeling where the wall was. I haven't talked much about it, but the ball was right on the edge of the sun when I spotted it; there was no sky between the sun and the ball. If the ball had been a few more inches to the left, there's no way I'd have caught it.

"I remember catching it, trying to turn my glove so the ball wouldn't pop out when I hit the wall. All those things happened in slow motion. But I do know one thing: I never would have made that catch without all that practice. Never would've gotten near it."

What's this? A mob of 10,000 screaming A's fans waiting for us at the Oakland airport. It had to be a mirage.

"I can't believe we're in Oakland," said Sal.

But we were. Unfortunately, the home field advantage didn't help us the next day, when Jack Billingham and Clay Carroll combined on a three-hitter. I thought we'd locked up the Series the following night when three pinch hits helped us rally and beat the Reds 3–2 with two runs in the bottom of the ninth.

One game away.

It was all up to me now. Game five. It wasn't to be. Pete Rose, just one for fifteen up to that point, hit my first pitch of the game over the 375-feet sign in right. Well, I thought, Daddy said it was gonna happen, and it just did. At least I got that runner off base real quick. Menke added another dinger in the fourth. Tenace's fourth home run (tying a Series record) and a two-run pinch single by Marquez, his twelfth hit in twenty-two at bats, got us a lead, but I couldn't hold it and, for once, neither could Rollie. We lost 5–4.

The next day it wasn't even close. We lost again, 8–1.

Game seven. A crowd of 56,000 on hand. Baseball like it oughta be. Blue Moon on the mound against Billingham. But Williams wasn't sitting pat, not now. Epstein, 0–16, was benched; Alou, one hit in six games, was dropped down to the sixth spot; Tenace, switched from catcher to first (the Reds were stealing us blind), was moved into the cleanup spot.

Odom took a 1–0 lead into the fifth. Perez doubled, Cesar Geronimo walked, and the count ran to 2–0 on Davey Concepcion before Williams signaled me in from the pen. Why not? We weren't playing any eighth game. I proceeded to walk Concepcion and load the bases, bringing up pinch hitter Hal McRae. I knew McRae well; he hit a lot like Rudi, sprayed it around. He liked to go the opposite way. I had to keep the ball tight; inside, he wouldn't be able to take me deep.

So much for that theory. McRae belted my first pitch 400 feet to deepest center field. All I could think of was, "Not now, not a grand slam in the World Series." But Mangual, back to the wall, made the catch. Perez tagged up and scored. Then Rose drilled a ball deep to right center. Again, Mangual hauled it in. Nobody said a word in the dugout. I finished the sixth and seventh innings, but Williams had seen enough. Every ball the Reds hit looked like it'd been launched by NASA. "I know you're getting guys out, Cat," Dick said. "But you're damn near scaring me to death. I gotta make a change."

Guess who saved it? Fingers, of course. Guess who knocked in the winning run? Tenace, of course. He doubled home a run to make it 3–2. It ended that way as Rollie coaxed Rose into flyin' out to Rudi in left. The Oakland A's, twelve years after Charles O. Finley bought himself a ball club, had finally won a World Series.

Inside the locker room we gave each other champagne showers. I'd never seen Mr. Finley so happy. "My first two or three years the barbs bothered me," he yelled to no one in particular. "But not anymore."

Sal and I grabbed the World Series trophy, holding on for dear life, cherishing a victory over a team nobody thought we could beat. To this day, beating the Reds' butts in that Series remains one of the true highlights of my career. The long-haired, mustachioed men from Oakland who weren't supposed to be in the same class with Cincinnati, had proved a point. It's not how you look, or what you say, it's how you *play*.

"Mr. Finley," we yelled over the din, "we'd like to get miniatures of this if we could."

"Miniatures?" asked Finley. *"Miniatures?* Hell, no. Everybody gets the same size." And we did. The trophy is in my living room today. As I said, the first time around, the man spared no expense.

Meanwhile, the champagne flowed. Funny thing was, though, in all the excitement, none of the players got real drunk. The two biggest casualties were Dick Williams' son and Epstein's wife. Now, to be honest, I've got to take more than a little credit for what happened to the little Williams. I kept passing the bubbly in his direction. He got so looped I had to stand him in a cold shower and dress him myself before heading to the airport.

As for Epstein's wife, all I know is that when I walked out of the locker room, she passed out in my arms. I put her down on the sidewalk and hustled back inside to find Ep.

"Hey, Mike," I said. "You better go outside."

"For what?"

"Your wife's passed out on the sidewalk."

Epstein gave me one of those you-gotta-be-kidding-me looks, took another glance at the madcap celebration. Another look at the door leading to his wife.

"Ah, let her die. . . ."

On the charter home we certainly made up for lost time. It got pretty crazy. Finley was the craziest, leading a parade of jazz musicians up and down the aisle, playing the same "Sugar in the Morning" over and over again. But by the time we neared Oakland, the only sugar that folks wanted was in their coffee.

Just as we were about to land, Finley stopped at the seat where Duncan and Reggie were sitting. The way I got it later, Duncan and Finley had a rather rough exchange of words. Charlie said something about "knowing" Dave. Dunc responded with a comment to the effect that Charlie didn't know any of us, and never really cared to.

Mr. Finley just shrugged his shoulders and kept on singing. But like a mule, he never forgot. On March 24, 1973, Dave Duncan was traded to Cleveland for catcher Ray Fosse. So much for champagne celebrations.

Ever get into one of those grooves where dreams and reality meet, and you're floating on a cushion of air, above the crowds, in total command of every possible situation?

Well, that's exactly how I felt on the mound for much of the 1973 season. Above the crowds. In total control. About 250 innings worth of feeling, if memory serves me right. I lost just five times in twenty-six decisions that summer, an .808 percentage, upping my two-year win-loss record to a stunning 42–12. It didn't matter whom I faced. Almost everything I threw was either on the black or just off the edge. Fact is, I guess the only thing I missed all year was the victory parade after we won our second straight World Series—this time in seven wild games over the New York Mets. I skipped all the post-Series festivities to get home to Helen and the kids—whom I hadn't spent any time with in six weeks—and, truth be told, to get in some dove hunting. When you're hot, you're hot, and I was itching to see if my skill in one sport had rubbed off on another.

Naturally, Mr. Finley threatened to fine me $1000 if I didn't show up to "help promote baseball in the Bay Area."

"Mr. Finley," I said, "if we haven't promoted baseball by winning two straight World Series, then we'll never do it." Never heard another word about any fine after that.

And anyway, I needed a break. Talk about an *intense* season. Streaks, gripes, groans, moans, bad breaks (including my thumb), Panamanian pinch runners, a World Series where a player is fired, our manager tells us he's quitting, and we threaten to walk out over a ticket snafu that leaves our wives in fear for their lives.

But don't let me get ahead of myself. Let's roll the videotape back to spring training for a second and take a look around the clubhouse. Epstein's nowhere to be found. He's been traded, no, *given* away, to Texas for reliever Horatio Peña—a swap of twenty-six home runs, seventy RBIs, eleven game-winning hits, and a .270 average for a 2–7 record, fifteen saves, and a 3.20 ERA. Not exactly the kind of trade that made Finley famous. But it just so happens that Mike had the misfortune of going 0–16 in the World Series. So off he went, unhappily, into oblivion. (The man's 1972 stats weren't even listed in our 1973 media guide. His World Series at bats were eliminated too; it was like Epstein never existed. Of course, Peña's stats were all there in black and white.)

And who's the black guy making all those funny catches in center field? Billy North, that's who. Billy came over to Oakland in a trade for Locker, and as it turned out, he proved to be just what we needed at the top of our lineup. A versatile switch-hitter blessed with great speed and instincts in the outfield and more pop in his bat than he got credit for. Especially from our announcers. I remember them talking about Billy, saying things like, "Here's Billy North coming up to the plate. If he was in a boat, he couldn't hit the water that's how bad a hitter he is. . . . Ooops, there's a base hit."

The only worry we had about Billy was his "hot dog" style.

Or so we thought. Watching him catch flies in the outfield, glove at shoulder level or below, Billy looked about as laid back as any ten surfers put together. "Billy," I told him one day, "we don't care how you catch it. Between your legs. Behind your back. Up your nose. Just don't miss it." And to his credit, he rarely did.

Meanwhile, the club and front office were in chaos. The first of three ticket managers to resign that year walked out. Our entire switchboard staff quit one day in a dispute over salary. The team was playing like it'd been set in cement, losing five of our first six regular-season games, outfielders were bumping into each other in the field like the Keystone Cops, runners getting picked off bases. I wasn't helping matters much; it took me six starts to win my first game. Vida and Blue Moon weren't exactly burning up the league either. Vida had a sore arm and was struggling and Moon went winless in his first five decisions. (It got so bad that at one point a lot of us shaved our beards and mustaches to change our luck.)

Finley didn't put up with this circus atmosphere for long. He traded for Deron Johnson, a veteran first baseman who could hit. Williams immediately plugged Johnson into our lineup as the DH. First game out, Johnson got a couple of hits and drove in four runs in an 11–4 victory as I went the distance. From that point on, the club started picking up steam. Executing. In May, I pitched twenty-six innings without allowing a run; by mid-June I was 8–3 with just two earned runs in my last fifty-one innings. Now in my ninth year in the big leagues, it was all coming together: I had three pitches—fastball, curve, and slider—and I could spot them all, especially the slider, within a three-inch circle wherever and whenever I wanted. In succession I shut out California, Kansas City, and Detroit, bringing us back within shouting distance of league-leading Chicago.

By mid-July I'd rattled off nine straight wins and raised my overall record to 15–3—good enough to earn the starting nod for the American League in the All Star Game. But I wasn't the only Oakland player having a four-star season. Five other A's made the team that year, including Fingers, Jackson, and Bando. Fingers, beginning to tap deep into his enormous potential, was nothing short of sensational, pitching two, three, four, and sometimes even six innings at times, picking up save after save. Knowles, Holtzman and Blue, now recovered from his arm problems, were also having starlike seasons.

As it turned out, even suffering the most damaging injury to date in my career didn't slow me down. Pitching in the All Star Game, I fractured a thumb attempting to catch a one-hop shot back up the middle off the bat of Billy Williams. I missed the next five weeks of the season only to return and win six of my next seven starts, boosting my record to 21–4—my third straight season with twenty or more victories. (Since April 28, in fact, I'd gone twenty and three.) We clinched the pennant in late September on a home run by Bando, his twenty-seventh of the year, as Vida won number twenty. Once again, it was playoff time. An encore performance of our 1971 league championship series against the Birds of Baltimore. A chance for some sweet, sweet revenge.

It certainly didn't happen in the first game, as Baltimore routed Vida 6–0, making it four straight postseason wins by Baltimore over Oakland. I got the call in game two, and thanks to four home runs, two by Big Sal, I beat the Birds 6–3. Two games—a win and loss—later, I was back on the mound again in the fifth and final game. This time I was matched against Doyle Alexander; yes, the same Doyle Alexander who pitched so magnificently for the Detroit Tigers down the stretch in the summer of 1987.

You'd never have known it was such a crucial game by looking into the stands. The game was played before just 25,000 fans, the smallest crowd in league championship history. But crowd or no crowd, we weren't about to be denied. Rudi knocked in our first run and we scored two more in the fourth to put us in the lead 3–0. I didn't have my best stuff that day, and later Jim Palmer said he thought they'd get to me. No way. This was special, a game I *wanted* to pitch. I held the Orioles hitless for four innings and gave up just five hits for the entire game. After the game even their manager, Earl Weaver, had something nice to say: "He's got his doctorate in pitching now," he said. "He had his B.A.; then he went on and got his master's. Today, the way he pitched, he earned his Ph.D."

After the World Series against the Mets—who were making their first appearance since the "miracle" of '69—I could have written a dissertation on the effect of disruptive influences on the family unit, the unit in this case being the Oakland A's. The only semipeaceful game was the opener, which we won 2–1 as the incomparable combination of the world's two worst dressers

(Holtzman and Knowles) combined with the "Cartoon Kid" (Fingers) to do the job. Holtzman, a twenty-one-game winner during the year and truly a master on the mound, went the first five. Rollie chipped in with three and one-third before the call went out to Knowles. We were now ahead in the Series one game to love.

Game two is when all the fireworks began. It went down in the books as the longest World Series game to date (four hours and thirteen minutes), but it's forever remembered by baseball fans as the day Charlie Finley fired our reserve second baseman Mike Andrews.

The stage had been set back in September when Williams and Finley tried to activate infielder Manny Trillo for the Series. Because Trillo had been picked up after the September 1 deadline, he couldn't be added to our postseason roster without permission from the Mets. Permission denied, said the Mets. Charlie complained, but nobody listened. That left Andrews, who'd drifted over from Boston after helping the Sox win a pennant in 1967, as our backup, backup second baseman behind Greenie and Kubiak. Now I know what you're thinking. Who in the hell *needs* three second basemen? Normally, I would say, absolutely, you're right, nobody. Except Williams. Greenie wasn't hitting—when I pitched, he used to tell Williams to let me bat ninth so *he* could bunt me over—so Williams played Russian roulette around the bag. Greenie would play long enough to get an at bat or two, then somebody would pinch-hit, and Kubiak would go out to play second. When Kubiak's turn to hit came up, Dick would pinch-hit for him and send another guy out to second. That guy, in this case, became Andrews in the twelfth inning. The scoreboard read: Mets 6, A's 6.

What happened next is all part of Finley legend and lore. Andrews happened to make errors on successive plays (missing a ground ball with two outs and the bases loaded and then making an errant throw) which led to three of the four runs the Mets scored in the twelfth inning. It made no difference to Mr. Finley that we were behind 7–6 when Mike messed up or that we made three other errors that day. No, we ended up losing 10–7, and Finley wanted a scapegoat. In Finley's office after the game Mike met with the irate owner and the team doctor, Harry R. Walker, for almost two hours. In their presence Andrews was coerced into signing a medical report that stated that he was now being put on the disabled list because of a "chronic" sore shoulder known in medical mumbo jumbo as "bicep groove tenosynovitis." Chronic my ass. Chronic as of the twelfth inning on Sunday. Andrews later said Finley had threatened "to destroy me in baseball" unless he signed the doctor's statement.

That did it. We'd lived with Finley's cost cutting, his dime-store business dealings. But this, this was the most despicable act I'd ever witnessed in baseball, a cruelly blatant attempt to railroad Mike out of his career. I spoke out loud and clear, telling the national media that Finley had another thing coming if he thought we were going to stand by silently and let this happen. The other guys felt exactly the same way. Ironically, it was just what we needed to pull us all together. On Monday we walked onto the practice field at Shea Stadium with Mike's number 17 taped to the sleeves of our uniform "in memory" of Andrews, now exiled to his home in Peabody, Massachusetts. Williams got hot because of all the camera crews hanging around. But it was pretty apparent he'd tired of Finley's act too. That night, in a private team meeting, Dick told us his plans for the future. Shockingly, they didn't include the Oakland A's.

"I won't be with you guys next year," he said. Mouths dropped open all around the room. *What the hell was this? In the middle of the World Series?* "It's not because of the team. Not you guys. It's between me and Charlie. I can't put up with this shit anymore. We're doing everything we can to win, and he's doing everything he can to keep us from winning. So win or lose, it doesn't matter to me. I'm out of here. I'm gone."

We all took a deep breath. Nobody said much. What the hell could you say? It was a total shock. We might not have liked Dick at times (no, make that we *definitely* didn't like Dick at times), for the way he treated us, but we always liked the results of those actions. The winning. The trophies. The respect.

I talked to Mike on the phone just before game three, and it gave me the mental boost I needed. I was about to pitch against Tom Seaver—19–10, 2.08 ERA, in front of a wild Shea Stadium crowd of 54,000 in the first New York night game in Series history. I always tell kids that if they ever have a chance to get some film of Seaver pitching to grab it. He and Jim Palmer come as close to perfection as any two pitchers alive. I knew I couldn't give up any runs that night because Seaver, a big-game power pitcher if ever there was one, wasn't about to get cuffed around.

And if the Andrews-Williams-Seaver scenario wasn't enough to worry about, a couple of more logs were soon tossed on the fire. First, warming up before the game, I ran into a guy on the field I knew, a promoter who worked for daredevil Evil Kneivel. He wasn't supposed to be down there, but hey, it's none of my business. . . .

"Cat," he said, "how you feeling tonight?"

I told him fine, considering.

"You guys gonna win tonight?"

I told him we were gonna try.

"Great," said the guy, "because I got $50,000 on you and the A's tonight."

The words couldn't come to my mouth fast enough.

"Well," I said, "then get the hell away from me."

Log number two arrived in the form of the thirty or so folks who had bused up from Hertford to see me pitch. Daddy was on hand; so were my brothers, cousins, local politicians, and the like. Not that I minded having them there. I loved it. But you know, you always want to do your best in front of those you love the most. I remember looking over in the stands and seeing Daddy, a wooden match in his mouth, chewin' away. He had a habit of chewin' on one while he smoked. First inning I'm told he chewed six right down to nothing. Mainly because the Mets were lighting me up. I don't know, maybe I tried to smoke the ball by people instead of pitching smart. Whatever. On the second pitch of the game, third baseman Wayne Garrett hit a towering home run to right. Felix Milan followed with a single, and Rusty Staub singled through short on a hit-and-run. Dick came to the mound and tried to calm me down. It didn't work. My next pitch—a slider I released at the wrong height— bounced wildly in the dirt past Fosse. Now we're down 2–0. "Now," I told myself, "you *really* can't give up any more runs."

And I didn't. Williams pinch-hit for me in the sixth, when we scored a run to tie it. We eventually won it 3–2 in eleven innings on a base hit by Campy and with some gutsy relief from Rollie.

"Tomorrow," said Greenie, "we'll have to find something else to get us going."

It didn't take long. Right after the game we had another open rebellion on our hands. First thing out of Helen's mouth when she saw me was, "You guys shouldn't play tomorrow." I'd never seen her so angry.

"You know where our seats were," she said. "Way up above home plate in the second deck. We sat right on the railing, and I swear, Jimmy, I thought I was gonna fall off. The people up there were so rude I couldn't believe it. Couple of the girls just got up and left and took a cab back to the hotel."

Something wasn't right. We'd all got tickets the day before, and the wives were supposed to sit right behind our dugout. Now Helen's telling me she spent the better part of four hours surrounded by belligerent Mets' fans. The Mets' wives had been given front-row seats in Oakland; now our wives had been shipped up to the stratosphere, high above home plate, worried out of their wits. "The rumors about the Mets' fans scared us half to death," Jill Fingers later told the papers. "We were afraid that if we waved our banners, we'd get bopped on the head or something."

What the hell was going on?

Tenace finally figured it out. Seems somebody had pulled a switcheroo—using our wives' tickets for his own personal entourage. I wonder who it could have been?

Next day we had another meeting. Face-to-face in the locker room with Finley. You talk about one pissed off bunch of ballplayers. Nothing's worse, believe me, than having to worry about the safety of your wife. No, I take that back. There's nothing worse than hearing about how dreadful it was sitting right on the upper-deck rail, getting insults tossed in your face by people with the IQ of a turnip. So now we're talking forfeit. I mean it. We were ready to chuck it, lock, stock, and ball bag, and show Finley once and for all that you can mess with us, but don't start messing with our families. I could just see the next day's headline: "Amazing! Mets Tie Series as A's Walk Off . . . Finley Ticket Switch Ignites Forfeit."

"We ain't gonna play, Charlie."

At first Finley couldn't believe his ears.

"What?"

"You heard us," we said. "We ain't gonna play the game. We're not going out on the field. Forget it."

"Now, guys, wait a second. Let me explain . . ."

"We ain't playing, Charlie."

You could see the sweat forming on Charlie's forehead. He knew he had made a mistake, a big one, and he was scrambling to make it up to us. "Listen, guys, it won't happen again. Honest."

It'd better not, we said. And our wives had better be behind that dugout come game time, or—no ifs, ands, or buts—we are history. Charlie could suit up some of his friends and play.

True to his word, our wives were back where they belonged. And, thanks to a ruling by Commissioner Bowie Kuhn, who found the sudden nature of Andrews's injury dubious at best, so was Mike. He got into the game as a pinch hitter in the eighth inning of an eventual 6–1 loss to left-hander Jon Matlack. Mike got two standing ovations—one before he hit, another after grounding out to third. Everybody in the park got right up to cheer—everybody, that is, except Finley, sitting in green jacket and hat under a blanket near the Oakland dugout. Then I guess he figured what the hell. He clapped softly a couple of times. Then more boldly. Finally, he started waving a green and gold pennant like a ten-year-old kid. Which, I guess, is how he acted at times.

The Mets took a 3–2 Series lead the next day on a three-hit shutout (2–0) by Jerry Koosman and Tug McGraw. I think all the commotion had finally caught up with us. So now it was my turn again, game six, a rematch with the great Tom Terrific.

But before we went head to head in Oakland Williams took a long look at his color-coded charts and started making some changes. He had to. One run in eighteen innings was nobody's idea of the way to win the World Series. So Tenace went from first back behind the plate, Deron Johnson started at first, and cagey veteran Vic Davilillo went out to center. The best move, however, was the one Dick didn't make. He left Reggie in the cleanup spot. During the regular season Reg'd hit thirty-two homers and had driven in 117 runs, but aside from one four-hit day early in the Series, his bat had been silent.

This time, however, he rose to the occasion, lashing out three hits, two of them doubles, and we won 3–1. I beat Seaver again, one pitch at a time, giving up just four hits over 7⅓ innings, retiring eleven straight from the first to the fifth. I was down to my last five outs, but Dick came and got me after a pinch-hit single by Ken Boswell. The Mets managed to score once, but

Rollie—pitching for the fifth time in six games—coaxed Cleon Jones into flying out to center field to end the game.

Jon Matlack versus Holtzman in game seven. For the second day in a row, the Mausoleum was a madhouse, a sea of chants and cheers. And here we were, facing the man who was truly the Mets' ace at the moment—a pitcher who had allowed no earned runs in his last twenty-six innings and just one—as in *uno*—in his last forty-two. Not a terribly pleasant thought for a team that had hit 147 home runs during the regular season and none so far in the World Series.

But that's what made the A's so great. We'd always find a way to beat you. And that's just what we did against Matlack. In the third inning Holtzman, a surprisingly good hitter, doubled. Then Campy homered to left for a 2–0 lead. Rudi added a single. With one out, Reggie came to the plate, riding a high from the day before. As I said, when he's hot, nobody can stop him. Not Seaver. Not Matlack. Nobody. Matlack made the mistake of hanging a curve, and Reggie jumped all over it. It landed 400 feet away for another home run and a 4–0 lead that the Mets never touched. Reggie was awarded the MVP, but it could have easily gone to Knowles, who pitched in all seven games, or to Rollie, who worked in all but one. Or to Campy. Or to Sal. Or . . .

Within minutes of our win, champagne in one hand, resignation letter in the other, Dick Williams announced that he was leaving as manager for "personal" reasons. Dick had gotten an offer to manage the Yankees, which would keep him closer to his family in Florida. He'd been our leader for three straight years—a longevity record in the history of Finley management. Most of all, he taught us how to win. I must admit that it was sad to see Dick go. Little did I know that, even more sadly, I would be next on the list.

10

FISHING FOR CATFISH

"If Cat had stayed, we would have won again in 1975. He was a quiet guy, but he was the backbone of the team. He never rattled, never let a loss get him down. He was always there for us."

—Joe Rudi

To throw a new twist on an old phrase, some folks might say that Mr. Finley bought the farm after I signed a free-agent contract with the New York Yankees on the last day of December 1974. After all, once I left the A's and free agency became a legitimate option in 1976, Finley would end up losing Reggie, Rollie, Vida, Sal, Rudi, Holtzman, and a host of other disgruntled players. Conventional wisdom suggests that if Finley had handled my situation fairly, with a little more grace, it might have kept others from jumping ship. The Oakland A's team that was good enough to win three straight World Series might have stuck together and taken a run at the Yankees record of five in a row. But we'll never know, will we?

The real reason we won't know—and here's the twist—is that Finley *didn't* buy the farm when he had the chance. Not the proverbial one. No, this one was real. Very real. Three hundred of the most fertile acres in all of North Carolina.

Backing up a bit, early in 1969 I borrowed $120,000 from Mr. Finley to buy that particular plot of land, promising to repay the debt at a rate of $20,000 a year plus 6 percent interest for as long as it took. The acreage in question was just a few hundred yards east of where I live today but miles ahead in soil content and productivity, its rich black dirt fed by the Perquiman's River.

A great buy. Or so I figured. But come June, Finley started hounding me and my dad for his money back. All $120,000. Right now. "But I'm supposed to pay you in installments," I said. To which he responded, "I know, I know, but I'm buying a hockey team and a basketball team, and I need the money."

I told Finley the truth. I didn't have the money. Not at what he was paying me a year ($75,000), and I wasn't about to go robbing Peter to pay Paul. Not after all my daddy taught me. But Mr. Finley was in one of his Charlie O. (the mule) moods. He wanted his money back. End of conversation. For a while, at least.

Then the calls started. Day and night. Night and day. Only on the days I pitched. Of course, Finley denied knowing I was pitching. This from the man who knew how much popcorn they sold every night, what lights were out in the rest rooms.

"Cat," he'd say over and over again, the same raspy voice, "do you know who this is?"

"Yes, sir, Mr. Finley."

"I . . . need . . . my . . . money."

It never varied. Or ended. "I . . . need . . . my . . . money." I'll admit it; it got to me. Try having your boss call up just before a sales presentation. See how you do. That's why, as I mentioned before, I started eight games in August and lost every one, ending the season 12–15. It got so bad that when I went to the ballpark I wouldn't take any calls. *"I . . . want . . . my . . . money."*

Finally, at Daddy's urging, I sold all but thirty acres to a longtime friend, Tommy Harrell, and built my present house on the remaining land. It's no coincidence that Harrell has since been voted the outstanding vegetable farmer in North Carolina and annually grows some of the finest corn, soybeans, and peanuts in the state. If not for Mr. Finley's attitude, I'd still have those 300 acres and be making a far better living off the land because of it. Am I still pissed off? You bet I am.

Which, in a roundabout way, brings us to the circumstances surrounding my departure from Oakland. A move that didn't have to happen. I never wanted to leave. Not in a million years. I loved the club, my teammates, and could have easily ended my career there. I'd have forgiven and forgotten if Finley would have asked me just once what it would take to keep me happy.

"Mr. Finley," I would have said, "you agree to buy back the land I sold tax-free [at a cost of perhaps $600,000] and I'll stay and play in Oakland for the same money I'm making now."

End of conversation. End of argument. But contrary to what

Mr. Finley says today, *that* conversation never took place. And for only one reason. Right up until the bitter (and I do mean bitter) end, Finley never once made a serious offer for my services. He wanted no part of me, not when it came to money. And it cost him dearly.

On February 11, 1974, I signed the standard major league baseball players contract, one that would pay me $100,000 a year for the next two seasons. Typically, the first contract Finley mailed to me I returned unsigned without comment. (I could have made more money baling hay.) The second contract I received—for a far more equitable sum—I signed, requesting, as an addendum, that Mr. Cherry seek IRS approval to defer $50,000 of my salary into insurance annuities. Much as Mr. Finley protested later, he knew I wanted to defer $50,000; either that or he can't read his own writing. As copies of letters sent to Mr. Cherry (letters Mr. Cherry has in his possession) attest, Finley went so far as to request minor revisions in the wording of the contract as to exactly when the $50,000 would be paid. Finley himself added the words "to be paid during the seasons as earned" before returning the contract—unsigned—to Mr. Cherry.

Of course, Finley did have other things on his mind at the time. Arbitration, for one. As the '74 season approached, I was about the only big-name player who'd signed; the rest of the so-called stars, tired of Finley's cold-blooded "take it or leave it" style of negotiating, had filed to have their disputes heard before an independent arbitrator—a new wrinkle in baseball. Yes sir, Finley's legal beagles sure had their hands full that spring as nine angry A's—Reggie, Sal, Holtzman, Fingers, Knowles, Rudi, Tenace, Kubiak, and reserve infielder Jack Heidemann—all filed for arbitration.

So it was in the presence of federal arbitrator Howard S. Block in San Francisco that the "Ice Man" finally began to melt. One by one Jackson, Bando, Holtzman, Knowles, and Rudi all won big raises—thousands of dollars more than Finley had been willing—or wanted—to pay. Reggie got the biggest raise—from $75,000 to $135,000—but the others did fine, too: Bando went from $60,000 to $100,000, Holtzman from $55,000 to $93,000, Rollie from $48,000 to $65,000, and Knowles from $50,000 to $59,000.

Now all we needed was a manager. Williams, it turns out, had been hired by the California Angels, his dream of managing the Yankees canceled by Finley's demand for high-priced player compensation. So, here we were, three days before training camp, the two-time defending World Series champs, and we still don't know who's the boss. Charlie answered that question the next day. Reaching into his bag of tricks, he rehired Alvin Dark to manage our club in 1974.

To say Dark was a darkhorse candidate is like saying Pat Paulsen is gonna be our next President. Alvin had been in golfing exile in Miami the previous 2½ years, something of a forlorn and forgotten figure in baseball circles. After being fired by Finley in the wake of the Krausse airplane incident, Dark had managed Cleveland for a brief period in 1968 before settling in Miami.

"Yes," said Finley at the time of the announcement, "he's managed the club before. Yes, he was fired. Yes, he's back. And yes, he expects to be fired again some day." Any more questions?

No, but after we started off slower than a pregnant water buffalo, Charlie had some answers. "I'm playing to *win!*" he screamed at Dark one day. "If you don't start playing aggressive baseball, I'll kick your fucking ass out of here. We won two years without you, and we can win again without you!"

Overall, Alvin did a solid job. He knew baseball, maybe too much, because he was always trying to outsmart the other team, and sometimes he ended up outsmarting himself. I remember one night Alvin pulled some move that backfired. Sal 'bout had a fit. He started kicking over trash cans, swearing, screaming at the top of his lungs: "Dark couldn't manage a damn meat market." After which I casually mentioned to Sal that the market manager in question had been standing right behind Bando the entire time.

"Ah shit," said Sal, "now what am I gonna say."

"Well, tell him he can't manage a meat market."

So Sal trooped off to Dark's office where he was met by a man with tears in his eyes. "Sal, you . . . really . . . don't . . . think . . . I . . . can . . . manage?"

Alvin looked so upset that Sal couldn't yell anymore. "Shit, I didn't mean it, Alvin," said Sal, hoping to make the best of a bad situation.

But Alvin would have none of it: "Sal, you . . . really . . . don't . . . think . . . I . . . can . . . manage?"

Adding to our woes, Charlie, after taking it in the shorts—

and wallet—from the arbitrator, started cutting costs. Out went
the stadium decorations. No fireworks after home runs. Half-
priced nights were shaved down from twenty to four. No family
discounts. No ball girls. No sponsors on TV telecasts. No
stamps for fan mail, for goodness sake.

So maybe it was money. Maybe the man who had boasted
that he'd made millions in insurance was desperate for my
measly $120,000; maybe the $25,000 he would have saved in
taxes had he not deferred the $50,000 into annuities made the
difference between red and black ink in his ledger. Either way,
by the All Star break he still hadn't paid me the other $50,000.
And I was beginning to get a little *upset*.

I ran into a player representative, Jim Kaat, just before the All
Star Game. I knew Jim and trusted him. I whispered to him how
I was gonna be a free agent and then watched his eyes grow to
the size of saucers.

"No you aren't," he said.

"Yes I am," I replied. "I don't think Mr. Finley is going to
pay me that money he owes me."

"Get your lawyer to write him a letter," Kaat advised, "but
don't write too many letters. He might change his mind."

All during August and September, Mr. Cherry fired off
letters to Finley, asking him to sign the deferred compensation
agreement. Not once did Mr. Cherry get a straight answer. One
time Finley contended that he was ready to commit but he
feared his wife, the secretary of the club, wouldn't sign the
paper. Another time Finley complained that he was worried
about other A's wanting the same clause in their contracts.

Mr. Cherry finally got tired of all the stalling and took my
case to the Major League Baseball Players Association in New
York. On October 4, 1974, this telegram arrived at the offices of
Charles O. Finley & Co., 310 South Michigan Avenue, Chicago, Illinois:

This wire is sent on behalf of James A. Hunter. Pursuant to
paragraph 7(a) of contract between Mr. Hunter and the
Oakland Club, please be advised that contract is termi-
nated due to Club's default in making payments in
accordance with said contract and its failure to remedy said
default within ten days after receiving written notice
thereof. Because of the impending playoffs and World
Series, the effective date of termination shall be the day

following the last game played by the Oakland Athletics in 1974.

Richard M. Moss, General Counsel
Major League Baseball Players Association

That last day turned out to be October 17, 1974, after we beat the Dodgers 3–2 to win our third straight World Series four games to one. A few weeks earlier we'd swept to our fourth straight American League West title. I'd won the title-clinching game, my league-leading twenty-fifth win of the season against just twelve losses. My stats were the best in baseball: 318 innings, twenty-three complete games in forty-one starts, an ERA of 2.49, a career-high (at the time) six shutouts, 143 strikeouts, and only forty-six walks. After the Series, I would win the Cy Young Award over Ferguson Jenkins.

But those stats were the regular-season story. They didn't mean diddly in the opening game of the playoffs. At least not to the Baltimore Orioles. Yep, those guys *again*. This time they bombed me 6–1 on the strength of homers by Paul Blair, Brooks Robinson, and Bobby Grich. Equal opportunity pitching at its best (or worst). Thanks to back-to-back shutouts by Holtzman (a 5–0 five-hitter) and Blue (a 1–0 two-hitter), however, I was back in business for the fourth game.

Just before Blue's masterpiece I'd been handed a message: "Mr. Finley wants to see you."

I walked into Finley's office to find American League President Lee MacPhail and Commissioner Kuhn in attendance. "You know all these guys," said Finley.

"Yep."

"I wanted to call you up here to pay you all the money I owed you. $50,000."

"No," I said. "Mr. Finley, you pay it the way the contract reads and everything will be just fine."

Finley started throwing a fit, making a scene. "See, Mr. Commissioner," he yelled. "What can I do? I offer him the money, and he won't take it. What can I do?"

What he did was ask everyone else but me to leave the room. Well, I figured, this son of a gun is finally gonna pay me. With maybe, just maybe, a grand or two of interest tossed in for suffering. Wrong. Finley never said another word about the money. All he talked was baseball.

"Jimmy, we're gonna win tomorrow. You're gonna pitch. We're gonna hit 'em. Then it's on to the World Series."

Which, when you think about it, is pretty much what happened. I edged Cuellar 2–1 in a rematch of the first game of the playoffs, pitching seven shutout innings of three-hit baseball. Cuellar didn't allow a hit during his 4⅔ innings but he lost the game on nine—count 'em, nine—walks and Reggie's RBI double off reliever Ross Grimsley in the seventh. When all the shouting and celebrating had died down, someone figured out we'd held the heavy-hitting Orioles scoreless from the eighth inning of the first game until the ninth inning of the fourth game—twenty-seven innings, fifteen without a runner ever advancing to second. Pitching, defense, and timely hitting. The Oakland way to play.

Welcome back to the 1974 World Series. The fussin' and feudin' A's (New York Times columnist Dave Anderson blithely suggested that the A's might be better off wearing green and gold bathrobes and carrying gray pails and water bottles) against "Team Together," the Los Angeles Dodgers, the winningest bunch in baseball that year (102 victories). All straight hair and Hollywood smiles.

Well, at least we lived up to our image. Dodger first baseman Billy Buckner helped matters along by suggesting to all the world that only a few of our guys could make their precious little Dodger roster. Riiiight. We didn't say so at the time, preferring to keep words to ourselves, but Buckner made a big mistake by telling us we couldn't play.

Finley, on the other hand, was once again the center of a three-ring circus. When he wasn't telling Dark who to play where—actions that caused Tenace to brand Dark a "puppet" —he was fending off questions about my contract dispute (which had now gone public in a big way), a pending divorce from his wife, Shirley, and a $2.5 million lawsuit filed by Mike Andrews.

The really big excitement, though, came the day before the Series was set to open in L.A. We really hadn't had a good fight in a while. Way back in June, when Reggie and Billy North went at it in Detroit, Reggie took the first shot then—and, unfortunately, missed. Billy did a quick tap dance—bam, bam, bam—all over the big fella's face. Now it was Rollie and Blue Moon who squared off in the locker room.

At the time, Rollie's marriage was in a mess, his wife leaving, returning, leaving, who knew what. Moon wouldn't leave it alone. He kept digging into Rollie's personal life—basically an off-limits area when the word is out that a guy's having trouble at home. Rollie took a lot before he started swinging.

Moon countered by slamming Rollie's head into a locker. Blood started spurting everywhere. I played paramedic, stepping between the two pitchers and pressing my hand against the gash on Rollie's scalp until trainer Joe Romo could rush over.

Did the fight bother us? Nah, not really. As Holtzman so aptly put it at the time, "This isn't the College World Series," he said. "With 27,000 bucks on the line, I hate everybody."

The next day Holtzman and Rollie, recovered from the five stitches he received in what he called a "nothing" fight, did a number on the boys in blue, combining for 8⅔ innings of two-run baseball. Along the way we showed the tough-talking Dodgers a thing or two about the A's. Like how a team with the second-lowest batting average in the league in '74 won its third straight pennant. The Dodgers out-hit us, but we scored runs on a blast from Reggie, Campy's suicide squeeze (scoring Holtzman, who had doubled and advanced to third), and a throwing error by Dodger third baseman Ron Cey. So there it was, 3–1 going into the ninth. But then Jimmy Wynn homered and Steve Garvey singled to put the tying run on first with two outs. Dark decided Rollie needed some relief. So he went to the bull pen. To me.

I'd relieved in one game in the previous five years, but Alvin was playing one of his hunches. I'd been up in the fifth inning getting in some throwing when the phone rang. It was Dark. How do you feel? "Great," I said. Next thing I know it's the ninth inning, Garvey's at first, and Big Joe Ferguson is lumbering up to the plate, 56,000 Dodger fans yelling themselves blue in my face.

"This guy can't hit your curveball with a boat paddle," said Alvin as I arrived from the bull pen.

"That's great, but he's gettin' fastballs today."

"Fastballs?" hissed Alvin. "What do you mean fastballs? He can't hit a curveball. Why do you want to throw him fastballs?"

"Because, Alvin," I said patiently, "I ain't got no curveball today."

Five pitches—five fastballs—later, Joe Ferguson went down on strikes.

The Dodgers evened the score the next day when relief pitcher Mike Marshall, who had won fifteen games and saved twenty-one others during the regular season, picked our "designated runner" Herb Washington off first base to kill a ninth inning rally. You never heard of designated runners? Another Finley experiment. Our first one, Alan Lewis, was called the Panamanian Express. He actually knew how to use a bat and glove, but unfortunately, when Alan got to us his legs already had a few too many miles on them. He wasn't near as fast as Washington, the world record holder in the sixty-yard dash at one time. Herbie, you might say, traveled light. He didn't know any baseball and didn't care to learn much. He was the only guy I ever knew who made $100,000 a year in the game and didn't so much as own a bat or glove. But when you could run like Herb, who needed equipment? Herb was so fast that we told him just to make sure the pitcher came set. Well, Marshall, one of the smartest pitchers around (as he loved to tell you), caught Herb leaning and we ended up losing 3–2. So now it was the Dodgers who were back on track, as we headed up to Oakland all tied at one game apiece.

From there it was as easy as one, two, three. Three games, three strikes, and the Dodgers were out.

Strike one. Game three. I shut down the Dodgers and Greenie tied a Series record for double plays (three).

Strike two. Game four. Bando's bloop single keys a four-run sixth, and we win 5–2. Once more Greenie's a wizard around the bag, diving, making sensational stops, always in the right place at the right time.

OTHER VOICES—DICK GREEN

"I was a major part of our pitching strategy. Maybe they don't do it anymore, I don't know. I was very involved in every pitch we threw. We had charts, color-coded things that Williams kept, that told us where a runner would hit a certain pitch. Not only with nobody on, but with men on base, ahead in the count. Fosse and I gave signals to each other all the time before every pitch, and I'd

*tell Campy, who didn't understand the charts too well, or
sometimes I'd yell over to Sal. That's how much we got into the
game. That's why Cat was such a winner. He was into the game
all the time. He knew he was out there two, three hours a night,
at work, and was plumb serious the whole time."*

Strike three. Game five. Fosse strokes a two-run homer. The
Dodgers tie it. In the seventh, Buckner gets pelted with debris,
garbage, Frisbees, and even, unfortunately, a few stray whiskey
bottles. Play is stopped. Instead of warming up, Iron Mike
Marshall, now pitching in his one hundred thirteenth game of
the year, his two hundred eighth inning, joins in on the
discussion about the vulgarity of our fans. He fails to throw one
warmup pitch.

Rudi, once described as "the quiet man in a noisy place" and
now the finest left fielder in baseball (one error in '72, only two
in '73) just stood in the batter's box and waited. He knew what
was coming. "I figured he'd try to sneak a fastball by me
inside," Rudi said afterward. That's exactly what Marshall
tried, and Rudi smoked it deep into the stands in left for the
Series-winning homer. Rollie, who had a hand in every win,
was awarded the MVP.

I skipped the victory parade in Oakland and headed home to
go hunting and wait for Mr. Cherry and Dick Moss to convince
Commissioner Kuhn to excuse himself from our fight with Mr.
Finley. During the World Series, Kuhn had suggested in a press
conference that he was considering mediating my dispute. Moss
quickly challenged the commissioner, saying in no uncertain
terms that Kuhn had no business or authority—to rule on
contract disputes between a player and an owner. The Basic
Bargaining Agreement stipulated that an impartial arbitrator
would rule on all such cases. Moss, a Harvard Law graduate and
former member of the legal staff of the Steelworkers Union, and
a man who would turn baseball upside down in 1976 when he
won the landmark Andy Messersmith free-agent case, was right
on the money as usual. So on November 26, 1974, at the offices
of the Major League Players Association in New York, 375 Park
Avenue, Marvin Miller, executive director of the association,
the owner's attorney John J. Gaherin, and independent arbitrator Peter Seitz heard my case.

I'll say this for Mr. Finley: He stood his ground right up until the end. Joe Flythe, a senior attorney in Mr. Cherry's office, remembers calling Finley just before the hearing, and asking one last time, "Are you willing to talk about this?"

"I've got the money for him," sniffed Finley. "You can have it any time you want. I'll send it to you. Wire it to you. But I'm not going to defer it."

Ask Mr. Cherry about Finley today, and this is what he'll say: "I'll tell you something about Finley. He would never write you a letter. He'd call me at night at all hours, every hour. He said, 'You let him sign I'll give him $50,000 and we'll take care of the farm.' Next day Joe [Flythe] and I would get together and write him a letter and call his attention to what was said. Of course, we kept a copy of everything. When we got to the hearing, we asked him about it. He denied everything. Finally he got so bad about it we pulled out the letters and showed them to him. He knew then that we had it all, and he just sat right back down in his chair."

But right or wrong, Finley wasn't going to go down without a fight—even if it meant stretching the truth from New York to Oakland. At one point Finley did just that, telling Seitz that he never saw, read, or signed my contract. The conversation, as I remember it, went something like this:

Seitz: "What do you mean you didn't sign it? That's your signature, isn't it?"

Finley: "No sir, that's not my signature. My secretary can sign my name just like I can."

Seitz: "Do you mean to tell me you took and never read this contract, never signed this contract?"

Finley: "You're perfectly correct, Mr. Arbitrator. Never seen it. Never read it. Don't know anything about it."

Seitz just slipped down a bit in his seat, pulled out his pipe, and began puffing away. Later, when I took the stand, Finley tried to stare a hole right through me, a major league psych job, legs crossed, dark eyes glued to mine.

It wasn't ten minutes after we both had testified that Finley must have sensed trouble. In the hallway outside the hearing room he buddied up to Mr. Cherry and Mr. Flythe, hinting that I could have my money—no breach of contract. But by then it was too late. On Monday December 16, 1974, by a 2–1 ruling (Seitz and Marvin Miller holding for the majority), I was awarded free agency. A simple technicality—Finley's refusal to honor my contract as written—and, I believe, Seitz's displeasure with Finley's answers, had put me in the unique position of being the first major league ballplayer in history to have the option of signing with *any* team I wanted. After nearly ten years of being an A, a decade of growing up with Greenie, Reggie, Sal, Rollie, Campy, Rudi, and all the rest, after ten long years of what Mr. Finley had once so aptly termed "sweat and sacrifice," the front door had opened. And I walked right through it. Not that I had any idea where I was headed. "We don't have a team anymore," I told Helen that night. "We don't belong to nobody."

The next day, while the commissioner prudently placed an "embargo" on negotiations until he had time to review the decision, Finley made one last move. He called Flythe on the phone. "Joe," he said, calling Flythe by his given name for the first time. "We ought to be able to work out our differences. What is it you want?"

"Mr. Finley," said Flythe. "I think the arbitrator has already decided."

"Oh Joe, that doesn't matter. Let's just get our differences behind us and we'll settle this thing."

We never did. At that point it was over. Finley had burned a bridge, and I wasn't about to swim across the river. I didn't know where I'd pitch next, but, thankfully, I knew the conditions:

1. A five-year contract, fully guaranteed, with substantial deferred money into the 1990s, making sure my future—and that of my children—would be secure even if I didn't save a cent of my salary.

2. I wanted to stay in the American League (where I knew the hitters) and away from artificial turf (where ground balls turn into base hits).

3. I wanted two $25,000 annuities for Todd's and Kim's college education.

No sooner had Kuhn lifted the embargo on December 18 than the phone started ringing. One of the first calls came from Ohio, and a gruff sounding voice on the other end said, "Cat, this is Thurman Munson. We need you here in New York. We can't get enough pitching in New York. We got the hitting, but we need the pitching. And, anyway, I always wanted to catch you, though I'll probably never catch the ball. They'll just hit it all the time."

We laughed. I would quickly learn that that, in a nutshell, was Thurman Munson. Sarcastic, secretive. We joked around some more and said goodnight. I liked the idea of playing for the Yankees—the tradition, all the world titles they'd won. But I kept my mind open. Had to. The phones were ringing off the hook somewhere else—at the law offices of Cherry, Cherry, Flythe & Evans in Ahoskie, North Carolina.

OTHER VOICES—J. CARLTON CHERRY AND JOE FLYTHE

It's a sultry summer day in Ahoskie, North Carolina, the second largest city (5500) in northeastern North Carolina. Mostly black and poor, Ahoskie is a dusty farming/textile town whose claims to fame include Lady Bird Johnson's whistle stop train tour to promote a national beautification project and the fact that one of Ahoskie's own was killed while flying with the Blue Angels flying team. It has a particularly proud past in baseball. Enos Slaughter played in these parts; so did the Perry brothers, Gaylord and Jim.

J. Carlton Cherry and Joe Flythe file into a narrow back room of their law offices, at 119 West Main Street, a quaint, two-story former bank building with Greek pillars out front. Inside, a visitor is taken to a back conference room, no wider than a rodeo chute, that is dominated by law books and a long walnut table. In a red leather chair sits senior partner Cherry, eighty-one years old, balding, with the regal look of an English barrister. Flythe, as he was in '74, is on Cherry's right, the ex-U.S. Air Force captain with a sharp mind for detail.

No, sir, neither Cherry nor Flythe would ever be convicted of impersonating hayseed attorneys. Their client list includes the

Georgia-Pacific Corporation, Planters National Bank and Trust, and Perdue Chicken. Both Cherry and Flythe have banged on a few tables in their time, mostly during $300 million gas and oil deals. So they knew a negotiation when they saw one.

On the table before them are three tattered file folders yellowed with age. The folders are filled with reminders of a three-week period in December of 1974 when Cherry and his partners presided over the biggest free-agent auction in sports history. Stapled to one folder are the business cards of two of the more prominent players—New York Yankee president Gabe Paul and Clyde Kluttz (field director, player development, New York Yankees). Inside the folders, scribbled in pencil, are numerous notations: Catfish's Social Security Number, Marvin Miller's office phone number, Cat's home phone, and the Yankees' address (Yankee Stadium, Bronx, New York 10451). A legal pad offers these musings: "KC will pay $3.3 million in package," "Call Pirates. $500,000 for farm trust or lease purchase." Dollar signs and decimal points abound. So do lists. One list has San Diego on top. On another it's Kansas City.

"The first man to call was Kansas City owner Ewing Kauffman," recalls Mr. Cherry. "Mr. Kauffman made a statement I'll never forget. He told us, 'I would like to have Catfish. God gave me the ability to manufacture and distribute drugs. I know my business. God gave Catfish the ability and skill to pitch a baseball, and he's the best.'

"We were seriously considering going to Kansas City to meet with Mr. Kauffman because that first day we didn't have any other appointments. But the very next day the phone started ringing. Everybody wanted us to come and see them. Finally, we decided to set up appointments, and they'd just have to come to see us here.

"We really didn't know what to expect. Cat had given us no dollar figures. 'Just see what you can do,' he had said. Almost everybody in baseball called or came down. Walter Alston, John Fetzer, Harry Dalton, Ruly Carpenter, Haywood Sullivan, Joe Brown, Peter O'Malley. The most exciting day was when Gene Autry, the California Angels' owner, arrived. The whole town of Ahoskie turned out to see 'The Cowboy.'

"Some clubs just called. Donald Grant of the Mets was that way. He didn't want to come down. He just said, 'I've got two million dollars I can spend. See if we can work out the terms.' The newspapers were printing that the Mets didn't have enough *interest to come down here. But the phone worked just fine when folks were offering that kind of money.''*

Now it's Flythe's turn to talk. *"Peter O'Malley came to town with Al Campanis for the Dodgers,"* he says. *"They had the best offer Jimmy got the whole time. They had $3 million. 'Spend it like you want,' they said. 'We want Cat for two years.' Three million dollars for two years . . . Can you imagine such a thing? That knocked our heads off.*

"We had no idea the man was worth that kind of money. We knew the Dodgers at the time were the wealthiest team in baseball. They had the money. They had it in the bank. It floored me. I had no idea they would offer that kind of money. When Jim turned it down, I said, 'What's wrong with that man?' I never asked him, and he never told. But he said from the beginning, 'I don't care to go to the Dodgers.' "

"I don't know what it was," says Cherry.

"I don't either," Flythe says.

By Thursday morning December 19, the dance card at Cherry, Cherry, Flythe & Evans was getting right full. Twenty-two teams had drafted me (all but the Orioles and Tigers participated), and the opening round of interviews looked exactly like this:

Thursday, December 19

MORNING
New York Mets
New York Yankees (Clyde Kluttz)

AFTERNOON
Boston Red Sox (Haywood Sullivan,
Dick O'Connell, and John Harrington)

Friday, December 20

MORNING
San Diego Padres (Peter Bavasi)

AFTERNOON
Texas Rangers (Bob Short and Dan O'Brien)
Kansas City Royals (Joe Burke and Ewing Kauffman)

Saturday, December 21

MORNING
Los Angeles Dodgers
(Walter Alston, Al Campanis, and Peter O'Malley)
Philadelphia Phillies (Paul Owen and Ruly Carpenter)

AFTERNOON
Cleveland Indians (Ted Bonda and Phil Seghi)
California Angels (Dick Williams)
Milwaukee Brewers (Mike Hegan and Bud Selig)

Monday, December 23

MORNING
Montreal Expos (John McHale and Jim Fanning)
Minnesota Twins

AFTERNOON
New York Yankees (Gabe Paul and Clyde Kluttz)
Atlanta Braves (Eddie Robinson)

Friday, December 27

MORNING
Pittsburgh Pirates (Joe Brown)

AFTERNOON
Houston Astros (Spec Richardson)

Saturday, December 28

AFTERNOON
Cincinnati Reds (Bob Howsam)

"Jimmy," Mr. Cherry told me that first day, "you don't have to drive over here every day if you don't want to." I wanted to, covering the fifty miles (one way) in my gray, mud-caked Ford pickup, a plug of Red Man in my cheek. I walked into Mr. Cherry's office every morning and listened. I wanted to know exactly what each club was offering, sense their attitude, to feel a man's handshake, to look owners and general managers straight in the eye. After all, this was the biggest decision of my life, and much as I admired Mr. Cherry, if it came down to two or three clubs, I wanted the advantage of knowing every bit I could about those men.

The scene outside on Main was crazier than the first day of huntin' season. People parading around everywhere. Owners jetting in and out on private planes. Newsmen staking out the front steps with minicams, watching all the owners and ex-teammates pass through. Gaylord came over to talk about Cleveland. Mike Hegan flew in on behalf of Milwaukee. San Diego sent Johnny Mac and Bill Posedel to persuade me to pitch for the Padres. I saw Posedel the morning after our meeting. He laughed and shook his head. "Shit," he said, "I love this place. I bought the whole town of Ahoskie drinks last night and it only cost me $2."

The first hint of just what kind of money we were talking about came from, of all places, the Cleveland Indians. Until then we were only guessing what I might be worth on the open market. Who knew? Then Ted Bonda, the Indians' executive vice president, wrote Mr. Cherry saying the Indians were "vitally interested" in acquiring my services. Indeed they were. To the tune of a $2.4 million offer over ten years.

"I can't believe it," I told Helen after the offer was made. "I've always heard Cleveland's the cheapest club around. I think we may be on to something."

The other opening bids on December 19 were hardly chicken feed. The Yankees were talking $1.5 million for five years, and the Mets phoned in an initial offer of $2 million for the same period. The Red Sox then offered a five-year $3 million package deal that afternoon. On Friday morning, the next day, I learned the Padres were also willing to consider five years at $3 million or more. Texas talked about a huge farm annuity, $150,000 a year salary for three years, plus $30,000 a year for fifteen years. The Royals checked in next with one of the best and most complicated offers: a six-year contract worth $825,000 in total salary, a farm equipment purchase option, $5000 per year per child for college, plus—and this really caught my eye—$50,000 a year for life. If I lived to be 70, the proposal was valued at some $3.5 million. I about screamed, "Where's the pen?'' but then I thought of something. One not-so-minor detail.

"How about if I die?" I asked.

"Well," said General Manager Joe Burke, "that's the end of the contract."

"How about my wife?"

"Well . . . we won't have to worry about that, will we? You'll be dead." Burke meant it as a joke, I'm sure, but as soon as the words left his mouth, mentally I crossed Kansas City off my list. Later the Royals graciously added $30,000 per year for life for Helen, but the damage had been done. I wouldn't be going back to Kansas City.

Slowly but surely the bidding increased, up and up and up, forcing quite a few of the weaker wallets to fold. The first to go were Minnesota, Atlanta, Houston, and Cincinnati. General Manager Howsam telegrammed the Reds' regrets: "After careful consideration of all the ramifications and involvements . . . the dollar and economic factors are so big that it would not be fair to our present players, our fans, or the club itself to continue."

On Monday, December 23, an intriguing letter, dated December 20, arrived at my post office box in Hertford. It said in part, "I naturally feel that the arbitrator, in making his decision, exceeded his authority and jurisdiction . . . However, I hereby offer, without qualification, to purchase and own the annuity on your life as you requested on or about August 1, 1974

"My purpose . . . is to demonstrate to you that while . . . the position I took was a correct one, I believe you know that I never intended to 'do you out of $50,000,' as you charged in the press." It went on to express hope that the courts would overrule the arbitrator and to say that a contract to play for the A's in 1975 was being sent to me. In closing it said, "During the years you have spent in the Oakland Organization I have valued your friendship, and if I prevail in court, I hope that relationship will continue to be close . . . I hope you will be joining us, in Oakland, as a member of the World Championship Team in 1975." It was signed Charles O. Finley.

The man never quit.

A few days later, after a couple of more rounds of high-stakes poker, ten clubs remained at the big table: San Diego, Boston, the New York Mets, the Dodgers, Philadelphia, Kansas City, California, Milwaukee, Montreal, and Pittsburgh. It helped, however, to read the fine print: The Mets, for example, while quietly covering all the bases—a $1 million bonus, a $250,000 farm loan, and five years at $150,000 per—left themselves some loopholes. If I happened to win less than eighteen games, it would cost me 10 percent of my salary; fifteen games, 20 percent. The Pirates' package included salary ($750,000 over five years), $1 million in insurance and annuities, $400,000 in deferred money (choice of stocks or T bills), and a limited partnership stake in five new Wal-Mart Stores.

One day blended into another. The faces changed, as did the offers, but still no decision. The owners seemed to enjoy the auction, the notoriety associated with putting their money where their mouths were, the opportunity to stand out on the law office steps and detail their proposals to the media. I'm not naive enough to think I wasn't a prize catch—there weren't too many Cy Young Award winners going up for bid every year—but my free agency was about much more than Catfish Hunter. It was about power. And ego. And, yes, in the days before collusion, about putting the best possible team on the field.

Christmas passed. New Year's was just a day or two away, and we still hadn't heard anything more from the Yankees. Club President Gabe Paul had made an early offer—$1.5 million for five years—only to find out from the newsmen camping out on Cherry's steps that $1.5 million wasn't worth a mention on the six o'clock news. "Well," said Paul, "I guess I'll just head back to New York then."

Clyde Kluttz had other ideas. "I think I'll stick around and see what I can do," he said.

What Clyde Franklin Kluttz did was check into a motel in nearby Elizabeth City and play a waiting game. For two weeks he read the papers, watched television, and then, as the sun began to settle, made his rounds around Hertford. One by one he'd suggest to family and friends—in his honest, neighborly manner—that New York was where I ought to be. Every other day or so he'd stop by the house and tell me the same thing.

"What about living in New York?" I'd say.

"I hated it, too," said Clyde, "but people are people. The city's fast. You wouldn't want to live downtown. Get a place in the country."

"But what about San Diego?" I said.

"A fine place," Clyde contended, "but how many players from San Diego ever made it to the Hall of Fame?"

"How about Steinbrenner?"

"Listen," said Clyde, "it can't be any worse than playing for Finley. You're going to get more press. You can handle the media. They've never been a problem. If you do well up there, you'll make more money off the field. That's where everything is happening."

I knew Clyde was selling New York, but I also knew he'd never once lied to me. Good or bad, he told me the truth about everything. Now it was up to me to make a decision.

December 30, 1974

Another telegram:

> As per our conversation one minute ago, we wish to add $200,000 to our offer payable in cash upon signing.

> New York Mets M. D. Grant, Chairman

That night I had a long talk with my daddy. The 100-mile trip was wearing thin, and, more important, deer season was almost over, and so far I hadn't so much as set one foot in the woods.

"Ain't you getting tired of this stuff?" asked Daddy.

"I'm gonna sign with someone tomorrow," I told him.

"You sure?"

"Yep. I'm not gonna take this mess anymore."

The following day, New Year's Eve 1974, I came downstairs early as usual. Helen was in the kitchen. I told her I was headed off to have breakfast with Clyde. "I'm gonna sign with someone today," I said. "I'm gettin' tired of driving over to Ahoskie every day."

I met Clyde at the Tomahawk Motel in Ahoskie. At that moment, if someone had pointed a gun at me and said, "Sign," I'm sure it would have been with the Padres, plain and simple. Despite the National League location and the distance from Hertford, the Padres had a lot of things working in their favor: (1) natural grass, (2) they'd showed how much they wanted me (Peter and Buzzie Bavasi had sent a steady stream of letters to me and Mr. Cherry, thanking us for the meeting, suggesting schools, making me feel wanted), (3) the presence of Johnny Mac and Posedel, and (4) Mr. Kroc's money. Rated right behind San Diego were Kansas City (Mr. Cherry's first choice. He and Kauffman had struck up a fine friendship, but while I loved the people, I disliked the artificial turf); Boston (natural grass, great tradition, not quite enough money); and the California Angels, for American League clubs. The only other National League teams I seriously considered were Pittsburgh (superb offer, struggling team, fake turf) and the Mets.

Clyde looked up from his coffee. "Cat, I'm gonna be leaving today to go hunting. Looks like we're out of it."

He stared me straight in the face. He took another sip. Then he spoke again, slowly, with feeling. "Jimmy," he drawled, "what would it take for you to come and play for the Yankees?"

We threw some figures around. I told him flat out that the $50,000 insurance policy for Todd and Kim to attend college was nonnegotiable; so was fifteen years of deferred money ($100,000 per year) and five years' salary—guaranteed. The salary and other perks, like insurance annuities, could be worked out. Provided the Yankees were willing.

"Well," said Clyde Franklin Kluttz, a smile on his face, "I don't know if they'll give it to you, but let's go find out."

The first thing I did was drive over to 119 West Main and lay *my* cards on the table. Joe Flythe's chin almost hit the floor when I said, "I'd really like to play for the Yankees. If I can get near or the same amount of money as the other clubs, that's who I want to sign with. See what you can work out."

OTHER VOICES—JOE FLYTHE

"How did I feel when Jimmy said he wanted to play for the Yankees? I'll tell ya how I felt. I felt like saying, 'Why in the hell didn't you say so from the start?' Ha! Ha! Ha! But I didn't say anything. All I did was drop my head, go back and get on the phone and try to get the Yankees up from a million and a half. Gabe Paul said that was about the best they could do. He'd call occasionally saying things like, 'If you ever change your mind and want to talk . . .'

"I called Paul the morning of the 31st. I told him we had been authorized by Mr. Hunter to sign with you for this amount of money. He said you might as well tell us exactly what you want. So we told him—the bonus, deferred compensation, insurance for the children. Certain figures we had to have. Problem was money was tight. Mr. Steinbrenner had bought the club a year before, but he was barred from baseball for making illegal campaign contributions. He couldn't help if he had wanted to—and he wanted to. Paul said he had to use the telephone. He came back on the line and said, 'That's more money than we want to pay, but we'll do it.' "

When I found out the Yankees had accepted our offer, I called Helen to tell her the good news. I fairly shouted, "I signed."

"Yeah, I know," said my childhood sweetheart, "with the Yankees."

"How did you know? The news isn't even out yet. Who told you?"

"Nobody. I knew when you left this morning you were gonna sign with the Yankees. As much as you talk with Clyde Kluttz and everything."

"Yeah, well I wish you would have told me. Would've made it all a lot easier."

By the time I returned to Cherry, Cherry, Flythe & Evans, it was close to noon. We gathered in the back room, around the walnut table, preparing for a plane flight to New York. For tax reasons, the Yankees wanted the contract signed in 1974 and weren't going to waste any time announcing it, a press conference was called at the Yankees' temporary offices across the street from Shea Stadium. Just as we were about to slip out the back door into a back alley to avoid the cameras in front, the phone rang. It was Buzzie Bavasi. Straight from that ship-to-shore radio conversation with Mr. Kroc. The Padres, already at $4.5 million for five years, far and away the biggest offer, were upping the ante again. Big time.

"Mr. Kroc said if you come to San Diego, you can write your own check," Bavasi told Mr. Cherry.

That's when Mr. Cherry had to explain the part about Bavasi being five minutes too late, about me already giving my word to the Yankees. To say Buzzie went crazy is like saying McDonald's sells some hamburgers. But to his credit, once Mr.

Bavasi cooled off, he sent a most gracious note to Mr. Cherry. ("Just wanted to tell you how much we appreciated the way you handled the Jim Hunter matter . . . You were nothing but fair, and that's all any of us can ask. With kindest regards . . .")

At Suffolk Airport, some thirty miles from Ahoskie, George Steinbrenner's personal plane was waiting. Five of us jumped in—Mr. Cherry, his son Tom, a partner in the firm, who did such a super job of handling all the entertaining and scheduling of appointments, Joe Flythe, and another partner, Ernie Evans, who's now a farmer. Waiting inside was Cleveland attorney and Yankee minority owner Ed Greenwald. In the forty-five minutes it took to fly from Suffolk into a blinding snow storm in New York, Greenwald wrote out a ten-page addendum to the standard players contract. I'd never seen a man work like that in my life. He'd write out a phrase on a yellow pad, and we'd talk about it. He'd write another phrase. We'd talk about that.

The whole way up we were like kissin' cousins, right up to the time we got to the ballpark. Then, suddenly, the lawyers started arguing so much I had to walk away and get some fresh air. They'd find me, show me a paragraph, and I'd initial my approval. Meanwhile, the press waited and . . . waited . . . and . . .

Finally, Greenwald got down to discussing paragraph seven, the one that would guarantee me $3.48 million over ten years.

"Well," he sighed, setting down his pen, "I'm not going to mortgage this club for one player."

I couldn't believe what I was hearing. Here we'd come all this way, accepted an offer, and now the Yankees were changing the deal. Joe Flythe cut Greenwald right off. He wasn't gonna stand for any nonsense. There were plenty of other clubs out there— one West Coast club in particular—that wouldn't have blinked at guaranteeing my future.

"If you can't guarantee at least a five-year salary and $100,000 a year for fifteen years, we might as well get right back on that plane right now," said Flythe, "because Jimmy's going to sign with someone else. He can make twice the amount of money from other clubs."

"Well, let him make it."

That's all Gabe Paul needed to hear. Normally the most mild-mannered of men, he turned to Greenwald and in a tight voice said, "Wait a minute. I don't give a damn about your club. Give the man what he wants."

What I received, considering the year and circumstances, was phenomenal: $100,000 a year for five years, half of it deferred; $53,462.67 a year in insurance annuities for ten years; a $100,000 signing bonus; fifteen years at $100,000 per year until 1994; $25,000 college endowments for both Todd and Kim; $200,000 in attorney fees; plus a brand new Buick every year for five years.

At the press conference, Clyde Kluttz was introduced and began to cry he was so happy inside. An aide to New York Mayor Abe Beame gave me a dime-store fishing pole as a present. It was an emotional time to be sure, but I had other business to attend to. As soon as the press conference ended, I was back on that plane. I was getting up bright and early the next morning. Had to. I wanted one last shot at deer season.

11

QUESTIONS WITHOUT ANSWERS

Oh and four.

As in uh-oh and four.

As in no wins and four losses. As in an earned run average (7.47) that belonged on the fuselage of an airplane. As in here I am in the pressure capital of the world, and the New York press is lighting up the barbecue so it can roast me for dinner.

In Oakland, if three local reporters showed up in the clubhouse at the same time you figured somebody either (a) got fired or (b) it was an off day for the Raiders. For years Ron Bergman of the Oakland *Tribune* was the only writer who ever traveled with the team. Ron always did a real fine job, although later when all the bickering and off-field shenanigans started up, I felt he and other local writers spent a little too much time covering what was happening off the field—parking tickets, trouble in a bar—things I don't think were any of their business. But I probably should thank him anyway, seeing as how he helped prepare me for New York. It's just that I thought I'd seen everything in Oakland. Turns out I hadn't seen anything. I know for sure I'd never seen the A's play field hockey in the hallway. Sure enough in spring training in '75, Mel Stottlemyre was out in the hall banging away. Mel got released in spring training (he was near the end of a fabulous career), but back in New York some guys played shots-on-goal with baseball bats, rapping each other on the shins.

Spring training 1975 had been one long interview. "Hey, Cat, do you think you're worth all that money?" "Hey, Cat, can the Yankees win the pennant now that you're in New York?" "Hey, Cat, are you going to do anything different here than you did in Oakland?" Good questions, actually, things I'm sure every Yankee fan wanted to know. And I'll say this: I had a lot more answers then than I did after I opened the season with a loss and kept losing until the end of April.

There were explanations, of course. Yes, I was pitching differently—both mentally and physically. I guess, like a lot of the writers, fans and my teammates, I got caught up in the hubbub, started thinking I was supposed to win every game. One night near the end of an atrocious April, my new roommate, Lou Piniella, and I had a talk.

"I'm finished trying to strike out twenty guys every game," I said.

"Whaddya mean, Cat?" he asked.

"I'm overthrowing, trying to earn the entire contract in one outing. I'm not myself, not pitching like I can. I'm trying to throw every pitch as hard as I can."

Lou told me what I already knew: "Relax"—stay with the style that had produced 161 wins over the previous ten years.

Looking back, I guess there were a couple of other unpublicized reasons. One was about five-eleven, 215 pounds, had a squatty body and answered to the name of Munson. The other—tall, dark-haired, thick-boned (and skinned)—was better known as Sweet Lou.

Yes, sir, Thurman, Lou, and I spent a whole lot of time together the first month of the season. A pinstriped version of the Three Musketeers. We all stayed at the Sheraton Centre Hotel on Seventh Avenue in New York while our families waited for the school semester to end. Talk about "boys' night out." Almost every night we'd hit the town for dinner and drinks before heading over to our favorite late-night eatery—the Stage Deli, on Seventh Avenue. I guess we were never home much later than 2 a.m., but not a whole lot earlier either.

One night after a day spent playing golf, we hit one of our favorite Italian spots, wearing, quite naturally, golf shirts and slacks. Everybody is dressed in suits and ties but us. The owner knows us, though, and seats us without comment. Suddenly, just as we begin to order, all activity in the room stops. Suspended animation. Our heads eventually turn to see a gentleman who's pulling off his gloves at the front door. As he stares out, the waiters and busboys are holding their breath. The man keeps staring out, nods his head once, and then walks slowly to a special table. Still nobody moved. What the hell is this? It is only after the man has turned to speak to his dinner guest that the room returns to normal. Then, one by one, every one in the restaurant—all except you-know-who—gets up and kisses the man on the cheek. I glance over at my golfing buddies. "Thurm," I said, "this is the last time we eat in this place."

When my record dipped to 0–4, it was time to take some immediate action. So one night, after returning to the Sheraton bleary-eyed, I dialed the number of a contractor named Buddy in New Jersey. "Buddy," I said, "this is Catfish Hunter. Remember that home we talked about you building for me in New Jersey? I want you to start tomorrow." Half an hour later, the phone rang again. It was Buddy.

"Cat," he said, "did you just call me?"

"That was me," I replied.

"Okay," he said, "see you at seven."

"Seven? No way. That's too damn early."

"Forget it," said Buddy, showing no sympathy. "You woke me up at 2:30 in the morning. I'll be back to wake you up at seven. See ya."

Speaking of wake-up calls, somebody should have sent one to the Yankees that season. Bill Virdon was our manager, and early on, it looked like we had the cut of a contender: Bobby Bonds, Elliott Maddox, Roy White, Thurman, Chris Chambliss, Graig Nettles, and Lou as the DH or in the outfield. But my slow start combined with key injuries to Maddox (knee), Nettles (leg), and White (foot) destroyed what rhythm we had. I finally got back on track with eleven wins in my next fifteen decisions, including six straight complete games in May and June, but other than me, Thurman, who would finish the season hitting at .318, and the hot-hitting Chambliss, the Yankees were hardly living up to the tradition of Ruth and Gehrig. It was more Larry, Moe, and Curly.

I was shocked by the contrast in team attitudes in Oakland and New York. The A's always believed they could find a way to win; in New York the '75 team never believed. Oh, they talked a good game, but that's it. Mention what it took to win, and it went in one ear and out the other.

Well, I took only so much of that horseshit before blowing my stack. It came after a particularly disgusting 5–4 defeat to Baltimore, our sixth in a row. I snapped after the game, saying how fed up I was with players going through the motions and picking up paychecks. I could understand physical mistakes, but mental errors, lack of hustle, poor defensive baseball—ah, it made my skin crawl.

"The Oakland A's made things happen," I said. "They didn't wait around. At Oakland we had guys who got on base and then would make the other team throw the ball, make a bad throw. The Yankees want to make sure they don't pull a muscle, they want to make sure they get well, but you've got to make things happen. You can't just sit back. You've got to do something."

Big impact that speech had. Wrapped around the All Star break, we lost fourteen of nineteen to trail Boston by 6½. The fourteenth loss was mine, 1–0 to Texas, a team I'd one-hit 6–0 several days earlier (88 pitches, 0 walks, 4 strikeouts) to raise my record to 12–8—my fifteenth complete game in seventeen starts. But after the 1–0 defeat, I just dragged a pink tub of ice across the floor and then sat down at my locker and soaked my elbow, feeling as low as Thurman, who sat in front of his locker for twenty minutes, undressed, and then sat some more, head buried deep in his hands.

Thurman. If I ever had to choose sides for a pickup game, he'd have been my first choice. No doubt about it (with Reggie a close second). Thurm played the game harder than any man I've ever met. He played in pain. He played with purpose. Most of all, he brought out the best in those around him.

Like so many others, I, too, found Thurman to be a walking contradiction, a shy, sensitive man who was never comfortable around strangers, particularly the working press, a group Thurman thoroughly intimidated, coming across as one mean son of a bitch. Which he certainly was, at times. Other times, however, out of the public eye, he oozed affection, especially around kids. The man was as devoted a dad as you'd ever want to meet.

The thing that was so confusing about Thurm was that if he liked you, he'd rag on you. "Look at that shit he's wearing," he'd growl as some sportswriter would walk by. The writer would think, oh, what an ass, but it was Thurm's way of saying he liked you. If Thurman *didn't* talk about you, forget it. He wanted no part of you. Hell, everybody else called me Catfish. Not Thurm. He called me Blowfish because, as he said, "Your cheeks puff out when you pitch." And, he could take some shit, too. Any time I'd see a fat person, I'd roll down my window and yell, "Hey, Thurman, we'll be right back to get you!" But overall he was a very protective man who used his gruff exterior as a defense mechanism, a shield of sorts, to keep folks away. The perfect cover for a rough childhood that had left him insecure over love and caring for others.

Thurman was born in Akron, Ohio, the son of a cross-country truck driver, a man who showed little or no love for his son. (I later discovered how little when I was told that at Thurman's funeral, the man walked up to the casket, chuckled, and walked away.) Thurman went on to win a scholarship at Kent State before signing with the Yankees in 1968. His minor league career consisted of just ninety-nine games, and when he was brought up for good in 1970, he hit .302 and won the Rookie of the Year Award. Thurman, I quickly discovered, had a real wild streak in him, a fearless fascination with speed and danger. He liked living on the edge. You could see it in the airplanes he flew, the guns he carried. I remember one time, a Sunday morning early in my first season when we were still living at the hotel, Thurm and I were driving to Shea Stadium. (We played at Shea that year while Yankee Stadium was being renovated.) Well, ol' Thurm's doing about sixty down Broadway when some guy tries to cross the street in front of him. Bad move. Next thing I know Thurm's got the car *on* the sidewalk, chasing the jaywalker down the street, bumpity, bump, bump, pedestrians flying all over the place as they scattered out of the way. "I'll get him! I'll get him!" screams Thurman. Finally, he pins the guy against a wall.

So what does the guy do? He reaches down into his suitcase.

"Gun!" I screamed. "He's got a gun!"

Thurm jammed his car into reverse and hauled ass off to Shea, laughing the whole way.

Another gun story. One night after a game at Shea we're walking out to Thurm's shiny new car. And I mean *new*. Less than 100 miles. So you can imagine Thurman's reaction when he saw that his windshield had been smashed. He went third-degree crazy, screaming, "I'm gonna kill the fucker that did this! I'm gonna kill 'em!" Next thing I know the trunk is up and Thurman's pulling out a .357 magnum and waving it around like this is Dodge City instead of Queens. Bam, bam, bam. He starts firing shots at a nearby fence. I figure half the Fourth Precinct or whatever will be over here in two minutes.

"Damn it, Thurman," I said. "There's people over there." He finally calmed down but not before trying to run over a few people on the way out of the parking lot.

By the time early August rolled around, Virdon should have been running for cover. Injuries, a disappointing season from Bonds, and bull pen problems combined to put Bill's head on the chopping block. But to his credit, he never hid behind a closed door like some managers do. He just treated us the way he had all year—as equals, no favorites. Bill didn't care if you played one inning or nine, you were a Yankee.

Take Walt (No Neck) Williams, for example. No Neck wasn't a starter mainly because he couldn't hit a curveball to save his soul. Bill gave him every chance to prove himself. Walt would walk by Virdon every day chirping, "I can hit the curveball, I can hit the curveball," and Virdon would reply, "But, Walt, you haven't hit a curve all year."

So Walt went to work. For one week straight he came out for early batting practice and hit nothing but curves. Once again he was ready to press his case. "Bill, if I can hit a curveball, can I play?"

"Walt," said Virdon, "if you can hit *my* curveball, you can play. Come on out tomorrow."

Sure enough, there was No Neck, a fine little left fielder, digging in the next day against Virdon. Bill warmed up with a few fastballs, and No Neck damn near tore the cover off the ball.

"Curveball," said Virdon.

Now, Bill's curve was controlled more by gravity than anything else. American Legion level at best. Still, poor Walt got himself all tied up in knots. "Sorry, Walt," said Virdon. "You still can't hit the curve."

Sadly, some players didn't like Bill's all-for-one, one-for-all attitude. Guys like Thurman and Nettles felt that because they played every day, they deserved preferential treatment. Maybe they did. But not in the eyes of Bill Virdon.

And if you wanted to argue about it, Big Bill would be glad to accommodate you. He was one of the macho men, a handsome, well-built ex-major league outfielder who prided himself on his physique—particularly his well-muscled chest and forearms. I swear at times Virdon was so preoccupied with how his forearms looked, walking around with them thrust out in front for fine view, that you'd swear he polished those babies at night. I remember one time Bill pulled Pat Dobson from a game—Pat was none too pleased—and afterward Pat popped off to the press. How dare Virdon replace him with Sparky Lyle, who was struggling at the time. How dare he this. How dare he that.

The next day, I walk into the clubhouse and see this huge coffin in the middle of the room. Word was that shortstop Fred Stanley and reserve catcher Ed Hermann—an accomplished woodworker and the man responsible for corking Nettles' bats—were gonna shape the coffin into a bar for Stanley's van. Sounded good.

Later on Virdon strolls by, shirtless, his chest popping out. Team meeting, he says. Everybody gathers around. Everybody except one player.

"Where's Sparky?" asks Virdon.

No sooner had the words left Virdon's lips than we hear this *creaaaking* sound. Up goes the coffin lid. The occupant was stark naked. Black rings were painted around his eyes.

"You raaaang, skipper?" said Sparky Lyle.

Virdon liked to die, he was laughing so hard. "Get outta there," he said before turning his attention to another pitcher. The smile was gone as he said, "I just want you to know I'm the manager and I can manage as well as anyone in this room." He moved in front of Pat. "There's one guy who's been disrupting this ball club, and some of you guys are beginning to follow him around." He took another step closer to Dobson, forearms at attention. "As for you, Mr. Dobson, you're a real good pitcher, and if you want to pitch, you're pitching Saturday. If you don't want to pitch, let me know, and I'll get somebody else."

Virdon was on a roll now. "And if it takes a tow truck to get you off the mound, I'll get one. But . . . [and here Bill turned and made a muscle with his biceps like Charles Atlas] . . . I don't think I'll need one. Do you, Mr. Dobson?"

Dobson never said a word.

Well, as it turned out, it wasn't Pat who got towed away. It was Virdon. On August 2 he was fired and replaced by Billy Martin, who had been fired by Texas a few days earlier.

Welcome to the roller-coaster world of one Alfred Manuel Martin. In my next 4½ years in New York, Billy the Kid would be hired twice, fired once, resign once, win two World Series, punch out a marshmallow salesman, withdraw into alcohol and self-pity, and, ultimately, live to be hired and fired by Mr. Steinbrenner five more times in the next eight years. But for all his boorish behavior and insecurities, Billy Martin was still the best field manager I ever played for. He always made something happen, and strategy-wise—maneuvering his bench in the late innings, getting the most out of a makeshift lineup—Billy was without equal. Best of all, he only played it one way: to win. His first speech, short and sweet, contained just such a theme: "We're gonna win," he told us. "We're gonna play ball. And we're gonna do it my way."

But, for all his managerial genius, Billy couldn't work mathematical miracles in 1975. Too much time, too many games had passed. By late August we were in third place, doin' a fast fade. On August 26 I moved my record to 18–11 by beating the late, great Oakland A's 7–1 for the second time in five days. It was my fourth complete game in a row, a span in which I allowed only three runs, struck out twenty-eight, and gave up sixteen hits—all singles. Was it special beating the A's? Bet your butt it was.

"I tried to show Mr. Finley I could still pitch," I said at the time.

On September 3 I won number nineteen, my twenty-sixth complete game in thirty starts (an 8–0 whitewash of Detroit), tying a Yankee complete-game record set by Carl Mays back in 1920. Another shutout, 2–0 over Baltimore, came four days later in front of 200 home folks who had bused up from Hertford to see what turned out to be my seventh shutout of the year—a career high. What's more, for the fifth season in a row I had won twenty or more games, becoming only the third American League pitcher in history to accomplish the feat—the others were immortals Walter Johnson and Lefty Grove.

My brothers told me about the record over the winter; I'd never even known about it. I've never been a records person, concerned about stats or streaks. All I ever wanted to do was pitch well enough to win every game I could. But now, in the afterglow, it was nice to know that, somehow, I'd bridged a gap between generations. It made me feel very very proud.

With eighteen games left, our record stood at 75–71. We were just three games ahead of Cleveland in a dogfight for third place. Billy made it clear that he definitely didn't want to finish fourth. Hell, he still had his sights set on first. Could I pitch against Cleveland on *two* days' rest? Well, when the manager says, Can you pitch, I pick up the ball. I'd never turned down an assignment in my life and wasn't about to start now. So, on forty-eight hours' rest, I pitched. Yankee Stadium was freezing that night, temperatures dropping down into the high thirties.

Amazingly, I lasted seven innings, and we won 6–2, my twenty-second victory of the year. Afterward, the combative, never-say-die Martin boldly announced that we were still in the race, even though we were eleven out with thirteen to play. Some members of the press questioned the wisdom of pitching someone who had already thrown twenty-eight complete games, the most in the American League, and 310 innings. I held my tongue. "Whenever they ask me to pitch, I pitch," I said. "I guess if he asked me to pitch every day, I wouldn't say no." In truth, I didn't know what the impact would be.

The next time out I went nine again, overcoming homers by Powell and Rico Carty—the first four-baggers off me in eighty-six innings—to beat Baltimore. In my final start of the season I lost 3–2 to Cleveland, throwing another nine, my eleventh complete game in a row. I ended the season with a record of 23–14 (most wins in the league and the most by a Yankee pitcher since Whitey Ford won twenty-four games in 1963) in forty-one starts. I had pitched 328 innings, also tops in the league. Incredibly, I'd pitched all but eighteen innings of the games I'd started. As it was, I'd completed thirty games (the most in the American League since 1946) and had an ERA of just 2.58. I finished second in the Cy Young voting to Jim Palmer. All and all, a helluva year, especially on a third-place club. Unfortunately, I would pay a helluva price for it.

In 1976, we moved into the "new and improved" Yankee Stadium. The House That Ruth Built had received a $100 million facelift, and, to a lesser degree, so had the team now playing in it. Martin was in full control now, and he started molding the club in his image, putting an emphasis on pitching, speed and defense. It paid big dividends as we walked away with the division (a 10½-game spread) before beating Kansas City in the playoffs. For the first time since 1964, a new American League pennant was flying over the Stadium.

It was one of those total team efforts. Instilled with Martin's infectious attitude and Thurman's leadership behind the plate, this Yankee team *believed* it could win. We pulled for each other. We got great seasons from guys like Mickey Rivers, who arrived with pitcher Ed Figueroa from California in exchange for Bobby Bonds. An equal to Campy in the leadoff spot, Mickey went on to hit .312 that year, drive in sixty-seven runs, and score ninety-five more. Fig added nineteen wins, Thurman won the MVP, Sparky saved twenty-three games, Nettles banged out thirty-two home runs and ninety-three RBIs, and White (.286) scored a league-leading 104 runs.

The year 1976 also heralded the return of New York Yankees' principal owner George M. Steinbrenner III. Not that George had ever really been away. On April 15, 1974, George was indicted by the federal government for making some illegal contributions through his shipbuilding company to former President Richard Nixon's re-election campaign. Mr. Steinbrenner pleaded guilty, took his medicine (a $15,000 fine), and went about his business. But then on November 27, 1974, Commissioner Kuhn took further action. He suspended George for two years, leaving Gabe Paul in charge of the Yankees. It proved a bitter pill for George, one he never fully swallowed (witness the private plane at Suffolk Airport). On March 2, 1976, however, George was reinstated by Kuhn.

George, obviously, has been the center of controversy in New York for years. A perfectionist, he's famous for exploding at employees over the tiniest mistakes—a dirty ashtray, the wrong address. It's easy not to like George, his meddling, the pressure he puts on all those around him—especially managers—to win.

Of course, you're always under pressure when you play for Steinbrenner's Yankees. It comes with the territory; that's the way George is. If you're not in first place, he's calling to ask why, offering suggestions, or—worse—taking action. Even if you're in first, he's calling, tellin' you to keep on winnin'. Or else . . .

So, with that in mind, as I write this my buddy Lou Piniella has been fired as manager and kicked upstairs to general manager. Once again, Billy is back, trying to recapture the magic of '77 and '78. Personally, I think George made a serious mistake by firing Lou as manager of the Yankees. But you know what? It's George's money and, therefore, his call.

What I do know—and like—about George is his belief in loyalty and paying a price to win. Off the field he's a good-natured guy, one who's taken his fair share of grief from his players over the years. Like the time we got lost driving from the airport to our hotel in Arlington, Texas, home of the Rangers. Somehow we ended up near Dallas. George was on this trip, sitting right up in the front of the bus.

Nettles, never one to suffer fools graciously, couldn't resist. Most of the time, Nettles would start fights or arguments and then mysteriously disappear in a Puff (his nickname) of smoke—à la Dick Green. Nettles was famous for easing controversial statements into a conversation. "I never said that," I'd say. "Oh, yes, you did," he'd answer, hoping to piss off a third party.

This time, however, Nettles took center stage. "Hey, busie," he screamed from the back of the bus. "What the fuck is going on? We going to one of George's daughters' colleges or something?"

Steinbrenner jumped up so quick you'd have thought he was sitting on a hot seat. "Who said that?" he yelled, eyes ablaze.

Nettles pulled back some hanging travel bags in front of his face. "I did. Nettles. Nettles said it."

George sat right back down. It wasn't worth an argument. Not in front of the whole team.

Later I found out that George had quietly donated thousands of dollars to the University of North Carolina, particularly the school's baseball team. One year I came up from Hertford and fed the team barbecue, and George was there and we had a wonderful time. The next year, no George. I asked around and found out why: His second daughter wanted to attend UNC, but someone in the admissions office had turned her down. I knew George had immediately crossed Carolina baseball off his Christmas list, providing me with the perfect opportunity to stick a needle in his side.

"Mr. Steinbrenner, you going to Carolina this year?" I asked before the barbecue.

"Hell no!" he bellowed. "You know why?"

"Why no, I don't. I had a guy ready to bring all that barbecue up again this year."

"Yeah, that was delicious . . . But I ain't going back!"

"Why?"

"You know why!"

"No, no I don't. Why?"

"You didn't hear about my second daughter going up there and them turning her down?"

"Turned her down! All the money you put up there, the lights . . ."

"Yeah, gave them all the lights!"

"They turned her down? I can't believe that. With her grades? Why?"

"I don't know."

"Bet the damn guy got fired."

A smile crossed George Steinbrenner's face. "Damn right! There was hell to pay around there. I made sure the guy was gone the next day! Ha. Ha. Ha."

George couldn't have been any happier as we opened the 1976 season by taking fifteen of our first twenty starts. I shut out Milwaukee on day one, 3–0, a pretty and precise three-hitter. I lost my next three, struggling to 3–5 by mid-May. Worst of all, I had a problem. My right shoulder was beginning to hurt.

In spring training I'd felt the first twinge of tightness. Even today I don't know the exact source of the pain. Maybe I didn't stretch enough. Maybe I pitched too many innings in 1975. Maybe this. Maybe that. The upshot was severe pain and discomfort whenever I raised my elbow up toward my shoulder.

So began an unending two-year cycle of questions without answers, poking and prodding by doctors, pain, disillusionment, disgust, frustration and anger. The end, really, of my five-year run as the premier right-handed pitcher in the American League.

I finished the remainder of '76 in fits and starts. One day I was up, untouchable. Like the day in May against Boston when the linescore read eleven innings, zero runs, three hits, three walks, five strikeouts, 106 of the nastiest pitches I've ever thrown. Great stuff. Better location. We won 1–0 in front of 43,000 at the Stadium. "As good a game as I've ever pitched," I said afterward. "Everything was in the right spot." Just ask Dwight Evans. I got him three times on strikes on nine pitches.

But there were increasingly more troublesome outings. Days like June 13, when my record fell to 7–6, my ERA rising to 3.69. "I just didn't have it," I said. "No zip on the ball." By August 8, I was no better than a .500 pitcher on a team running away with the division thanks to Figueroa, Holtzman, Dock Ellis, and Doyle Alexander. I lasted just 4⅓ innings against Baltimore, my quickest exit in 1½ years. An Al Bumbry single, a tape-measure blast by Reggie, now playing for the Orioles, and again, more questions. Some people blamed the muddy mound; others said I wasn't warming up long enough. Some insisted I throw more breaking pitches; others wanted more fastballs; others suggested I was pitching on only one side of the plate, whereas in the past I'd used the entire surface.

The most common reaction was to question all the innings I'd pitched down the stretch in 1975. The thirty complete games. Well, maybe. Maybe not. But whatever it was, Billy had nothing to do with it. I knew that much. He was just trying to win back then. What I did know was that for the first time in my entire life, from the frontyard days in Hertford to the bright lights of New York, I was hurting, truly injured. But where? How? Why? Which way to turn?

I really didn't know.

In August my win-loss record continued to bounce back and forth over the .500 mark. The biggest highlight—the only highlight, really—was a 2–1 victory over Milwaukee, my sixteenth victory of the year and two-hundredth of my major league career—making me only the fourth pitcher to win 200 games by the age of thirty-one. I couldn't help but be pleased with the company I was keeping—Cy Young, Christy Mathewson, and Walter Johnson. "Maybe you're a better pitcher when you work once a week," said Munson, a twinkle in his eye.

Thurm and I had grown increasingly close as the year wore on. By now our families had settled about a mile from one another in Norwood, New Jersey, a rural, low-key community about thirty minutes from Yankee Stadium. Helen and Diane, Thurman's wife, became fast friends. Early in the year, when Diane was still back in Canton with the kids, Thurman hardly ever left our house. He'd come back from a game and fall asleep on our living room couch. He loved it because he said he could wake up and make his calls and never get out of "bed." Thurman's the only ballplayer who ever slept on that couch. In the process he and Todd grew mighty close. Todd loved Thurman to death; Thurman felt the same way. "He's gonna look like me, Cat," he'd laugh. "Short and fat. He's gonna be a catcher just like me."

Thurman went so far as to give Todd an autographed catcher's glove. Every chance he could—in the front yard, pregame at the Stadium, in the clubhouse even—he'd take the time to toss the ball with Todd.

On game days, the two of us and Nettles (my across-the-street neighbor) would drive in together, mixing baseball, business, and current events. Thurman loved to talk about real estate, his wheelin' and dealin', how he was going to be a millionaire, or close to it, by the time he was thirty. He'd bought a big ol' $300,000 custom-built home, four, five times the size of my place.

"Yeah, well," he said when I asked him why he needed so much space, "I might stay here all year 'round."

"No way," I said. "All your business is in Canton."

"I don't know," he said. "I'm going to make it big enough to do either one."

He made it big enough in '76, all right. Won the MVP Award after hitting .302. I finished a disappointing 17–15, my lowest win total since 1969. I'd done my job, working 299 innings in thirty-six starts, but going into the playoffs against Kansas City, I wasn't sure which one of me was going to show up on the mound.

First game, the old Cat was back as I handcuffed Larry Gura and the Royals with a five-hitter, my game in such a groove I never went to a three-ball count once during the entire game. We split the next two before the ball came back to my court. Unfortunately, the new me showed up, the uncontrollable me, and we lost 7–4 despite two dingers off the bat of Nettles.

It was 2–2 now. But as any Yankee fan can tell you, we won it all the next night on Chambliss's dramatic bottom-of-the-ninth home run off Mark Littell. But even the champagne and sweetness was short-lived. We never got rolling in the World Series and lost four straight to the "Big Red Machine" from Cincinnati. I'm sure I said "Wait until next year," but had I known what next year was going to be like, I might have held my tongue.

12

DIAMONDS IN THE ROUGH

The Reverend William Kalaidjian cleared his throat before addressing the masses who had gathered to worship. "We pray," he began, speaking to the 43,785 who were attending our '77 home opener. "We pray this year from your great heaven we receive the world championship."

Well those prayers were answered, all right, thanks in large part to the unforgettable Reg-gie . . . Reg-gie . . . Reg-gie show in the South Bronx. You know the story. It's legend by now. Three first pitches, three different pitchers, three home runs. We defeat the true-blue Dodgers in six. Hip, hip, hurray. But Lord, it was a struggle.

From the first chants of Reg-gie . . . Reg-gie . . . Reg-gie in our home opener, after Sparky and I combined on a 3–0 shutout of Milwaukee, to the last final huzzahs, it was baseball like I never want it to be again. We got our diamond rings, but like diamonds in the rough, you had to look long and hard to find the sparkle in this season.

Physically, the downward spiral that had begun in '76 continued, accelerating at an alarming rate throughout the season: a line drive off my left instep in the home opener against the Brewers put me on the twenty-one-day disabled list, from April 13 to early May; my aching arm got so sore that if some mugger had yelled, "Reach for the sky or I'll shoot," I'd have been dead; and, later, there was a mysterious late-season pain in my groin that went from being diagnosed as a hernia to an I-don't-know to, finally, seminal vesiculitis, an inflammation of the sac near the prostate. In other words, a urological infection. Whatever the latter was, it kept me on the shelf from September 10 until the second game of the World Series. That's when Billy made the controversial move of pitching me on, oh, thirty days' rest. He said it would set up his rotation for the rest of the Series. So I took the ball. The result won't make my highlights film.

But beyond the physical pain—and it was terrible—was the mental hurt. The fights, the feuds, the snubs, the bickering and backbiting, the incessant demands to be traded. You needed a scorecard to keep track of the tantrums. Munson was pissed because we were short a catcher. Figueroa, Cliff Johnson, Nettles, and Munson were all moaning about a trade. Roy White, relegated to a reserve role after so many years as a starter, just walked out of our World Series celebration saying, "I'm not part of our win, so why should I be a part of the celebration?" Billy was damn near fired four different times— in March, May, June, and July—while the rift between Reggie, Martin, and Steinbrenner grew wider by the day, the hour, the minute. And, of course, the press did its New York best to inflame the situation. I guess with so many writers, all of them couldn't write good stuff about the team, so some of them were looking for the bad stuff, what I always called "dirt" about a person. And some of those writers seemed to be driving a steam shovel at times. When I played with the A's, at least we were united by our dislikes: the low pay and Finley. In New York, it was different because so many members of the '77 Yankees honestly couldn't stand the sight of one another, team or no team. And in the center of the controversy stood one man: Reginald Martinez Jackson.

No sense going into any deep, dark background here. Reggie had signed with the Yankees in 1977 after spending the 1976 season in Baltimore. The numbers were a cool $2.9 million for five years. In fact, it was Mr. Steinbrenner who had asked me to do him a special favor in the fall of 1976, when Reggie was playing with Baltimore. I figured I'd better call Mr. Cherry and check this out.

"Mr. Steinbrenner wants me to go to Baltimore and get Reggie Jackson," I told him. "He wants him. What should I do?"

Mr. Cherry had just one question: "Can you handle Reggie?"

"If anybody can do it, I can," I told him. Still, I never went.

As I said, I've always admired Reggie. He's one of those rare, radiant athletes who come along once, twice a decade. Who rise to the occasion. Always has. Always will. For that reason we called him Buck back in Oakland. After Mays. It was a nickname I know Reggie cherished.

Sure, he was full of himself at times. He loved that locker by the door. With Reggie you've got to let a lot of talk go in one ear and out the other. Like his habit of counting his "roll" of hundred dollar bills in other people's faces. Like bragging about his body. One time he popped off, challenging umpire Ken Kaiser, a man best measured by a seismograph, to a fight.

"So you think you're tough," said Kaiser, picking up the six-two, 210-pound Jackson by the crotch, like a pro wrestler, lifting him over his head, and setting Reggie down, ever so gently, in a trash can.

"I do believe you're a little strong," said Reggie.

"Don't you ever mess with me again," Kaiser said.

Unfortunately, Kaiser wasn't around in spring training when Reggie's mouth started putting in overtime. I read where Reggie felt I never supported him, never said a word to ease his transition to New York. Who could get a word in edgewise? When I joined the Yankees, I went out of my way to become one of the guys. I never bragged about my contract. I never showed anybody up. I did my job, tried to help the club win, just like twenty-four other guys did.

With Reggie it was the same but different. He wanted to fit in, be part of the team, but his ego got the best of him. He just talked too much, that's all. He liked to talk, and everything he said the press wrote down. A lot of times you talk and don't know what you're saying, and in that respect, Reggie got caught with his pants down. In Oakland he'd talk and talk and talk and the writers would write part of it and then just listen. Not New York. Not with twenty to thirty guys hanging on every word. Not with five, six papers covering the team on a daily, sometimes hourly, basis. Sometimes Reggie even put his foot in his mouth while talking with us. I remember one night ten of us were in this hotel bar in Detroit when Reggie literally started crying in his beer. Tears were running down his cheeks. "If I was white, I'd own the world," he said, before adding: "and if I looked like Quirk, I'd own the world," referring to Kansas City catcher Jamie Quirk, who is movie-star handsome.

Chambliss, who is black, couldn't believe his ears. Neither could I. Everybody'd liked to have died then and there.

Chambliss turned to Reggie and said, "Reggie, you know what you'd be if you were white. Just another damn white boy. Be glad you're black and getting all the publicity you do, getting away with all the shit you do."

In Oakland, that kind of self-important psycho-bullshit might have been excused as "just Reggie." In New York, egos have a tendency to expand in direct proportion to the size of the city. Feelings get hurt. Wounds are opened. Reggie, for some reason, felt we were all square pegs trying to fit into his round world. It caused problems. Major problems. Particularly with Munson.

Thurman's main gripe about Reggie was money. Not his— Reggie's. Thurm was none too pleased with the news that Reggie had signed for $2.9 million, and as time passed, the money angle got a lot of ink in the local papers. But nobody ever quite got the story right. Sure Thurman was pissed off, but not about how much Reggie was making. No, he was mad because he felt that Reggie was a liar. Plain and simple. All Thurman ever wanted to know, man to man, was what Reggie's contract called for. Nothing personal. After I had signed, Thurman had had a clause inserted into his contract that automatically made him the highest-paid Yankee—whatever anyone else made, Thurman was to receive $1 more. So, obviously, Thurman had a keen interest in knowing Reggie's numbers, although I believe he could have cared less what Reggie made; he was all for people making money. He just wanted some hard facts to use in discussions with George.

Now maybe it was none of Thurman's business what Reggie made. If so, Reggie should have told Thurman just that. Instead, according to Thurman, his lawyer went to Reggie's lawyer, then Munson's agent to Reggie's agent, but I don't believe Reggie ever told Thurman what the exact numbers were. More than once driving into the ballpark Thurman told me how he'd quietly questioned Reggie about his contract. "I don't think he's ever told me the truth," said Thurm. "I like him as a player, but I can't stand the fact he lied to me. He won't tell me the truth. I know, because I've caught him in a lie two or three times."

(Reggie and Billy weren't exactly exchanging Valentines either. Billy went out of his way to treat Reggie as anything but the established star he was, a man with MVP, RBI, and home run awards to prove it.)

It didn't help matters much that we started out 2–8. Then Billy began pulling his lineup out of a hat, and we won five straight. I came off the disabled list just long enough to get hit on the same foot again, two inches away from my earlier injury. I pitched miserably in May, lasting 2⅓ innings against Seattle, then missing a start because of shoulder stiffness. In my next start I lasted just one inning. Talk about fun. Five runs, all earned, one walk. My fastest exit since June 1970. My ERA now stood at 5.76. I was losing it, and I didn't know where to go to find it.

"He's in a depressed state," Thurman told the press.

In some respects, my failures were slightly obscured by the avalanche of publicity that followed Reggie's infamous "straw that stirs the drink" story in *Sport* magazine. It all began in a game on national TV when Reggie missed a fly ball down the line in Boston that went for a double, and Billy totally lost it. He stood up and started screaming like he wanted a big piece of Buck when Reggie trotted into the dugout. I think Ellie Howard, former Yankee catching great and our first-base coach at the time, knew it too, and he quickly stepped between them. I went down to the bull pen. Billy saw me later and said, "You scared we was going to fight, so you went down to the bull pen?"

"No," I said. "I wanted to go down there. I thought you might want to use me in relief."

"Oh, I forgot about that," said Billy. "I thought you just ran down to get away from the fight."

What fight? Believe me, Billy's brawling image aside for a second, it wouldn't have been much of a fight; Reggie would have wiped the floor with Billy.

The result of all this: more and more meetings with Steinbrenner, awkward apologies, a team rift a yard wide. On and on and on. George wouldn't let Billy alone. Calling, advising, directing, deciding. Billy, a street kid, couldn't cope with Mr. Steinbrenner's interference. It got so bad one time Billy—with George still talking—just ripped his phone right out of the wall.

Me? My motto at the time was: If you can't pitch, don't bitch. Heck, I spent so many hours in the training room that I coulda qualified for some kind of first aid certificate. Thank goodness for Gene Monahan. He's got to be the best trainer I've ever seen. Gino did everything he could for me; he must have rubbed three layers of skin off his hands, all the massaging and rubbing he did to my shoulder. The only thing he wouldn't do is lie. If you said "Don't tell the owner or don't tell the manager" you were hurt, it rubbed Gene the wrong way. "I got to," he told me. "It's my job."

I always believed that my job was to play baseball. Not to worry about outside influences. But that's half of what playing baseball in New York was all about. Money and who hated whom seemed to make up the majority of the other half. Meanwhile, my struggles continued. One week, no pain. The next week, zip. No control. No velocity. No nothing. I got letters from everywhere, folks suggesting all different kinds of cures. I was willing to try anything short of taking advice from a Medicine Man. Heck, I even tried drinking gallons of cranberry juice. Nothing helped. Six times I gave up back-to-back home runs in a game, including twice in one game in one of the most pitiful performances of my career. It happened on June 17 against Boston. I faced just six Red Sox hitters, and four took me out of the yard tying a major-league record for most home runs allowed in one inning. Rick Burleson led off the game with a homer. Fred Lynn followed with another. Then I managed to record two outs before Carlton Fisk and George Scott connected.

Billy did his best to cover for me. He should have won an award. "He feels good," he said. "He hasn't pitched enough yet. This is still spring training for him."

But actions spoke louder. I became a once-a-week pitcher. My form, for the first time in my career, deserted me. I was opening up too quickly. I pleaded with Thurman to scream at me to stay on top of the ball, knowing full well I couldn't, my shoulder so tight that scratching my ear was a difficult undertaking. I never knew when I would pitch. Finally, my frustrations and anger rose to the surface.

"Pitching rotation?" I said one day in answer to a question. "I don't think we have one. I think you go from one day to the next around here not knowing who's going to pitch. At Oakland, we knew three weeks ahead who was going to pitch. Over here, you know one day ahead. That's it. You can't prepare yourself to pitch. If you pitch every six days one time, four days another time, seven days another time, you're not going to get into a groove. You're not going to pitch well."

And I didn't. Not that it mattered. After Reggie and Billy made their peace, the club jelled and we won forty of our last fifty games, charging from five games out on August 10 to win it. Nobody could stop us. Sweet Lou (.330), Rivers (.326), Munson (.308), Jackson (.286), Chambliss (.287), and our sweet-fielding, soft-talking second baseman Willie Randolph (.274) all had sensational years. Nettles bombed twenty-nine home runs. Sparky, after getting out of Billy's doghouse, caught fire and had a Cy Young season: 13–5, twenty-six saves, a 2.17 ERA.

Sparky. He had the perfect temperament for a reliever. He never worried. Never had a sore arm. Just give me the ball, that was his attitude. He taught Ron Guidry his slider. That's all Sparky ever threw—slider, slider, slider. Slider.

Off the field, he'd do anything. He was like Dick Green in Oakland. Sparky loved to get naked and plop down on birthday cakes (at last count, he'd spoiled seven). In the locker rooms after games, with women reporters walking around, he'd parade by with a towel under his *arms*, leaving "home plate" fully exposed. Another time we caught Sparky walking naked out his hotel room door with nothing in his hands.

"Guess you guys figure I'm locked out," he said. What followed was vintage Lyle. He began to laugh his crazy laugh, jump up and down like an ape, and wave his arms. If you've ever seen Sparky with his clothes off, it's not a pretty sight. Funny, yes. Pretty, no. But we all stopped laughing when Sparky reached behind him with his left hand and pulled a room key out of his ass.

"See," he said. "I got a key. Ha! Ha! Ha!"

In many ways, those incidents, the jokes, the needling, the gallows humor, are what kept me sane in '77. Then, of course, there was Lou Piniella.

Lou and I go back a long way; to 1969, to be exact. Lou was a rookie outfielder for the expansion Kansas City Royals, the team that American League owners replaced in Kansas City when Charlie flew the coop. Lou was already rattling the fences with his short, compact stroke. In his first game, in fact, Lou banged out four hits, which got him all sorts of headlines. I got my first look at him during a doubleheader in Kansas City. He had drilled a long home run off Nash in the first game before stepping into the box against yours truly in the nightcap.

Poking around for a soft spot, I tried to sneak a fastball by him low and away. Lou just reached down and gulfed it over the leftfield fence some 400 feet away. Over the years this homer would grow and grow in stature, Lou's voice deepening oh-so-serious-like as he'd fondly recall the day: "I hit that ball so hard, fans thought it was starting to thunderstorm. Hit off the top of this building, that building, the sound was so loud I thought they called an air raid."

"Lou," I'd say, "you never had enough power to make much noise."

"Whaddya mean? It ricocheted off the roof and bounced around so much George Toma [the Royals' famed groundskeeper] came running out with the rest of the grounds crew and started putting out the tarp."

Occasionally, I'd counter such obvious drivel with this little diddy: "Lou," I'd begin, "how about the time I struck you out and you threw the bat down to third base. Then you went into the training room, lay down and started praying. 'Dear God, please put me out of my misery. Let the stadium fall on me. Anything. Just put me out of my misery.' "

Or when the mood struck and I really wanted to get Lou's goat, I'd do this:

Lou: "Remember that one I hit off you in Kansas City?"

Me: "Don't remember."

Lou: "You remember. Municipal Stadium. Fastball. Down and away."

Me: "Don't remember it."

Lou: "Whaddya mean? The grounds crew thought it was a thunderstorm . . ."

At this point, I'd resort to my never-fail reply: "Jim Fucking Wohlford."

Jim Wohlford is the player the Royals moved into left field right after Lou was traded to the Yankees. Over the years, Wohlford, who now lives in Visalia, California, and who was a solid major league outfielder, has been unwittingly immortalized in every bus, locker room, hotel room, coffee shop, bar, bathroom, and any other venue Lou and I ended up in together. Whenever Lou dug the needle too deep—and believe me, he was one of the best at it, particularly on the subject of home runs allowed—I'd just say the words "Jim Fucking Wohlford." It always bought me a moment or two of peace.

Then if Lou started up again, Nettles or Munson, or Whitey Ford, our pitching coach in '77, would fire another round.

"Hey, Lou," Whitey would begin.

"Leave me alone, Whitey. You're just a teeny little guy who pitches those silly fuckin' pitches. You never beat nobody anyway."

"Lou, I got just one thing to say," Whitey'd answer sweet as sugar. "If it wasn't for expansion baseball, you'd never have made it."

That's what I loved so much about Lou. He dished it out, but Lord, he could take it, smiling away, laughing along with us. Had to. He provided such an inviting target.

I mean how this man dressed in the morning is beyond me. He went on the road a lot of times with a suitcase full of dirty clothes. First thing he'd do after check-in was call the valet and get his laundry sent out. Of course, sometimes the stuff wouldn't come back until after the series was over, or Lou left something at home, or he needed some laundered item, so he'd go out and buy a whole new wardrobe. One time in Seattle he didn't have any shoes, so off he went down the sidewalk—barefoot—into a local shoe store. Funny thing was the salesman wouldn't let Lou buy any shoes because he'd left his socks somewhere.

And gamble? Lou would bet on anything. Horses, dogs, stocks, trotters, jai alai, which bird would fly off the wire first. You name it. One time he and pitcher Don Gullett were at a jai alai track in Florida. Piniella was like a daddy to Don, so anywhere you saw Lou—racetrack, dog track, anywhere—there was Gullett coming up right behind him. Lou would always say, "Don, give me some more money," followed by, "Give me some more," followed by Gullett's inevitable lament: "Lou," he'd say, "I ain't got no more either." Now, all the jai alai guy had to do was catch a serve for Lou to win $10,000. That's all. Just catch a serve. Naturally, he did everything but, and Lou lost ten grand—and most of his marbles. We're talking major tantrum here. Screams, ice and chair throwing, begging to get thrown out. And it wasn't long before he got his wish.

And when he won, oh, Lou loved to tell you every last juicy detail. How this horse inched outside, the jockey did this and that. You'd have thought Lou was the only guy in America who ever booted home a winner. But when he lost? Forget it. Not a word.

One day in Florida, I found out he lost big, and I mean B-I-G. So I rushed to my car and drove to this place I noticed on the way to the park. It sold hay. I bought as much as I could fit in my trunk and then came back and stuffed his locker right up to the top. Lou, being the observant man he is, noticed as soon as he walked in the locker room.

"What the hell is this?"

Our legendary clubhouse manager, Pete Sheehy, rest his soul, sauntered over. In a buttery smooth voice he said, "Lou, you win at the track last night?"

The jig was up. "That damn Catfish," said Not-So-Sweet Lou. "He heard I lost, didn't he?"

"Lou," I said. "Why don't you just feed 'em hay. It's a helluva lot cheaper than money."

More Lou: He had this curious little habit of always touching his hair and smelling it while he talked. A habit. Nothing more, nothing less. He'd do it on the bus, in the clubhouse, unconsciously rubbing two fingers together in his hair and then smelling them. I loved to catch him in the act. Embarrass the hell out of him in front of other people.

"I just want to know one thing, Lou," I'd say. "Just what does it smell like? I want to know. Where'd you have your head for you to keep smellin' it like that."

And when Lou wasn't gambling, sipping some Jack Daniel's or playing a game, you could count on him to be doing one thing: complaining. He was the Yankees' answer to Rollie Fingers. Lou could find a dark cloud in every hotel, bus, coffee shop, pair of shoes in the world. Especially shoes. He loved to complain about his feet. One day in spring training, he borrowed my 9½'s and wore them one full inning before opening the complaint department. (Lou's problem was he's a perfect 9¾.)

"Damn feet still killing me," he said. "Cat, you don't have enough damn toes on that right foot of yours to break this damn shoe in."

So out he goes into right. Sure enough, he flips off one and then the other, doing his personal impression of Shoeless Joe Jackson. Then he slings both shoes—my shoes—over the fence.

"Those damn things were killing my feet," he said, barefooting it back into the dugout.

"That's nice, Lou," I admitted. "But those were my shoes."

"Ah, I don't give a damn. I'm not wearing them anymore. And neither are you."

Of course, there was one thing that wasn't funny about Lou: his ability as a ballplayer. He was as disciplined and dedicated an athlete as you'll find. I can't count how many times I woke up in the middle of the night to find Lou practicing his swing before a hotel mirror. "I got it, Cat! I got it!" he'd yell. "They can't get me out now."

"Lou," I'd mumble, "go to bed."

Thanks to the teachings of Charlie Lau, who changed Lou from a power to a line-drive hitter, Lou learned to hit the ball to all fields. In New York he was one of our toughest outs, and he never, not once, ever quit on the field. That's why Lou, contrary to Steinbrenner's opinion, was such a good manager. His players know he won't ask them to do anything he hasn't done himself. Except, of course, bale hay.

Lou's personal profile aside, our playoff series against Kansas City boiled down to this: Sparky's 5⅓ innings of shutout relief in the pivotal fourth game as we held on to win 6–4. Spark had come on in the fourth, runners at first and third, two outs, the dangerous George Brett at the plate. A couple of sliders later, Brett flew out to left. The Royals got all of two hits the rest of the way. We won it all the next day on another dramatic three-run 9th inning comeback.

Chris, son of a Navy chaplain, had to be one of the finest guys you'll ever meet, a guy other players—black, white, blue— looked up to for leadership. Normally one of the most mild-mannered men, Chris spoke his mind when it mattered. We called him "Snatcher" because he liked to snatch the ball out of the air at first base.

In the Series, against Los Angeles, Gullett pitched his heart out in the first game. In most of his time in New York, Don never went more than two, three starts without reinjuring his shoulder. But no matter how much it hurt, he never complained. This time, however, he reared back and found the Gullett of old, going 8⅔—leading the game 3–2. But when he walks Steve Yeager to put runners on first and second with two out, Billy goes to Sparky, winner of the last two playoff games. Lyle immediately gives up a bouncing single to Lee Lacy. Now it's 3–3 and extra innings. We eventually win in the twelfth when Paul Blair singles home Randolph, who had doubled to open the inning.

Willie's been the heart and soul of the Yankees since I left. He's changed some since then, matured, but back in the late '70s he had a hair-quick temper. You didn't have to say much. I always kidded him about not being able to play. Something along the lines of, "It's gonna rain, Willie, looks like you won't be in the lineup today," because for a while there when it rained Willie scratched himself from the lineup. He was afraid of getting hurt, pulling a muscle, on a muddy, slippery track.

But I'll say this: Willie and Nettles worked harder than any two infielders I've ever seen. They took twice as many ground balls as other players. Willie was the type of guy you get on him and he'd accept the challenge: "I'll show ya. I'll show ya," is his attitude.

The next night Lasorda comes to the game in the company of a priest. I should have been saying my prayers. I hadn't pitched a single inning since September 10, out with that hernia-urinary tract infection. My win-loss record reads 9–9 with a 4.72 ERA—by far the worst of my career. My arm was a question mark, but Billy was in a bind: His pitching rotation required that somebody other than his regular starters—who needed an extra day of rest—start game two in New York. That somebody was me. "I don't have anybody else," he said. "You're my best shot."

"Then give me the ball."

The press and some of my teammates made a big stink about it—how dare Billy throw me to the wolves—but, hey, it didn't bother me. I'd rather pitch than ride the pine anytime. I figured even if I didn't win I was making a contribution.

It wasn't pretty. In the first, Reggie Smith lined a ringing double to right center, and Ron Cey followed with a blast into the Dodger bull pen in left. With two out in the second, Steve

Yeager hit another shot over Piniella's head in left. 3–0 Dodgers. The lead grew to 5–0 in the third when, after a Bill Russell single, Smith unloaded a cannon shot into the bleachers in right center. What could I say? I had done my best.

Reggie took over from there. His three home runs in the sixth game will live forever in baseball legend and lore. Didn't surprise me in the least; I'd seen too many of Reggie's shows in my time. As I said, when the man set his mind to it, when he got hot, they haven't built a ballpark big enough to hold him. It wasn't long after Reggie picked up his MVP Award that I ran into Mr. Cherry again. He remembered my boast about "handling" number forty-four.

"Cat," he drawled, "how you all doing handling Reggie."

I told him the truth. "Ah," I said, "I can't handle him." Then again, neither could the Dodgers. And we all had diamond rings to show for it.

13

MIRACLES . . . AND OTHER COMEBACKS

I guess it's best to begin the Miracle Year 1978 at around 7 a.m. on January 10, as Charles Woodard, the local druggist, and I were heading out of Hertford to do some duck hunting. It was a wicked winter day, the temperature a frigid five degrees, a cruel wind howling down with a vengeance from the north.

About forty-five minutes later, two huge oil transport trucks pulled up to the pumps at the Winslow Oil Company. At the time, Winslow Oil was located on the southern edge of town and overlooked the Perquiman's River. Shivering from the cold, the drivers began pumping fuel oil into the thirty-six-foot-tall storage tanks. Police and fire investigators never completely determined what happened next. They figure it was a spark. But what I do know is this: At exactly 7:50 a.m., one of the tanks, filled with 30,000 gallons of fuel, exploded.

Folks say it sounded like a sonic boom. It was heard as far as five miles away. The resulting fire and series of blasts—six tanks would blow over the next seven hours quickly turned one entire section of town into an inferno. The Winslow offices, with $600,000 in cash and receivables, were the first to go, burning up like crepe paper. Two employees barely escaped death, crawling on their bellies through the fire before throwing themselves into the river. An adjacent feed and seed store went up next; soon after, both tankers and three fuel service trucks were engulfed in flames. Meanwhile, the worst fire in Hertford history raged on and on.

Charles and I first saw the big black cloud of smoke from twenty miles away, deciding to hustle home as fast as we could. It was close to 10:45 when we drove back into town. By then, 125 firemen from seven different towns had been joined on the scene by several sheriff's departments, the North Carolina Highway Patrol, the Coast Guard, and U.S. Navy. Everyone there was saying a silent prayer that the wind would shift north, away from downtown. (Thankfully, those prayers were answered. The town was evacuated but saved from any serious damage.)

Pushing the accelerator of my pickup to the floor, I raced toward the center of the blaze to see what had happened. A second tank had blown at 9 a.m., fueling the flames. But now, thanks to all the men and equipment, the fire appeared to be under control. The only problem was the arctic weather; water from the hoses was freezing on the firemen's gloves and clothes. So I whipped my truck around and headed home. Ten minutes later I was back with every stitch of fresh clothing I could find.

I got right to the inner edge of the fire before one of the fire marshalls stopped me.

"Jimmy," he said, "you can't go in there."

"I've got fresh hunting gloves and clothes for the firemen."

"All right, go on, but be careful."

I drove slower now, feeling the heat. I stopped just across the street from where the Winslow offices once stood. "Here," I said to two firemen, picking up the hunting clothes, "take these."

It was 10:59 a.m.

A minute later two more storage tanks went off like bombs.

To be honest, I'm not quite sure what happened next. Fact is, I've never said much about the next few minutes of my life to anyone outside of Hertford until now. What it feels like to set a foot or two inside death's door and, miraculously, be pulled back out again, isn't something I've cared to bring up in casual conversations over the years. All I remember now is a voice screaming "The tanks blew!" and an ear-splittin' explosion and the sensation of someone pulling me down . . . down . . . to the ground.

The tops of both tanks, twelve feet in diameter, shot thirty feet straight into the sky. One landed in the river hundreds of yards away never to be seen again. The other rocketed over a house across the street, flipping like a flapjack. It crash-landed on nearby Grubb Street, spun and careened against the fire chief's pickup truck, shearing off a huge chunk of metal. Then the top kept rolling, out of control, up the curb, flipping one final time into the air. . . .

Before landing on top of me and two other firemen.

"Move," I thought, *"move!"* But I couldn't. Four hundred pounds of plate steel, three-eighths of an inch thick, twelve feet in diameter were crushing against my chest. To this day, I don't know how hot that top was. My only thoughts were: "I'm burning to death. Burning to death." That's all that registered. "I'm going to die. Right here, right now. My life is over."

Remember growing up and reading those silly stories about mothers who suddenly find the superhuman strength to lift a car off their injured child? Well, I'm here to tell ya' those stories aren't so silly. The two firemen were dazed and injured, unable to help. Somehow, some way, I was able to push that slab of steel off of us.

"Jimmy, Jimmy," a rescue squad member shouted as I stumbled away from the scene. "C'mon, help us move these guys into the van." I barely heard a word. I just stood like a statue staring at the blaze. A group of firemen arrived to cart the tank top away. It took five of them to move it.

"Jimmy! Jimmy!"

I started to run—I don't know where. My nephew said later it was back toward town. Back and forth, back and forth I sprinted, aimless, alone. Somehow I found my truck, crawled in, and barely moved a muscle for fifteen minutes. Doctors said later I was in shock, delirious. By the grace of God, I found my way home.

Inside the door, I fell apart. I couldn't stop crying. Feeling the same horrible sensation over and over again: "I'm burning to death . . . I'm burning to death."

Less than a month later, still shaken by the experience, I headed for Florida and spring training. My body hadn't felt right since the accident. I was thirsty all the time now. I had lost nine pounds in three weeks. Worse, while driving down to Lauderdale, I experienced a never-ending urge to go to the bathroom. I must have stopped that car every fifteen minutes. Helen and the kids were about ready to have me committed. I knew something was wrong; I headed straight to the training room as soon as I arrived in Lauderdale.

"Hey, Doc," I said, "every time I pass by a bathroom I gotta go. What's up? I'm pissin' myself to death."

The next day, February 16, Gino sent me over to see Dr. Sheldon Nassberg at Northridge General Hospital. "Do you feel bad?" he asked. I told him no. I told Nassberg I'd been drinking water like a fish, flushing toilets every half hour for the past two weeks. Nassberg, now co-medical director of the Diabetic Treatment Center at Holy Cross Hospital in Ft. Lauderdale, didn't need a crystal ball to tell this thirty-year-old man he had a problem. Even before the blood sugar test came back (at 500 milligrams per decilitre; normal is 80–125), he knew the answer.

"It's a wonder you haven't passed out by now," said Nassberg. "You're a diabetic."

Wonderful. Three weeks ago I was a happy, healthy, "normal" athlete. Then I'm almost crushed to death. Now I'm an insulin-dependent diabetic. I thought back to the explosion. Was it possible my disease—a chronic metabolic disorder that adversely affects the body's ability to manufacture enough insulin, the chemical needed to convert carbohydrates into energy, to combat excessive sugar buildup in the blood—had been triggered by that traumatic accident? During that terrible time, had my body chemistry somehow been radically altered? Nassberg said no. Among type II diabetics, whom he said account for 90 percent of those with the disease, such a reaction is possible. I was type I, what Nassberg described as "genetically predisposed" to contract an illness often set off by a virus. Either way, I was in trouble, because left untreated diabetes can lead to heart attacks, stroke, kidney malfunction, and nerve damage.

Great. Now what? My first thoughts were like those of so many others. I was surprised and scared. The ball game's over. It would take a miracle for me to pitch again. I can't play anymore. I can't do this. I can't do that. But thanks to the gentle teaching of Dr. Nassberg, I found out that there's much more "yes" than "no" associated with diabetes. With changes in diet, a monitored weight loss, and regular exercise, miracles could happen, I could—would—live a happy, healthy life.

"Your life's not over. Your professional days aren't over," said Nassberg. "As long as you take care of yourself, eat the right foods, take your shots, and manage the [insulin] dosage like you're supposed to, you'll be in better shape than all those people eating sweets. And you'll live longer."

None of this happened overnight, however. Even disclosing I had the illness was kinda tricky. At the time, the Yankees were negotiating with Texas for pitching, and naturally, the last thing they needed in the papers was mention of my illness. Nothing like pushing up the price of available talent. So the day after meeting Dr. Nassberg I entered Northridge General under the alias of "James Hunt." Only Mr. Steinbrenner and our trainer, Gene Monahan, knew the secret. And it stayed that way for ten days until the *New York Daily News* broke the story. Until that scoop I was a double agent—practicing with my unsuspecting teammates in the morning, learning a whole new way of life every afternoon.

Every day, Nassberg would visit my hospital room and we'd talk for ninety minutes. He explained that diabetes was part of *his* family history; that's why he tried to stay so skinny. "Ever go to an old folks' home and see any fat people?" he asked. "You won't see any. They're all dead."

Slowly I learned about the disease and how to control it through diet and exercise. I learned that today there are an estimated twenty-two million Americans suffering from diabetes; a majority of them are overweight men and women with a family history of the disease, or pregnant women with babies weighing over nine pounds. I learned to watch for symptoms— unusual thirst or hunger, dizziness, sores on the feet or body that don't heal. I learned that 50 percent of those suffering from diabetes in this country don't know it, primarily because doctors routinely take blood tests but don't always check blood sugar levels. I learned that type II diabetes can often be controlled just through diet and exercise.

Slowly we made some changes. Nassberg put me on a 3000 calories a day diet free of sweets and other junk food—a big blow for someone who grew up on Momma's cooking and ate dessert with every meal. I discovered sugar in places I never knew it existed.

"Can't do that," said Nassberg as I bit into a big apple.

"Why not? You said eat an apple. I ate an apple."

"But not a *big* apple," he cautioned. "You must eat small portions of everything. There's too much natural sugar in a large apple. Why do you think it tastes so good?"

Nassberg went on to teach Helen how to give me my shots. He warned me not to inject insulin into my legs or pitching arm on game days (it would be more quickly absorbed because of exertion, raising my blood sugar level). He showed me how to check my blood sugar level (four times a day), especially before pitching. "We don't want you passing out on the pitcher's mound," he laughed.

Above all, he gave me a glimpse of what my future would be like should I ignore his recommendations. "Right now you can probably go two, three years not taking your medicine right, not eating properly," he said. "You won't think it's affecting you. But what diabetes does is make your body a lot older than it is because everything has to work so much harder to keep your system clean. After those two or three years, you'll fall off quickly. Do things right, and you won't lose your eyesight all of a sudden. Or die."

I listened to every word. I became an "avid student" in the words of the good doctor. What else can you do? Soon my face began appearing on the sides of buses in Florida, promoting blood sugar tests. Today I annually travel around the country on behalf of Upjohn, a pharmaceutical company that's been researching the problem for years and is concerned about health and education. In cities like New York I go on radio talk shows and do TV interviews, trying to help people recognize and understand the varying degrees of diabetes. I remind them to ask their doctors for blood sugar tests. I talk about the benefits of exercise and weight loss, especially for type II sufferers, because a body free of excess fat responds to glucose more quickly. I talk about the value of eating natural foods. I encourage people to experiment with natural sweeteners such as unsweetened apple butter, and try to convince them to eat more green vegetables, such as string beans and peas. Most of all, I steer them clear of all junk food and diet drinks.

Last year in fact, in conjunction with Upjohn, all this information and much more was put into a twenty-page, four-color cookbook called *Cooking with "Catfish" Hunter*. It includes dozens of recipes for people with diabetes. Things like Seventh Game Black Bean Soup, Pennant Fever Pasta, Catfish Sole (a personal favorite: sole fillets stuffed with shrimp and crabmeat). For dessert, there's Pitcher's Mound Pie (apple pie with a crunchy whole wheat crust), compliments of Helen Hunter. I'm not one to hype too many causes, but this one's important. So if you want information about diabetes, call 1–800–232–3472. And for free copies of the cookbook, write P.O. Box 307-C, Coventry, CT 06238.

Over the hill.

Three words. A simple phrase. But one I heard over and over

the first six weeks of the 1978 season. The reason? Easy. My arm was basically shot. I couldn't raise it above my waist without pain. I was short-arming, pushing every pitch. Like all athletes, I'd always known my career would end one day. But the way I pictured it was much more humane and graceful—one day I'd just lose my stuff and step aside. I'd never *dreamed*—despite pitching 3228 innings in just thirteen years—that a bum arm would do me in. Sore arms happened to other guys. But now it was happening to me.

Was it ever. I lost my first start to the Brewers on a raw, windy day, lasting all of two-plus innings and giving up homers to Cecil Cooper and Gorman Thomas. Alarms went off all over the clubhouse. The questions started. Was it the diabetes? (No.) The shoulder and arm again? (Yes.)

"Are we panicking?" asked a writer.

"If you are," I said, "George will too."

Red flares went off again in my next start, a 6–1 loss to Baltimore. I allowed five runs in just 4⅓ innings. My ERA was now 15.63.

I could feel the guys pulling for me. And after I had beaten the Royals 4–2 on May 2, my first win of the year—and my first since August of '77—George sent a bottle of champagne to the locker room.

"It may be a little flat from standing on the shelf for so long," said the card. "Congratulations, The Boss."

A week later I rolled the dice again—they came up sevens as I handled Minnesota, 3–1. Then I completely crapped out. On May 21 I lasted all of forty warmup pitches. My shoulder felt like it was locked in a vise. I left in disgust and anger. "I can't throw at all," I told Billy. "My arm's killing me."

Where to turn? The club's answer was the disabled list and a trip to the office of Manhattan orthopedic surgeon Dr. Maurice Cowen. Cowen initially diagnosed a torn muscle behind the shoulder, prescribing rest, massage, and, perhaps, manipulation —the stretching of the arm and shoulder under anesthesia—if necessary.

It became necessary. In June I pitched all of one inning. Unfortunately, it was against a runaway train called the Boston Red Sox, who were leading the division by about ten games. Billy put me in a lost cause to test my arm. It was pitiful. I got ripped for four hits (homers by Scott and Lynn) and two runs before striking out Yaz with the bases loaded. Some folks speculated at the time that Yaz felt so sorry for me that he purposely went down swinging. No way. Yaz was too much of a professional to ever do that. He may have felt sorry for me, but he wanted to beat me.

Three days later I went back on the disabled list. My teammates tried to cheer me up by putting signs like No. 1 HYPE (for hypochondriac) above my locker. But deep down I knew they hurt, too. One Yankee spokesman was quoted in the papers as saying, "Cat may never pitch again." And honestly, I wasn't up for the debate.

Especially after I tried to throw batting practice to Todd in our front yard in Norwood.

There I was, pushing powderpuff tosses to home plate when Helen spoke up. She'd seen enough. "Why don't I pitch and you go and play the outfield," she said.

"Why?" I asked.

"'Cause I throw harder than you now."

I went to see Cowen the very next day, June 25. He was an interesting guy who loved to race $27,000 turbocharged Porsches. In his private practice he treated everyone from Little Leaguers to Martha Graham dancers. As the Yankee team doctor, he'd manipulated Gullett's arm in May and later did a similar procedure on injured Detroit star Mark "The Bird" Fidrych. Manipulation, said Cowen, was really nothing more than the stretching and adjustment of muscles. I figured, what the hell, I'll try anything once. At this point I told Cowen, "I don't care if you cut the damn thing off and glue another on." I wanted to pitch.

OTHER VOICES—DR. MAURICE COWEN

"Catfish couldn't cock his arm to throw. He was throwing the ball halfheartedly in front of his shoulder. I talked to a few physicians who had taken care of athletes. Manipulation, at that time, was somewhat popular. I figured it couldn't hurt him, so I put him in Lenox Hill Hospital.

"While he was under general anesthesia I manipulated his arm back into the cocking position—something I could never

have done while he was awake. It made this resounding noise—a
big pop! Someone in the room said, 'Ah, shit, we broke his arm.'
We immediately took an X-ray, but I honestly didn't think I had
broken it, because I hadn't used that much force. So I continued
to stretch the arm back and forth.

"What happened to Catfish was that the coracoacromial
ligament, a big ligament in the shoulder, had thickened and
swelled and wasn't allowing his greater tuberosity—a node, a
part of the bone that the muscle attaches to—to pass under it.
During the manipulation of the arm, a piece of the ligament
broke off, allowing the shoulder to move up into a cocking
position."

All I remember is waking up on the 26th and seeing Dr. Cowen
standing over me. In his hand was a wad of surgical padding
wrapped with tape. "Here," said Cowen, tossing me the
"ball." "Throw this."

I threw it.

No pain. Not even a twinge. "Hey, Doc. It doesn't hurt
anymore."

Cowen asked if I had experienced any pain during the
ten-minute process, even though I was under anesthetic.

"No, why?" I asked.

"Well, your arm popped so damn loud I thought I broke it."

That afternoon I played lob ball with Todd in the backyard in
Norwood. That night I kept my arm in ice, hoping against hope
that I wouldn't wake up with another ache. I'd always thought
something would happen, some miracle, and I'd be able to
come back and pitch.

Next morning: No pain.

Friday: Fifteen more minutes of pain-free pitching. For the
first time in two years, my arm felt normal. A miracle. All I
wanted to do was get out there and start pitching before it started
hurtin' again. The Cat was back.

But what was I coming back to? Defending World Champions
deep into a soap opera subplot as complex and controversial as
any on *Dynasty*. Including:

• The draining day-to-day saga of *As the Clubhouse Turns*
  starring Billy ("one's a born liar, the other's convicted")
  Martin and George (I'm the Boss) Steinbrenner.

Costarring a rebellious cast of characters including Jackson, Munson, Figueroa, Rivers, Lyle, and Nettles.
- A pitching staff in shambles. By the All Star break, no fewer than fifteen different guys had been on the mound. It got so bad minor leaguers were driving up from New Haven to audition for starting roles. First baseman Jim Spencer was warming up in the bull pen. And so many injuries. Gullet had four starts after his manipulation and then went back on the disabled list. Messersmith also was disabled, along with Tidrow and Figueroa. Rivers, Randolph, and Dent also were out of the lineup with injuries.
- A "cancerous" internal situation. Guys going through the motions. Munson, White, Lyle, Figueroa, Johnson, and Spencer demanding to be traded. Billy, stressed out, fighting a drinking problem. Thurman and Reggie still at each other's throats.

I guess the whole mess got started when George got worried about Billy's failing health, his increasingly haggard look, and offered him a graceful way to retire. Billy would have none of that and pushed even harder, putting more pressure on himself and the team. Particularly on Reggie, whom Billy perceived as one of "George's boys," a big-bucks free agent who had somehow to prove himself all over again to Billy—a thought that stuck right in Reggie's craw. All the animosity came to a head on July 8 in the tenth inning of a game against Kansas City in the now-famous "bunt" incident. Thurman was on first when third base coach Dick Howser flashed Billy's bunt sign to Reggie—who hadn't successfully sacrificed since 1972. Reggie, naturally, got insulted. He tried to bunt once and failed. Billy took off the sign. Reggie said screw you, and bunted again. He missed. Howser raced down and told Reggie to hit away.

"I want to bunt," said Reggie.

"Billy says to hit away," repeated Howser.

"I want to bunt."

Bunt he did, popping a third attempt foul for an automatic strikeout.

For some unknown reason Martin held his rage. It was assistant coach Gene Michael who told Reggie he was out of the game. Afterward Martin lost it, smashing a soft-drink bottle against the wall and heaved his clock radio into the hallway.

Reggie got suspended for five days, which seemed to ease the tension, and we started playing well again, chopping four games off the Red Sox lead and moving up a notch into third place, ahead of the Orioles.

Billy, however, just kept withdrawing more and more. It was no deep, dark secret that he was hitting the bottle pretty hard. All of us were concerned about his physical and emotional state. Billy had always wanted to be one of the guys. He wanted some of the guys to like him and he wanted others not to like him. I don't know why. You figure it out. Munson liked him for a while and then he got to the point where he didn't like him. Maybe it was because when Billy got to drinking sometimes he said things he didn't know he was saying about the guys that were sitting there with him.

But to this day, I never saw Billy come to the ballpark drunk. He may have left that way, but never on the way in. Drunk or sober, he finally lost it five days later, telling two local reporters at Chicago's O'Hare Airport that "The two men [Reggie and George] deserve each other. One's a born liar, the other's convicted." Martin was forced to resign in tears the next day, July 24, and was replaced by mellow Bob Lemon, a former Yankee pitching coach. Just twenty-four days earlier, Lem had been fired by the White Sox. Now he had a five-year deal to manage the Yankees.

Lem went quietly about his business, putting Thurman back behind home plate, Reggie fourth in the order, and Bucky Dent back at short. "Go have some fun," he said. And we did. He settled us down, put a blanket on the confusion and turmoil. We were still 14½ back of Boston.

I returned from the disabled list on July 17. By August the real Cat was back. (So was Billy, by the way. Just five days after Billy had resigned, Mr. Steinbrenner, taking a page from Barnum's book, had shocked all of us with an Old-Timers Game announcement that Martin would return to manage the club in 1980 with Lemon being kicked upstairs as general manager. Nothing would have surprised me at this point. He coulda changed our nickname to the Buccaneers and I'd have just looked for my pirate cap.) Meanwhile, the pain never returned to my shoulder. My first time out in August, I threw eight shutout innings and won. Then I beat Baltimore twice in back-to-back starts. In the first win, 3–0 over Jim Palmer, I had career stuff; my velocity and location were back to where they had been three, four years earlier. It was my first shutout in more than a year and my first complete game since August 1977. The next time out was a five-inning, rain-shortened win, after which the press started asking if I planned to play another year. That's how good I looked.

Oh, and the Red Sox were stumbling. By August 7 we trailed by just 7½ games.

By month's end I was 6–0 for August with a 1.64 ERA. Guidry, meantime, was an incredible 19–2. He got off to an 11–0 start, the best by a Yankee since 1960. The first time I saw Gator it was during the second game of a doubleheader at Shea Stadium in 1975. I won the first game, 2–1 I think, and then went inside to soak my arm, get showered, and change back into a fresh uniform. When I walked back into the dugout, I didn't know who was on the mound. He wasn't in the clubhouse before the first game. The team must have brought him up just to pitch that game. "Who is that skinny guy, the bat boy?" I asked. Pretty soon he started throwing strikes, throwing the ball right by people. During that season he threw it by *everybody*. Like a 159-pound version of Dwight Gooden. As time wore on, Gator and I got to be real close friends. He stayed at my house every fall and spring when his wife was home with the kids for school. Mostly we talked hunting and fishing.

On September 1 we trailed Boston by 6½. Soon after we outscored the Red Sox 42–9 (and outhit them 67–21) in a four-game series at Fenway, all part of a 16–2 tear that left us tied for the league lead on September 13. (Miracles, anyone?) Later, I beat them in the third game of another series sweep in New York. Rice took me deep for a 2–0 lead early, but then my fastball and sinker showed up. By the time the seventh rolled around, I said to myself, "I flat got 'em. Church is out." The way I used to feel.

Lem just kept rolling along, pushing the right buttons in his low-key style. "It's a lot of fun," he told his wife, Jane, over the phone one day. "It's better than sex . . . as I remember it."

Meanwhile, Gossage proved worth every penny of the $2.75 million Mr. Steinbrenner paid him to replace Sparky as our closer. The first time I saw Goose pitch was when he was playing for Chicago. Reggie was up and hit a one-hop shot off Goose's shin. One out later Munson lined a rocket off the other shin.

Goose fell down kicking both legs up in the air screaming. We about died on the bench we were laughing so hard.

But when he got on the mound the joke was on the hitter; Goose was like a madman. To look at him, you know he doesn't know where the ball is going, I don't care what he says. He doesn't know. He just rears back and throws and tries to pick up the target. Nothing fancy. I told him he was the only guy in the big leagues I wouldn't hit against. If I had to hit, I'd just forfeit my at bat.

In the last game of the regular season we had a chance to win it all. We played Cleveland one game up with one to play. My postmanipulation record was 10–2. Unfortunately, after this game it was 10–3; I lasted only 1⅔ innings, thirty-eight pitches. Andre Thornton and Gary Alexander hit big home runs, and we lost 9–2. In a one-game playoff the next day, however, in a shot heard round the world, Bucky Dent cracked a three-run homer, and we beat Boston 5–4. Some folks called it a miracle, but Bucky didn't surprise me hitting that home run. Heck, in Boston anybody's got a chance to be a hero with that "Green Monster." I liked Bucky; he certainly didn't have a whole lot of range, but every ball he got his glove on he made the play. And, anyway, with Nettles at third, he could afford to cheat up the middle a little bit.

In the playoffs we beat Kansas City in four, trading victories in the first two games in Kansas City. My turn came at home in the third game. You may remember it. George Brett hit a playoff record three home runs. Led off first with a homer. Reggie tied it. Brett hit another in the third. Hits by Thurman, Reggie, and Lou and an error put us up 3–2. Brett tied it in the fifth. Some people thought three home runs by one guy was noteworthy. Probably was. But to me it typified my style of pitching: three dingers with nobody on base, no other runs, and we win the game. Next year, in the first playoff game against Kansas City, Goose got a real good taste of what kinda hitter Brett was at the time. On the first pitch Brett hit a ball into orbit, I mean upper deck and gaining speed. I couldn't resist.

"Hey, Goose," I said.

"Yeah."

"Remember those three home runs I gave up."

He didn't say anything.

"That one went farther than all three of mine put together."

This time, however, Reggie answered in the sixth with a sacrifice fly and we won it 4–3 on Thurman's two-run homer in the eighth off Doug Bird. We went on to defeat the Royals.

In the World Series against L.A. we lost the first two and then won four straight. Reggie hit two more tape-measure blasts and drove in eight runs. Rivers hit .333, and Nettles played third base about as well as it has ever been played. Dent hit .417, drove in seven runs, and was named MVP.

I got the call in game six with us leading the Series three games to two. On the morning of the game I had breakfast with Lindblad, who had been traded to the Yanks during the middle of the season. He could tell my mind was on other matters.

"What's your problem?" he asked.

I told him I was worried about Daddy. Paul knew exactly what I meant. We had been vacationing together in Hawaii after the '77 Series when I called back to Hertford to see how things were going. "Not well," said my sister Elizabeth. She told me Daddy had just been diagnosed as having lung cancer. I was ready to jump on a plane right then and come home. "Don't," she said, adding, "There's nothing you can do now."

I looked up from my breakfast and told Paul my problem. "Dad's not feeling well," I said. "I think this may be the last season I get to hunt with him."

"We may not make it back, Cat. We gotta win the Series first."

"Hunting season opens tomorrow," I said, "and I plan on being in North Carolina at sunup."

Dad and I had been hunting and fishing together in the off-season since 1966. We'd walked and talked hundreds of mornings away, side by side, him offering advice about one problem after another. One year, I remember, I wanted to buy some more land.

"Don't need mo' land," said Daddy. "Got enough now. No need to go into debt for it."

"Thinking about building another shelter for the tractor."

"Don't need no more shelters."

We talked about me buying a big house on a lake near town. Daddy knew I wanted it. "It's no place to bring up kids," he said. "A farm is a place to learn what work is about, where you learn to appreciate what you get."

I found out later that day that Lou had some trouble with my timetable. Especially after he saw that airplane ticket sticking out of my back pocket. He ran around the locker room shouting, "Why don't we all take a twelve o'clock flight."

So I pitched that sixth game for Daddy all, I guess, except the first inning, when Davey Lopes hit my third pitch of the game into the bleachers in left, and a little bit in the third inning, when the Dodgers had two runners on and Reggie Smith due up. That's when Thurman waddled out to the mound.

"Well, Catfish," he said, "you better make sure you hit my glove exactly where I put it because you ain't got diddly squat tonight."

"Hey, Captain Bad Body," I said, "just get your ass back on behind the plate and catch it after I throw it. I'm in a hurry to git home."

One way or another I got Smith to ground into an inning-ending double play. I scattered six hits over seven innings, and we went on to win 7–2. The Yankees had their twenty-second World Championship, and I, in this season of miracles and other comebacks, had a reservation at the airport.

14

THE WALK OF LIFE

APRIL: Notes on the Bronx Zoo . . .

Gossage Out 6 to 8 Weeks;

Yanks Bow to Rangers, 5–0

JUNE: Hunter Is Annoyed at Uncertain Status

JULY: BILLY BOY IS BACK!

AUGUST: Coroner: Paralysis Hit Munson

SEPTEMBER: On the Road Going Nowhere with the Yankees

OCTOBER: Salesman Says Martin Hit Him

Yanks Oust Martin and Replace Him with Howser

The headlines and heartaches of my last season in New York hit with the force of a hurricane. Dave Anderson of the *New York Times* called 1979 a "nightmare" year for the Yankees, and for this Yankee it was truly one dark day after another.

Little did we know that the storm clouds were already forming when we arrived for spring training. Just ten days after the '78 season Bob Lemon's youngest son, Jerry, had been killed in a Jeep accident in California. We all knew Jerry was the apple of Lem's eye—his will to win. It was obvious from the time the pitchers and catchers reported in February that baseball had lost its appeal. "My heart's just not in it anymore," Lem told us.

I knew exactly what he meant. It was all too clear now that Daddy was dying of cancer.

My entire off-season was devoted to his care and comfort. I tried to get him to go hunting with me. Every day I asked. He always said no. "Well," I said, "what about just going for a ride?"

"I don't feel like it," said Daddy. "Goin' over those bumps hurts me."

"What if I just stay on the main roads?"

"No," he said, "it hurts too much."

I'll admit it, I had a hard time understanding this. If I was very sick, knew I was going to die, I'd want to go everywhere, do everything I could. But maybe it's different when you're the one feelin' the pain, the hollowness in your heart. But still I wanted to tell him, "Daddy, c'mon, let's go out." But I never did. Not once.

The only time he'd get in the car was when we traveled to Norfolk for his radiation treatments. I'd usually drive him when I was home. He'd sit as tall as he could, staring out the window, as we rode to the hospital. Ninety minutes down. Ninety minutes of treatments. Ninety minutes home. We'd go in cycles—ten days on, ten days off. Daddy sat silent the whole way, both of us hoping, praying, the radiation would somehow burn the sickness away. And for a while it worked. One week there'd be no sign of the disease; the next, however, it would be right back inside him again, eating away at his strength. His manhood.

But still he never complained. Not once. Not even later on when the cancer gained hold and filled his lungs with fluid, and a doctor in nearby Edenton was forced to insert a big, long needle into Daddy's back to drain out the fluid. Daddy just sat there, straight back, in an old wooden chair. From behind the doctor would stick the nasty needle into the lower part of the back, up into the lungs, and draw out the fluid. No novocaine. No pain killers. No nothing.

It was the tears, the tears that finally did the talking. Daddy had been a brick his whole life; I'd never seen him cry, not once, but now if somebody mentioned how so-and-so was sick, tears started rolling down his cheeks. The cancer had softened him up. I guess in the back of his mind he was thinking—he was thinking he was going to die.

Near the end, we stopped the treatments and put Daddy in a small hospital in Edenton. It wasn't much—a dozen rooms, spare but clean, with a country feeling. At least we could push his wheelchair to the window, where Daddy could see the corn growing tall across the way.

"Need some rain," said Daddy.

OTHER VOICES—PAUL LINDBLAD

"I guess we roomed together for about eight of the fifteen years Cat pitched in the big leagues. It's funny, we never talked much baseball, mostly about life down there in North Carolina. I felt like I lived down there half the time. Heck, I knew just about everything that was going on, who was purchasing what land, all the fussing and feuding going on between Cat's brothers. How big brother was mad at little brother, things like that. They couldn't wait for Cat to get home because he'd more or less speak to each one individually and straighten them out. They were all kinda hardheaded—just like Cat was. I would just laugh at the whole mess.

"As far as the arm trouble and his dad, well, as far as '78 was concerned, he just kept most all of that inside. Even at the worst, just before the manipulation, he never really felt sorry for himself. You could see a little change after he got the bad news in Hawaii because it was eating at him. But he'd really never spill his guts. He wasn't the type to do that. Helen couldn't even help him. I think Jim just learned to live with it and accept it as it was."

In spring training Lem pretty much left us alone. Too much alone. We didn't run as much as we should; we lost our spark, the edge we'd developed winning two World Championships. The loss of Blair, Rivers, and Tidrow, all traded away, didn't help matters much. The biggest loss, however, came in April when Goose got into a wild locker room brawl with our six-four, 225-pound reserve catcher, Cliff Johnson—a man who possessed the unique ability to do exactly the wrong thing at precisely the wrong time.

Cliff had to be one of the downright laziest ballplayers I ever saw in my life. I always called him "Fence Post" Johnson because one time he bought a bunch of railroad ties to make a fence out there in Texas around his ranch. "The only reason you want those ties, Cliff," I said one day, "is so that you'll be able to walk from one to another and lean on them." Cliff truly had all the talent in the world and could have been a good catcher, but he didn't want to catch. He didn't want to work. No, sir, what Cliff liked to do most was sit around and shoot the shit. Or get into wrestling matches with people and show how strong he was. Some time during the '78 postseason Johnson came up behind Ellie Howard and was gonna throw him into a big bucket of ice that was chilling the champagne. He picked Ellie off the floor, and before you know it, Ellie ended up in a locker. When he charged out, Ellie was on top and just grabbed Cliff like a baby and threw him across the room like a toothpick. "Don't ever mess with me again or I'll kill ya," said Ellie, and meant it.

Goose had been such a stud for us in '78, so dominating, that Lem and Billy found little use for Lyle. He was shipped off to Texas. But now, as a result of the fight, Goose was out of action for twelve weeks with torn ligaments in his right thumb. Without him, our bull pen contributed a grand total of two—count 'em, two—saves during the next three months.

That was only the beginning of our miseries. Lem eventually got fired, replaced by Martin on July 18. With Martin at the helm, I quickly became the odd man out in the rotation, the sixth starter on a five man starting staff that included Luis Tiant, Ed Figueroa, Tommy John, Jim Beattie, and Ron Guidry. And even though my arm felt fine and I pitched well enough to win three of my first four starts, my record read 0–3, and I was on my way to impersonating the Invisible Man. I felt like Billy knew I wasn't gonna be there next year and no way was the team going anywhere in '79, so he was gonna look at everybody but me.

"Hey, you hear Clyde's in the hospital?"

I told one of my teammates that, yes, I'd seen the story in the paper that day about how Clyde Kluttz, the chief Yankee scout, had entered a hospital for tests relating to a circulatory problem in his hands and legs. I called Clyde that night. Said he was doing fine, just a little tired.

The next morning I got another call. Clyde's dead. Cause of death: a blood clot. I couldn't believe it. Overnight I'd lost one of the most important, influential figures in my life. Clyde had been a second father to me since high school. A voice of honesty and reason. Now he was gone.

Clyde's sudden death shocked and saddened me, adding to my growing frustration. I'd never been one of those pitchers who could sit for a week and come back blowing heat; I needed work to stay in shape, to fine-tune my control. Time passed. Nobody said one word to me for three weeks. It wasn't my place to stand up and complain. But when the press started askin' around, countin' the days before my appearances (they reached eighteen at one point), I spoke up:

"Why don't you go ask the pitching coach and the manager," I said. "They probably have a lot more to say about it than I have."

"Who's supposed to tell you when you're going to pitch?"

"The pitching coach," I said. "But the pitching coach on this club knows less than anyone."

Tom Morgan, the man in question, didn't much care for my remarks. He insinuated in the press that the reason I wasn't pitching was that I wasn't healthy, my stuff was weak, I'd lost my control. He said my windup was all messed up. He claimed he looked at old films and noticed how I'd changed my windup.

"Show me where it's different," I asked Morgan. He never showed me nothin'.

So I decided to show them, all of them, that my windup wasn't at fault. I devised something of a secret plan of my own. The day before a scheduled start in Milwaukee I told Brewers' third baseman Don Money and ex-A's teammate Mike Hegan, also playing for the Brewers, to keep an eye on me during the game. "I'm gonna pitch like Tiant," I said. They both laughed and said I was nuts.

"Just watch me," I said.

Sure enough, the next day, El Catfisho was out on the mound twisting and turning, swiveling his hips like some disco dancer. I swear Money about died laughing in the batter's box when he saw me. I looked like the spitting image of Tiant. All I needed was a big fat Cuban cigar in my mouth and nobody'd have known the difference. I went six strong innings before, frankly, I got so damn tired of swiveling around I couldn't concentrate. I ended up losing another close one. My record now read: eight starts, five losses, no wins.

For those looking for an omen, the calendar showed exactly 100 days left in my career when I won my first game of the season, 3–2, allowing only four hits over six innings. Billy was back in the saddle by then. Bringing him back was George's idea, naturally, of how to give a toothless third-place club (we were ten games behind the front-running Orioles) a swift kick in the pants.

Billy and I got along fine (although I must say I was probably in the minority). We got into it hot and heavy only one time. Figueroa was hurt, Guidry was in the bull pen trying to replace Goose, and Tiant and John were proving to be the only consistent starters. Yet Ken Clay and Don Hood, two rookies, were showing up on the mound a whole lot more often than I was. Enough was enough. I walked into Martin's office one afternoon and spoke my piece.

"Why aren't I pitchin'?"

Billy was puffing on his huge Sherlock Holmes pipe, blowing little white rings of smoke into the air. "When do you want to pitch?" he asked.

When do you want to pitch. Like, *Oh, gee, I'm sorry, I didn't know you were interested.*

"Don't care," I said. "I just want to get into the rotation. Pitching every fourth or fifth day is the only way I can pitch."

Billy blew another ring. "We'll put you in there," he said, "but if you don't do the job . . ."

"Well, you'll have to put me in there more than once. Put me in there three, four times in a row. Then you'll know whether I'm doin' the job. I can't pitch one time here, wait two weeks, pitch 'nother time. No way I can do that."

"All right," said Billy.

But every time he said "All right," I pitched one time, then not again for two weeks.

The last time I saw Daddy alive was right after I beat Seattle on July 12—the date, as it turns out, of my last win in the big leagues. Shortly thereafter, I went home for the All Star break and it was almost too much to bear, seeing Daddy lying there, tubes in his nose, a shell of his former self. A couple of times on earlier visits, while I was standing right there, his lungs got so full of fluid he'd plunge into these god-awful spasms, shaking, and squeezing my hands until they had subsided. "It'll be only a matter of minutes now," the doctor would whisper as he walked in. But Daddy would hold on for another month and a half, lucidly talking to each and every one of us, remembering our names. "Just goes to show you, I don't know anything about it [his disease] either," said his doctor. "What I do know is that this man has the strongest heart of anyone I've ever seen."

But finally, the heart gave out. It happened two weeks after the All Star break. It was a Sunday morning, July 26. I was already at the park, in the training room, preparing to pitch.

Then Billy stopped by. "Cat," he said when we were alone, "I need to see you in my office for a minute." In his office Billy took a deep breath and started to talk. "I just got a call from one of your brothers," he said. "Your dad just passed away. I want you to go ahead and take a shower and go home. Stay as long as you want to."

Daddy had died. I left the clubhouse immediately and flew right home. All the funeral arrangements, the handling of the will, fell on my shoulders. I didn't mind; my brothers and sisters had all done their fair share while I was away.

So many feelings. So many different feelings. For a while I didn't care if I ever played ball again. It really didn't matter. And instead of crying in the house with family and friends, I found myself walking the fields, behind the old house, breaking down, crying on my own. I knew he was better off; the pain had passed. Some sons might have said, "Let him die to ease that pain." Not me. Daddy meant everything in the world to me, and pain or no pain, I had wanted him to live as long as he could.

I was back home in New Jersey on August 2 when Mr. Steinbrenner called.

"You hear about Thurman?" he asked.

"No."

"He's dead. He got killed in the worst way, crashed his plane and burned up."

Thurman dead? It couldn't be. Not now. Not right after Daddy and Clyde. Thurman? It was like George had said an oak tree standing tall in my front yard for the last thirty years had suddenly just fallen over. Oak trees don't just fall; Thurman Munson just doesn't die. Not now. Not this way.

Stunned, I walked across the street to tell Nettles the devastating news. Typically, he thought it was some kind of gag. "Right," said Graig. "What's the joke?"

"No joke," I said. "Thurman's dead."

Then the phone rang. Mr. Steinbrenner was on the line.

It was true. Practicing "touch and go" takeoffs and landings during an off-day that afternoon at Canton-Akron Airport, Thurman had lost control of his twin-engine Cessna Citation I—the damn thing never worked quite right to begin with—and crashed short of the runway. The plane immediately burst into flames, rolling until it struck a large tree stump. The *only* tree stump in the vicinity.

According to the coroner's report, Thurman was wearing a seat belt but not a shoulder harness at the time of the crash. As a result, he hit his head against something in the cockpit with such force that he was left paralyzed from the neck down; he was aware of the events unfolding around him but was utterly helpless, unable to move. Two of his passengers, a flight instructor and a friend, had tried unsuccessfully to get Thurman out. Both escaped with burns and minor injuries, from which they recovered.

Thurman was dead when the rescue workers found him. Cause of death: asphyxiation resulting from inhalation of superheated air and toxic substances. He was thirty-two years old.

Many of Thurman's teammates—Lou, Reggie, and myself in particular—had warned him about buying that $1.2 million Cessna. It was too much plane, we argued. It was an eight-seat passenger jet, and Thurm—who had been flying since '77—was familiar with Piper props. That Cessna was tricky, far more powerful, more sensitive than the Pipers Thurman was used to flyin'. But the number one thing in Thurman's life was his family, and as the Yankee tempers ran hotter and hotter, Thurman sought faster and faster ways to cool himself off—to get home to Diane, the kids, and solitude. "You get up there," he said one day, "and nobody asks you any questions." He was so proud of that plane, the "NY" logo on the side. He was always bugging Reggie, Nettles, Lou, anyone who would listen, to fly back with him to Canton. Every time he asked me, I told him no. "Ah, it's just as safe as anything else," he would say. "You might be safer, but I ain't goin'."

I can't remember just what words I used to tell Todd that Thurman was dead. I guess I just held him close and cried along with him. When he was done cryin', Todd picked up that catcher's glove Thurman had given him—the one he had played catch with time and time again—and put it on the top shelf of a closet. Never touched it again, either. Not once. I remember one day Paul found it and started fussin' with it. Todd roughed him up pretty bad. "Don't ever touch that glove!" he screamed.

Dealing with three deaths in a span of three months was beyond belief. You try not to let it affect you; you know you've got a job to do, a game to play, but Lord, it's a lot to ask of a man. Thank goodness for the guys out in the bull pen who helped me sort out my feelings. Who listened. Who made me think of my days at the Mayo Clinic and remember how bad I felt there until I looked around and saw I was the healthiest person in the place.

All I could think of now was that these deaths were some kind of message. An omen. Somebody was trying to tell me something. Telling me to straighten out my act; that maybe, just maybe, I was next. From that time on, I've gotten down on my knees every night and thanked God for my life; not for what I've accomplished or who I am. But simply for being alive, for making it through another day happy and healthy.

The happiest day of my final season came on a sunny Sunday in September when the Yankees—Mr. Steinbrenner, really—declared September 16, 1979, Catfish Hunter Day and went about retiring my number. Before the game, Reggie came up to me in the clubhouse with this big, beautiful gold trophy in his hands, a shiny replica of our World Series trophies, the one with all twenty-six team flags flapping in the breeze over a stadium. But this one was different—at least the inscription was. It said, "Jim 'Catfish' Hunter, September 16, 1979. From Reggie Jackson." But Mr. Steinbrenner wouldn't let Reggie present it to me on the field. "Now if that was from the whole club, I would do it," said George.

"What's the difference?" asked Reggie.

So Reg gave it to me in the clubhouse before we went on the field. It was a wonderful, warm-hearted gesture and one I'll never forget. Today that trophy has a proud and proper place right in my living room.

Looking back, September 16 reminds me of my "Day" in Hertford, the big brass bands, marching girls, pom-poms. And just as I did at the high school, I stepped to the microphone. Helen, Todd, and Kim were at my side. I thought about my proudest moments—winning twenty games or more for five straight seasons, my perfect game against Minnesota. The sellout crowd sat silent.

"There's three men shoulda been here today," I began. "One's my pa." The crowd burst into cheers. "One's the scout who signed me." Bigger cheers. "And the third one," I continued, pausing for a second, "is Thurman Munson." A wild, riotous ovation. They wouldn't stop. Fifty thousand people stood on their feet, stomping, whistlin'. Not so much for me—more for my father, for Clyde, and for Thurman. Cheering, I guess, for what friends mean in all our lives.

I'll never forget my last words as a Yankee.

"Thank you, God," I said, "for giving me strength and makin' me a ballplayer."

Then, on that sunny September day, with tears in my eyes and my family at my side, a thirty-three-year-old ballplayer stepped away from baseball and into the future. It was time, after fifteen years, to begin anew. Time, in the words of one popular rock group, to do "the walk of life."

15

BASIC TRAINING

"C'mon, hit it. Hit it. Ah, you missed the ball. Keep your head on it."

"But, Daddy."

"I don't care. You're missin' it. Swing the bat."

Paul Hunter, seven, scampers after a baseball that has rolled twenty feet away and tosses it back to his dad, who's flipping burgers on an outdoor grill.

"C'mon," says Jimmy Hunter, "let me see you swing the bat."

Paul Hunter assumes his lefthanded crouch, takes a tentative cut, and misses, head moving off the ball. "Hurry up, hurry up, chase it dowwwn," says his daddy. "Almost time to eat."

It's as clear as the crystal-clear blue sky above that class is now in session around the Hunter household. At various times, subjects range from the finer points of planting corn to hitting to the opposite field to keeping your elbows off the table. Because Todd will be leaving soon for Louisburg Junior College, near Raleigh (where he'll be playing third base), most of Hunter's days are spent educating Paul, a student of baseball, hunting, and fishing. Folks in Hertford can't help but compare the two: the freckled faced, husky little Hunter who proudly tells "Dad-dy" how today he killed a snake and a white raccoon with "my BB gun," and the local hero.

On this Saturday late in the summer, daughter Kim is off playing in a day-long softball tournament. Helen's there, too, yelling and cheering just like she did for Jimmy twenty-five years earlier. Jimmy is sitting in the living room telling a story when a knock is heard at the back door. It's a white-haired woman, in her sixties. "Is Catfish here?" she asks.

"That's me," says Jimmy.

"I got my daddy out in the car. He's eighty-one. Would you . . . ?"

"Be right there."

Outside, at the car, Catfish talks a little high school baseball, some farming. The conversation winds down.

"How about a baseball," says Hunter to the eighty-one-year-old man. *"Would you like that?"*

"That'd just be wonderful."

Hunter walks up toward the house only to be stopped when the man calls out his name. *"Yes, sir?"* says Jimmy. The man asks for a second ball, for his son.

"I'll see what I can find," says Jimmy.

Two minutes later he's back, two shiny new baseballs in hand. He autographs them both, waving as the car pulls away. *"Nice folks,"* says Hunter.

The family finally gets together for a quick dinner. Todd's racing to a date. Paul's bragging about the coon he shot. Kim's scolding Todd for leaving shampoo bottles in the shower. In short, your typical family meal. Soon after, the frequency with which a certain entree was once served in the Hunter household becomes the hot topic of conversation.

"Mom ever tell ya all we ever ate was hamburgers when we were first married?" asks Jimmy, clearly on the tease.

"What?" says Helen.

"Yeah, you know. Hamburgers. Hamburgers in the morning. Hamburgers for lunch. Hamburgers for dinner."

"Now, Jimmy, we did not . . ."

The kids, clearly loving this little debate, urge on their father.

"Sure did," says Hunter. *"Hamburgers and eggs for breakfast, hamburgers for lunch, meat loaf for dinner. Hamburger. Hamburger. Hamburger."*

"Did not."

"Did so."

"Well," says Helen, quite contrite. *"That's all we could afford back then. And besides, you like hamburger."*

That he does. He's also, in his retirement, taken a keen interest in gardening. He loves to slip behind the wheel of his red Ram pickup and give away some of the harvest. As he's doing right this minute, yelling for Charles, his prize bird dog, to git into the truck.

"Now, Jimmy, that's enough," says one neighbor as Hunter

pulls yet another cucumber the size of a small missile from a wicker basket. "Can't eat no mo' of these. You take 'em. Want some squash?"

"Well, just a couple . . ."

Next it's over to sister Elizabeth, same delivery, same response—"Jimmy, that's enough"—before Hunter heads out into the back roads of his farm, spitting Red Man into the styrofoam cup between his legs. Over the course of the next hour he points out bear tracks and a dozen deer, all the while keeping his eyes peeled for some young pups who had escaped their kennel earlier in the day.

"Fuzzbuster, is that you?" he drawls into his CB radio to brother Pete, in the process of growing a mustache. He goes on to tell you how brother Marvin is called Office One ("He works in an office all day"), brother Ray is Peanut ("He won a peanut trophy around here one year"); and brother Edward is Highway ("He used to work for the Highway Department"). And Hunter?

"This here's Silver Bullet," he calls into the CB. "Any sign of that dawg? No. Well, check the rivah. Mighta gone over there."

Sure enough, near the river, Hunter spots the escapee; in minutes, whipping around the dusty dirt roads of his farm, he collars the puppy. Just another day down on the farm.

I still get up with the sun to work my 600 acres of corn, soybeans, and peanuts. Farming, I guess, is a way of life, one you never quite get out of your system no matter how far prices fall. I know I coulda stayed in New York after I retired in 1979 and done some deals with all the promoters and businessmen making me promises. Heck, one corporation said I could live in one of them Park Avenue co-ops rent-free in exchange for publicity and acting as a company spokesman. "Where the kids gonna play?" I asked, knowing full well the answer was, "Nowhere, really." Central Park is nice to visit—the carousel's a classic—but as far as I know, you can't do much dove hunting without attracting a whole lot of unnecessary attention. No, North Carolina was home. I said I was gonna help Helen raise the family, and that's exactly what I was going to do.

Now farming, well, that's another matter. Daddy always told us boys, "Never farm. There's no money in it." I remember one year, sometime in the forties, Daddy told us after he settled with the owner of the land and paid all his bills, he made seventy-five cents for the whole year. And we'd tell ourselves, ah, Dad don't know that much about it. Well, when I retired, there was a little bit of money in farmin', but the last four, five years, for-get it. I shoulda listened to my dad. It's bad now and gettin' worse all the time. You don't know one year to the next sometimes whether you're gonna come out even, let alone make any money, what with interest payments eating up your cash flow, and prices dropping like a rock off some cliff. I mean, beans used to sell eight years ago for $9 to $12 a bushel. Now it's $4. Corn was $4 to $5; now it's $1.50. Up until this year, my brother Edward helped me, but he's got another job now, and I don't know if I can make it alone. Todd's a good worker; he'll do anything I tell him. But he's going off to junior college this year, and 600 acres is too much for any one man.

Ever farmed before? It's a lot like learning how to pitch or like raising kids. You need to know the fundamentals, have some basic training, before reaping any rewards. With farming, that means using a disk or tiller to flatten the land and spraying on different kinds of fertilizer before adding lime to neutralize the soil. (Soybeans got to have lime.) Planting begins about the end of March, first of April, so you can be ready to pick by the end of August, first of September at the latest. Corn goes first, then peanuts and beans. You have to be real careful with peanuts; if the ground's too cold, they'll rot. Paul Smith says my daddy was the best when it came to judging exactly the right time to plant peanuts. Be off a day or two, and it can cost you everything.

"Mr. Hunter," Paul would ask, "what do you think?"

"Well, Paul," my daddy would answer, "what do *you* think?" Paul said he wasn't quite sure.

"Well, if I was you, I'd go ahead and put them in."

"Thanks, Mr. Hunter. That's all I needed to hear."

Now, by the time the peanuts are in, the corn's coming up and you have to start cultivating it, keeping the grass and weeds down. When that's done, you check the beans for weeds. Then you spray the peanuts for these little green grasshoppers, called thrips, and the soybeans for the worms that like to snack on the pods. Sometimes you have to dig drains for your irrigation ditches because if the water stands, it will scorch the crops— burn right through the roots. And spraying? Ha, if you don't calibrate the flow just right, you can kill a whole crop. Farming also means watching the weather channels at night—and usually they're wrong—because if you spray and it rains right behind you, you've just wasted time and money.

June and July are my busiest months. I work the fields from sunrise until about four. Then I hustle inside, take a shower, and drive thirteen miles to Edenton. From there, a bus takes the American Legion team—I've coached first base the last three years—to our games. We usually travel about two hours to places like Snow Hill, Greenville, Rocky Mountain, and Goldsborough. We play twenty-five games a month, so most of the time I'm getting home at two or three, four in the morning, grabbing a couple of hours of sleep and then heading back out into the fields.

August is vacation month for most farmers. It is a breeze, really—a little sprayin' here and there, watching your peanuts, keeping an eye out for worms, baiting a hook for perch or catfish.

Right now I'm watching prices. Unless they go up—which they seem to be doing a bit—there's no way any individual farmer can survive. Heck, a new John Deere 4630 tractor will run ya almost $50,000, and that's naked. A decent accessory, like a cultivator, for instance, can add another $3000 to $4000. It seems the only way to make money these days is *not* to plant. Last year I didn't plant seventy-five acres, and the government paid me $324 an acre—a helluva lot better than losing money on the crop. Another year the government took 100 percent of my 200 acres of corn and paid about $200 an acre not to grow it. In the end I got the biggest check I ever got for farmin'—and I didn't have to drop a seed. It seems crazy, but as long as the government would rather store corn than give it to some hungry people in the states, or the world, for that matter, farmers are going to continue to limit crops. What else can we do?

So why do I keep doing it? With my deferred money and pension, I've got more than enough money to live on. Helen keeps askin' me, "If you're not makin' any money, why do you keep doin' it?" I guess, bottom line, it's because my daddy did it. And because I like seeing things grow, being outside workin' in wide-open spaces. I keep tellin' Helen I'm gonna retire at forty-five when I start drawing my baseball pension. She just laughs. "At this rate," she says, "you might have to retire at forty-five from farmin'."

OTHER VOICES—DAVE DUNCAN

"You know what's funny about Cat? I don't have any real strong memories of him. It wasn't like he was doing anything fantastic all the time. I handled him like I handled all the pitchers—had him learn to use his kinds of pitches and then anticipate what he wanted to use. It wasn't like I was directing him; it was more like I was trying to think along with him.

"With Cat, his out pitch varied from hitter to hitter, depending on the situation. He had excellent control of his slider and could take and run his fastball up on somebody with a little more velocity than he'd shown maybe a pitch or two before. Not an overpowering pitch—but just enough to get by the hitter. The hitter doesn't even realize the pitcher has just made a great pitch on him. And Cat could actually move the ball inch by inch. Control was his greatest asset. You'd see a guy swing at a ball one inch out of the strike zone. The next ball was two inches out. Then three. Boom. Boom. Boom. He had outstanding control all over the strike zone. See, most pitchers have a strong side of the plate where they have real good control. Very few people have excellent control all over the strike zone—in, out, up, down. Cat did.

"You know another thing about him? He never wanted to come out of a game. My conversations with him were never lectures, they were about what he wanted to do with the next hitter—to slow him down, to let him catch his breath. That's because he had great, great instincts. He was always mentally into the game. Very few times was he flat mentally. He was like a machine. A machine. He had what you look for in every pitcher—and that's instincts. And today you don't find it in too many. But they're in all the good ones. Some guys never develop those instincts, and believe me, they're impossible to teach. You can work and work and work and work. You can talk. You can educate. And you think you're making great strides. But until that guy walks across those white lines and has the presence of mind to use all the things you've taught him, you really haven't accomplished anything. Cat had that presence."

The day breaks dull and drizzly, and the fans are pressing tight against the backstop in Fort Lauderdale's Lockhart Stadium. The sun's not out, but Whitey Ford, Lou Piniella, Ron Guidry, and

Rick Rhoden are, so the only moans and groans are those coming from the pitchers and catchers out in right field. Hopalong Cassady, ex-Heisman Trophy winning running back at Ohio State and longtime Yankee spring training conditioning coach, is slowly stretching and twisting bodies into pretzels. Along the first base dugout, cameras in hand, Yankee caps perched on their heads, fans gather and scream like first-graders. "Whitey, Whitey!" "A picture here. Pleeaaease!" "Lou! Lou! Lou!" "One for old times' sake."

Old times' sake. Ain't that the truth. I felt the same way back in spring training in 1980, right after I had retired and was working with the Yankees' young pitchers, Double A and Triple A guys on their way up. So the full impact of my decision never really hit me until camp broke. Sure I was a coach, but how natural it all felt dressing every day, working out, sitting in front of my cubicle in the clubhouse. Then, suddenly, reality hit. Spring training had ended. I didn't want to leave; I musta said goodbye to everyone five times that last day. Finally, Pete Sheehy spoke up. "You gonna stay here the rest of your life?" he asked, smiling. Pete knew. He'd been part of the same scene for more than fifty years, and he never left it, dying in 1985.

Pete and I got real close back then. In '80 and '81 I actually lived in the clubhouse for two weeks until Helen arrived. Nobody really knew it but Pete and me, but after the players left I handled half the clubhouse chores, picking up the dirty clothes, wet towels, and hanging fresh uniforms back up in the lockers. Pete was slowing down a bit and I hated sitting around the hotel, so I stayed every night. I'd run over to the press trailer to get Pete his favorite liverwurst sandwich and we'd work until 7 p.m., cleaning, washing, polishing shoes for the next day. Then I'd take him out to dinner, a different place every night.

"Pete," I asked, "what do you want to eat tonight?"

And from somewhere in the locker room a gruff voice would call out, "Fish."

I loved Pete, who'd been a part of the Yankee tradition since the days of Babe Ruth. Most nights he'd call me over and tell me stories. Old guys, young guys. The greats, the not-so-greats. He loved ex-Yank Tommy Burns, who came from North Carolina. He loved ex-Yank Dan Pasqua, called him "my boy" because Danny had played for years in Pete's backyard in Jersey.

"Pete," I said, one time, "why don't you write a book?"

He just shook his head. "It'll stay right here," he said, pointing to his head. "It was said in the clubhouse, it's gonna stay in the clubhouse. I got it all right up here."

One of Pete's happiest days was when we gave him a World Series ring. At first he didn't want to take it. "You guys won that ring," he said, "I didn't do anything."

"Pete," I said, "you never got a ring before."

"I know," he answered, "I didn't want one."

So we *gave* it to him and tears came to his eyes. "You guys are something else," he said. I always say the same about Michael J. "Pete" Sheehy.

So every year now I drive back, pulled by the pace, the opportunity to teach and forget farming and fertilizer for six weeks. Whitey and I work at one of the back diamonds behind the left-field fence, drilling fundamentals into these kids' heads. Sometimes, I have to admit, it takes a mighty big drill. You see, a lot of young guys today just don't want to put the necessary work into playing the game. I see it at every level from high school on up. First thing I look at is the car. If the kid's driving a shiny new car, chances are he's not gonna work as much as it takes to be a real winner.

And pitching? Well, there's a big difference between throwing and pitching. There's a mess of throwers in the major leagues today. Guys like Calvin Schiraldi in Chicago, Bobby Witt in Texas, and yes, even Nolan Ryan in Houston. Back when I was pitching with the Yankees, Ken Clay was the worst offender. I often told him if I had your arm and my head on the shoulder of that arm, I'd win twenty games every year.

"Why?" said Clay.

"Because you don't know how to use it."

Clay was so clueless he'd get out in the outfield before a game and throw long distance for an hour. Naturally, that day he'd get called upon to pitch and wouldn't be able to get an usher out. Great arm, great slider, bad brains. He wouldn't listen to anybody.

Ryan is not so easily explained. Certainly he has a Hall of Fame fastball and as good a curve, and he is as good a thrower as there ever was in the game. But why does Nolan have a little more than a .500 record in his career? Walks (almost five per game) is one reason. But so are his strikeouts—almost 9.5 men per game. I think Nolan has always been more interested in striking you out than in getting you out. Watch and see sometime. How many 2–2 or 3–2 counts does he have during a game?

Know what happens? Infielders roll on their heels instead of up on their toes. Outfielders lose concentration. An entire defense starts to spectate like fans in the stands. Hitting is affected, too; players spend so much time standing around, waiting for someone to *finally* hit a ball, the whole rhythm of the game is disrupted. As hitters they become anxious at the plate.

Whitey Ford, on the other hand, was a pitcher, one of the best I've ever seen. Don Sutton is a pitcher. Fernando Valenzuela is a pitcher. Doyle Alexander, Frank Tanana, and Jack Morris of the Tigers are pitchers. They move the ball up and down. In and out. They mix it up. Unlike a thrower, who may breeze through the order the first time but get knocked out in a hurry when his fastball no longer finds the corners (he doesn't have the ability to move it around), a pitcher counterpunches. He takes a hit or two, then adjusts, changes speeds, moves away from trouble, recovers. It might be an inning or two before a true pitcher runs out of gas and gets knocked out.

So you want to become a pitcher? Or have one at home who dreams of making the big leagues? Read on. If not, well, you might want to skip the rest of this chapter. Of course, some fans might find it food for thought while watching the next NBC Game of the Week.

I know what you're thinking. Cat's gonna give us that standard list of what-to-dos. Read these books. Watch those videos. Not me. You want tips like those, go talk to Tommy John or Tom Seaver. I swear John can talk one hitter for an hour. It's the same way with scouting reports in the big leagues today. We'd get briefed before every series on the likes and dislikes of each hitter. "You can pitch so-and-so low and away," the scouts would say. Or, "So-and-so doesn't like the ball up and in." After a while, the scouting reports all started to sound alike: "Pitch 'em up and in, then low and away." It got so ridiculous I stopped listening.

My only question was this: "Where does he like it?"

The answer came. Fastballs away. Or curveballs in. "Well then," I'd say, "that's where he ain't gonna get it."

Simple as that. I worked quickly, pitching everywhere but near a particular hitter's power. And once I found a soft spot, a hole, bam, I pounded away until the batter adjusted. And believe me, not many did.

The best way to find that hole? Well, I've never before admitted this publicly, but my secret was something called the X pattern. Nothing space age about it. You just move the ball around the strike zone using the letter "X" as your guide. Sometimes I'd start up and in, at the top right of the letter "X." Then I'd dip low and away, to the lower left corner of the X. Other times I'd begin up and away, come back with down and in, back up and in, then low and away. I used the X my entire career, and nobody ever figured out I was pitching in a pattern. One time, Fosse, when he was catching for Cleveland, thought he was on to something.

"I didn't know you pitched that way," he said one day.

"What way?"

"You pitch in an X pattern. We've been watching you the last three or four games, and that's how you pitch."

"Is that right," I said, dummying up. No way I was giving away *that* secret. "Really? You're kidding? I never knew that. I don't think so."

I know. I know. I forgot one thing. *But Catfish, what about all those home runs you gave up?* True, true, true. I gave up tons of home runs. But did you know those 374 dingers came in 3449 innings of work—or one every 9.4752 innings pitched. That's less than one per game. And with a lifetime ERA under 3.30, I couldn't have given up all *that* many with men on base.

My strategy? With nobody on, throw strikes. Get ahead of the hitter. Make him hit your pitch; that's why you've got seven guys with gloves behind you. With one on, depending on the score, the inning, you adjust. You play a little more cat and mouse, chipping away at the black.

This attitude stems from two factors—Control and Confidence. Capital "C" on both. Because from Control comes Confidence. The easiest way to gain Control? One pitch at a time. Learn the fundamentals of the fastball first. Throw it and throw it and throw it until you can dot the "i" in strike at sixty feet six inches. Then go on to the slider or curve.

Of course, it's not all fundamentals. Arm speed, elbow up, wrist down, that sort of thing. No, to be a winner in baseball, you've got to use your head and legs as much as your arm. That means *really* running between starts; none of that stationary bike riding I see so many pitchers do today. You don't have to win any Olympic marathon medals, but get your laps in.

Another forgotten or ignored aspect of pitching is pregame preparation. In fifteen years I never varied my pregame ritual. I never went to bed early the night before I pitched, figuring, I guess, that I'd toss and turn all night and eventually end up with the same amount of sleep even if I'd hit the sack at 10 p.m. So I went to bed early *two* days before I was scheduled to throw. That way I always felt rested.

Did diet make a difference? I don't know, but I always ate fish, preferably flounder, if I could get it, before every start. A potato, green vegetables, brain food I guess you'd call it. Then I went to the park early, got my rubdown, played some cards and thought about my job. That's when I wanted to talk baseball. During those two to three hours on the mound every four days, my teammates depended on me.

And once I set foot on that mound, I didn't care if I was up ten runs or down ten runs—I wanted to pitch. To close it out. Sure it hurt to pitch sometimes, a lot of times, but as my daddy said, "You don't get anything by doing nothing." So I pitched. And the bigger the game, the better I liked it. Not that I was about to let anybody know I was excited. I approached every game the same way. One pitch, one hitter at a time. The rest was window dressing. Let others go on whoopin' and hollerin'. I thought about hitting the glove, throwing strikes, staying in control.

Speaking of which, what follows is some more basic training, a working man's guide to becoming a consistent pitcher:

The Setup. Your feet should be on the outer edge of the rubber, your shoulders straight and pointing toward first and third. This shortens the distance to home plate, keeping the "fast" on your fastball. As you wind up, raise both arms over the head and turn your back foot slightly into the push-off position. Be sure your foot stays in contact with the rubber for proper leg drive. Now lift your front leg, balancing your weight on your rear leg—making sure the back leg is flexed and up against the rubber to ensure proper drive to home plate. The ball should be hidden in the glove. Your front foot should land with the knee bent facing directly toward home plate. This brings your hips open, ensuring proper control of your body and thus your pitch. Your front foot—and this is critical to control—

should land in the same spot *every* time you pitch. Same spot. Every pitch.

Arm Action. Your pitching arm should be parallel to your shoulder on *every* pitch. Dropping down invites inconsistency. Fastballs are thrown best across the seams (for better control) with your wrist locked back until your arm reaches the release point. At release, snap your wrist down for extra speed and to put spin on the ball. Learn to control your fastball before using any other pitch.

The slider is another story. I learned to throw mine while pitching batting practice for Oakland in 1968. Somebody—the name escapes me now—yelled "throw it like you're throwing a football." I did and the ball "slid" a little bit. "That's a slider," somebody yelled. Sure was. I kept throwing it until it became my strikeout pitch to right-handed hitters.

It's actually an easy pitch to pick up. Throw it across the seams, slightly off-center. Make sure the wrist is "on top." Think fastball until your release point, and then tuck the wrist inward and make like Dan Marino, letting the ball slide out of your hand.

The curveball can be thrown with two distinct breaks— straight down or a sweeping movement—depending on where you place your arm. Again, to make the pitch, hold the ball across the seams and turn the hand in, toward the body. Make sure the wrist is tucked in and you pull down on the seams at the release point. If you're throwing the curve right, your pitching hand should end up hitting your opposite knee after releasing the ball.

You'd know all this if you happened to pick up the pitching pamphlet I co-wrote back in 1978. "Pitch like a Pro," was put together by former Yankee pitching coach Sammy Ellis, his then agent Dick Grimes, and me. It never sold a hoot, but still it contains valuable tips for pitchers—young and old. At the risk of putting anyone to sleep, here are ten helpful hints, courtesy of a quick trip back to "Catfish's corner":

1. Control—Control—Control—Control. The surefire way to become a winning pitcher.

2. Concentrate on pitching the ball through the catcher's mitt, not just to it.

3. Maintain eye contact with the target at all times.

4. Develop one pitch at a time (starting with the fastball). When you've mastered control of one, move on to another.

5. Pitching begins with the lower body. Proper leg drive comes from the back and legs, so get your body in shape before throwing hard.

6. Don't try to strike out hitters. Throw the ball to a spot and make them hit your pitch.

7. Learn to grip the ball properly without looking at it. Keep it down and develop the proper follow-through.

8. Learn to field your position, to cover first, and back up bases.

9. Keep the ball down.

10. Don't get discouraged. Play under competitive conditions whenever possible and never get too high or low mentally before or after a game. Pitch every game as if it's your last. You never know—it could be.

16

PRESENT AND PAST . . .
TOGETHER AT LAST

Diane Munson is a pretty woman with a perky personality. Eight years after the death of her husband she spends her days car pooling and supporting her children—Tracy, seventeen, Kelly, fifteen, and Michael, twelve—at high school and Little League games.

It's the night before Diane and her family will pack to fly to New York for Old-Timers Day, and apprehension is apparent in her voice.

"I remember when the Yankees had a chance to get Catfish," says Diane. "Thurman was really pushing. I remember he called information—and I'm not trying to make fun of the size of the town or anything because I'm really not sure what it is—but I know when he called and said I'm looking for a Jim Hunter, the operator said, 'Oh, yeah, Catfish,' and gave him the number immediately. They didn't even have an unlisted number. That's what down-to-earth people they are. Thurman got a real kick out of that.

"The three of them—Thurman, Catfish, and Lou Piniella—used to like to crack on each other constantly. Anything they could say they would. It seemed like they could get away with it because of the friendship they had. It almost seemed like if Thurman didn't like you, he wouldn't bother cracking on you. So although some people might see that as sarcasm, or maybe even hurtful, none of these guys did. They understood his makeup. How he hid a lot behind that.

"When Jim was first acquired, lots of people were naturally wondering what he was like. We had a nice clubhouse in our apartment complex and threw a big party, one that was—how do

I say this nicely?—progressing, and people were feeling very, very good. Anyhow, they got one of the young pitchers—I think Sparky had a lot to do with it—they got him totally loaded. He ended up getting sick in the clubhouse. Now keep in mind that this is a rented clubhouse, really nice. I was real upset because I was pregnant at the time and there was no chance that I'd be able to clean it up. Catfish and Helen are the ones who ended up cleaning it. You know, I'm still to this day amazed by that. He acted like it was no big deal. It just shows what kind of people they are.

"They're number one in my book because of the kind of classy people they are . . . a lot of people, since Thurman's accident, and, really, it's painful, but a lot of people have forgotten about me. Life goes on, and I understand that. But Jim and Helen have never forgotten me or the children.

"Thurman basically was an insecure person. It stems from his childhood. He had a tough one. His dad was a truck driver, and he was a real tough cookie. He was real hard. So Thurman had some real problems growing up, and I think he kept a lot of his insecurities inside. He had the kind of personality that he never wanted to talk about them, never wanted to show the hurt. He developed an exterior that was gruff, or whatever people wanted to call it.

"People whom he cared about saw an entirely different side of Thurman. He was the most two-sided personality I've ever known. He was the finest father I've ever seen. He spent time with the children before it became fashionable. He wanted to have a close-knit family, that was his number one priority, because he didn't have a good family life."

Diane Munson explains that this will be only her second trip to New York since her husband's death in 1979 and how daughter Kelly is anguishing over whether to attend a state softball tournament or fly to New York and experience firsthand Yankee fans' reaction to the mention of her father's name. "I didn't want to force her to go to Yankee Stadium," Diane says. "That's not right. I wanted her to make her own choice. I said, 'We're invited to Yankee Stadium. I'm sure there'll be a lot of friends he played with, plus I'm sure they'll mention your father. You decide what you want to do, and I'll understand your decision and I'll support you.' She just drove herself crazy for four, five days deciding what to do. Finally, she made the choice that she wanted to go to New York. Her reasoning was that she didn't have that many memories of her dad, and this was a time she thought she could hear some. I said, 'You know, Kelly, we're isolated from the Stadium, where they show little tapes. People get to see his persona, and they get to be a part of it every day at Yankee Stadium. But we don't. And we're there so seldom that when we are there, and they put those tapes on, and the fans still go wild—God, I'm getting choked up—it's still so amazing for all of us.' I think the kids should be a part of that. I think they should know what he meant to people. What he still means to people. In New York, they loved him. I want the kids to be able to feel some of that. And I don't want to make him a monument, but I want them to share in his legacy."

I definitely had what you'd call one of those checkered All Star careers. In six appearances (I was selected two other times but failed to pitch) I set All Star records for most games lost (two) and, surprise, surprise, most total home runs allowed (four). In 12⅔ innings my ERA was a trashy 6.39. Not exactly the Cat's meow.

Not that I didn't enjoy myself. Take my first experience—puhlleeze. It was back in '66, and Krausse, who also made the team, and I drove from K.C. to St. Louis. One problem. The game was scheduled two days before payday, and, at the time, Lew and I didn't have two nickels to rub together.

"Cat," said Krausse on the way over, "you think the league is going to pay for our hotel?"

"Hope so."

Well, we didn't hear anything, so the first day it was fast-food city. Once we got to the hotel we started ordering room service. We figured if worse came to worse, the hotel could always bill us in Kansas City. "Let's have room service instead," we said. On it went, the plates piling up, until, that is, word got out that the league was picking up hotel bills and giving us each $150 in expense money. Our hearts started pumpin' again.

We got the checks right after the game—a game I saw no action. On the way home we saw this real nice restaurant, a fancy place. "Think they'll cash this check?" asked Lew. "Hope so," I said. They did, and believe me, the food never tasted so good.

The next year I pitched my semifamous five innings before

Perez put me out to pasture. My disappointment continued in 1970 and 1973. In '70 I lasted one-third of an inning, giving up three runs on three hits. Three years later I started the game, only to have Billy Williams break my right thumb after I foolishly tried to barehand a hot shot back up through the box. I threw six innings in three more outings from 1974 to 1976, getting my hat handed to me every time out.

I recite this little bit of history so you'll know things haven't changed all that much since I retired and took up pitching in Old-Timers and All Star games. Still checkered. Except now I'm taking it on the chin from local high school varsity, and guys like Roy McMillan.

The high school reference dates back to May '87 and Hertford's annual grudge match between our 1964 State Championship team and the local Perquiman's High School varsity. We've been playing this game for about seven years now, but this year was special. Not only did the game represent the so-called closing ceremonies of Catfish Hunter Day, but Todd, a senior, was out at short and my brother Pete was coaching in the Perquiman's dugout. Even Paul got into the act, throwing out the ceremonial first pitch, a strike that smacked into the center of Francis's glove. A real family affair. I half expected to see Helen calling balls and strikes.

Fact is, it's a big game in these parts, and more than 2000 people were there to see it. A town, by the way, that from the looks of things that night has a whole lot less hick in it than most folks think. Sure, your fair share of good ol' boys—the weathered faces, huntin' caps, and coveralls—were on hand. But right next to them were young girls in designer jeans, the surf set on skateboards, and high school athletes in varsity jackets.

Freddie and Francis were there, too. So were Billy Nixon and Riley Williams. Hershberger even suited up—as our designated ringer. Bobby Carter was back on the bench, scratching out a lineup and figuring out ways to steal some runs. We'd need all we could get. The Perquiman's Pirates, true to form, were leading their league, primed for the playoffs. By game time, a standing-room-only crowd packed the stands, although I can't honestly say whether or not half of them weren't hoping to win that Remington shotgun they raffled off in the fourth inning.

In retrospect, I can't say we brought back any great memories of '64. Freddie Combs ripped the second pitch just foul—a true highlight—and then went down on strikes. Francis Combs followed suit. That brought me to the plate. I'd been taking semi-secret batting practice for days, the last time the night before with brother Edward, when I pumped about twenty balls out of the park. But that was practice. This was business. I swung and hit the first pitch hard—a little on the hands—to the curly-haired kid at short. He did his daddy a favor by throwing the ball up the line, but Alex Cox, the Perquiman's first baseman, made a fine swipe tag to retire the side.

Now it was my turn to pitch. I fanned the first batter—a message of sorts—then coaxed the next hitter to ground weakly to second. Trouble was, Riley's throw was wide, putting one on with one out. Now, the number three hitter stepped in. Looked familiar. Same kid I've seen so much around the dinner table the last seventeen years. I fired the first pitch right up under his chin. Might as well let him know it's serious. I wasted a changeup high on the next pitch before just missing with a fastball outside. Three and oh. Todd took his chances and swung on the next pitch, hitting a hard grounder to Freddie at short. Freddie made a nice play, but came up low on the throw for an error.

That was the beginning of the end. A handle shot to right, a coupla more fly-ball doubles that would have been caught back in '64. At the end of two innings we were down 6–0. It ended 7–2, and it wasn't pretty. I went hitless. At least Freddie homered.

So, with that humbling experience fresh in my mind, I headed out to play in three very special events and serve as an honorary captain at the 1987 All Star Game in Oakland.

The first event, the Old-Timers Baseball Classic in Washington, D.C., was just that: Classic. After one inning, the American League trailed 9–0. I started the second inning in place of Jim Perry and promptly threw two pitches for two outs. Next up was Roy McMillan, former Milwaukee shortstop now in his sixties. I figured what the hell, throw the ball down the middle of the plate. What can he do? I'll tell you what he did. He hit the ball over the fence in left for a home run. Orlando Cepeda was next. Another fastball down the chute. Another home run. Cepeda I could live with. But McMillan? Granted, Roy is recognized as one of the best defensive shortstops in

history, but a home run to a guy who hit .243 lifetime? Who had
sixty-four home runs in more than 6700 at bats, less than one
per 100 times to the plate? Granted, the fence was only 245 feet
away, but there's a matter of principle here. And pride. (Oh,
well. Nobody can ever accuse me of not being an equal
opportunity pitcher. I serve up gopher balls to young and old
alike.)

Thankfully, I got a measure of revenge my first time up in the
bottom of the second, ripping a single to left to load the bases.
When ex-Tiger Dick McAuliffe followed with a grand slam, we
trailed 11–4. My next time up (same inning; we were starting to
hit now) the score was 11–9, and Johnny Podres had replaced
Jim Bunning. I fouled off the first pitch and then bombed the
next one high over the center-field fence, 400 feet from home
plate, tying the score. "We know the ball is live now," quipped
Boog Powell. We eventually won a wild one 25–11.

But Old-Timers Games in Washington are one thing. Reun-
ions with ex-teammates in New York and Oakland are quite
another, as I would discover one memorable weekend in July.

One big team
Present and past
Together at last . . .

*By 10:15 a.m. the locker room buzzes baseball. Interview here.
A story there. The smell of cigar smoke and Father Time mixing
in a frat party atmosphere. On this sun-drenched Saturday in
New York, the Yankees of the '60s will face the Bombers of the
'70s as The Equitable Old-Timers Series, a twenty-six-game
traveling tribute to some of baseball's best, makes its only stop in
the Bronx.*

*In one corner of the Yankee locker room, Ron (Gator)
Guidry's locker has been usurped by Sparky Lyle, who's shaking
off the dull throb in his temple—a souvenir of an evening with his
buddy Dick Tidrow the night before. An enterprising radio
reporter presses a mike toward Lyle and politely asks how it felt
to win the Cy Young Award.*

*"Shit," says Sparky, "I got the phone call, figured it was
another near-miss. You know, tough shitsky. Oh, sorry about
that. Ha, ha, ha.*

"But then they told me I'd won the Cy Young, and I swear I jumped straight up to the ceiling, I felt so good about it."

"What year was that again, Spark?"

"Seventy-five, seventy-four . . . seventy-three. Shit, who can remember after last night." It was '77. Nobody bothers to bring it up.

Across the room Dave Anderson, the New York Times' esteemed columnist, has caught himself a Catfish; Hunter's left cheek is stuffed with chew. Between answers a stream of tobacco juice flows into a paper cup. The room revolves around this Pulitzer Prize-winning writer and a future Hall of Famer; nearby Paul Blair and Mickey Rivers are talking center field; Bucky Dent, Ron Blomberg, Dick Tidrow, and Elliott Maddox share memories from the 1970s; Bobby Murcer, Fritz Peterson, and Bobby Richardson dress in the same order they always have. In a back corner William Joseph Skowron pulls number fourteen over his back.

"Hey, that's Lou's [Piniella's] number," somebody says.

"That's right," says Moose, "but I wore it before he did."

Not ten feet away is former Yankee right-hander Mike Torrez, best remembered for his seventeen regular-season wins and two complete-game World Series victories against the Dodgers in '77 and, of course, his home run pitch to Dent while pitching for Boston in '78. Trouble is Torrez has forgotten; not the wins or the homer (never the homer). His shoes. In front of his cubicle he searches vainly through a gym bag. "Fuck, I knew I had them in here," he mutters to himself. Then loud and slow: "Son . . . of a . . . bitch." Hunter walks by.

"Give ya shoes away, too?" he chuckles, leaving Torrez to his troubles.

"Shit!"

The room stops, if only for a second, when the Clipper comes in, the silver hair set off by the blue sport jacket, white shirt, red tie, and grey slacks. Joe DiMaggio walks without pause into the Coaches Room, an off-limits enclave at the back of the locker room. Billy Martin joins him a few moments later, sipping a beer.

By now Hunter has a circle of reporters around him, firing questions about the Hall of Fame, baseball, beanballs. "It's parta the game," he says of a recent rash of knockdown pitches.

"But they shouldn't be throwin' at the head. In the American League, see, you can't go after the pitcher because of the DH. I think if you throw from the shoulder down, it's okay. But not at the heaaad."

And of his induction into the Hall of Fame this month?

"I still can't believe it. As a kid, I always dreamed of being in the big leagues. But being in the Hall of Fame, you never dream about that. You just figure, I guess, that the guys in the Hall are so much better. It's almost like they were looking down watching me and saying, 'Kid, it's going to take a long time before you can join us.'"

And just what emblem will appear on his plaque? The A's or the Yankees? *"I decided not to put an emblem on it,"* he says, in such a way that lets you know he's spent a long time thinking about it. *"I asked if I could get one of those hats you could spin around. You know, one emblem in front, one in back."* He laughs, and the reporters, taking notes, laugh with him.

In ten minutes the room empties onto the field, where a brand-new Yankee video, *"One Big Team"* plays on the giant screen in left center. Produced by Major League Baseball Productions, it proves to be a stirring montage of the men who made the pinstripes famous. Its main theme, repeated over and over again, goes like this: *One Big Team/Present and Past/ Together at Last.*

Mel Allen has the crowd in the palm of his hand as he moves to a microphone set up behind home plate. *"Welcome to the forty-first annual Old-Timers Day,"* he booms. *"We have a new format this year. One that will match the stars of the '60s against the stars of the '70s. The likes of Mickey and Whitey against the likes of Bucky Dent and Jim Hunter."*

After appropriate player introductions, Allen's voice veers to somber as the organist plays *"Auld Lang Syne."* Allen asks for a moment of silence for *"members of the Yankee family we have lost."* Surprisingly, there's no mention of the most tragic loss of all—at least in the eyes of the fans gathered today. It comes a few moments later, as, frame by frame, a tribute to Thurman Munson unfolds across the huge video screen in center field. Number fifteen slapping a base hit to right. Number fifteen smashing into a catcher at home plate. Number fifteen absorbing a blow himself and then rising, fist in the air, signaling that, yes, he'd held onto the ball.

Another picture on the screen. That of Diane Munson and her children in a private box behind home plate. The ovation builds and builds like a wave, stronger, washing over them. You can't help but wonder how Kelly Munson feels right now. Hearing the ovation. Feeling the love. How proud she must be. You know she has made the right decision.

Allen again. Final introductions. "Now I'd like to introduce the latest Yankee to make the Hall of Fame. No one ever doubted that he would make it. We're happy to have him here today. Let's have a real Yankee Stadium welcome for that gentleman farmer"—the ovation erupts, in one solid voice—"from North Carolina. Hall of Famer"—the sound has doubled, picked up steam, fifteen full seconds, from the heart—"Jim 'Catfish' Hunter."

I loved being back in the Yankee locker room. Pulling on number twenty-nine. Slapping backs. Spitting chew. Hangin' out. Shooting the bull with Whitey, Nick, the clubhouse guy, the writers. Seeing Sparky, Tidrow, Jim Spencer again. It's funny, the first question at these All Star Games, at least among the players, is never "How you doin'?" No, it's "Still got the same wife?"

One of the funniest parts of the day was seeing George strutting around wearing his hat with the words "Top Gun" in front. God, he loves that hat. Makes him feel like a fighter pilot, a macho man, dominant, the baddest dude around.

You think I was going to let Mr. Steinbrenner get away with that?

"What's that shit?" I asked, pointing.

Steinbrenner looked surprised. "What shit?" he asked.

I pointed to his head.

"Oh, Top Gun. I love it. That's me. That's who I am."

"You're no Top Gun," I teased. "You pay salaries, that's it."

"Yeah," said George, clearly swallowing the bait. "Well, they're damn big salaries. It's *my* club."

"It's not your club," I argued. "I can say whatever I want. I don't play for you anymore."

George didn't like that idea. "But I'm still payin' you," he argued.

"Yeah, I know," I said, smiling. "But you can't do anything about that."

George just laughed. He knew I was kidding. And you know what? He actually looked pretty good in that hat.

I'm introduced to the capacity crowd just after Lou, right before Billy and Whitey. Standing there, I look up into the stands as Mel Allen starts talking about Thurman while clips of his career appear on the center-field screen. I about cried when I looked up and spotted Diane in a classy black dress standing in a private box behind home plate. I don't know how she and the kids could stand it, seeing Thurman up there on the screen.

Only two men remain in the dugout now. The tension builds. Slowly, Number seven steps out onto the field, gingerly jogging across the grass before breaking into a slow trot. Mickey Mantle runs a step or two and then stops and walks slowly to the first base line. The noise builds, 50,000 strong; people can't stop cheering. There's no mention of Mickey's recent hospitalization, the heart scare a couple of months back. No need to; everybody knows. Prayers have been said. The roar continues, fading into the wind, and then starts up again. Louder. It's as if the fans are saying hello and goodbye to their hero all at the same time.

One Yankee to go. It's quieter than a Sunday church service as Allen says, "This man has just been voted the greatest living ballplayer." The words "Joe DiMaggio" get lost in the air. The Clipper jogs easily onto the field, waving proudly. I don't know Joe nearly as well as when he coached the A's, but it's common knowledge he's pretty sensitive about his place among Yankee greats. One time a few years back, he *wasn't* the last man introduced and he left early and boycotted the Yankee Old-Timers games for a couple of years. Whitey and Mickey just chuckled. "What the hell difference does it make, first or last?" asked Mick. "The people know who we are." To me, *that's* the essence of both men. What makes them special. Never, not once, have they put themselves above any player. You wore a Yankee uniform, you were a Yankee. Simple as that.

I got the starting nod for the '70s club. Bobby Richardson took an easy strike on the first pitch and then skied a lazy fly to left. Next up was Norm Siebern. Norm was nicknamed Smiley by his teammates when he broke in with the Yankees in 1956 because he laughed about as often as prisoners break out of Alcatraz. He fouled a couple off.

"Keep swinging, Norm," said Mel Allen over the P.A. "Catfish is always around the plate."

I threw the next pitch into the wheelhouse of this forty-four-year-old former first baseman/outfielder. The result is a drive deep into the gap in right center where fleet-footed Elliott Maddox gets on his horse to haul it in. Bobby Murcer walks to the plate. I knew Bobby would be by far the toughest out in the lineup. In batting practice he peppered the right-field porch like it was 1971 (.331 batting average) and 1972 (thirty-three home runs) all over again.

What the hell, I figured, he's forty-one, I'm forty-one, let's get that ball on up there. So I reared back and let one go. I'd say eighty-four to eighty-five on the radar gun, on the black, inside corner. Strike one. The crowd, hearing Jeff Torborg's glove pop, lets out this big "Aahhh!" Murcer got the message, wiggling his bat, smiling away. I come right back with another fastball, taking a few miles off, and Bobby rips it to right for a single.

Now it's time for Moose Skowron to bat. He was nicknamed after Mussolini by his grandfather, but anyway you slice it, Moose is a moose. The four-time All Star fouls one back and then hits a shot to deep left, where Rivers back-pedals to the track to make the catch. I'm happy. No runs, one hit, no errors. Every pitch a strike.

We end up winning the game 2–0 on a double by 1978 World Series MVP Brian Doyle. Not only did I pitch well, but I lined a rocket to left for a hit in the second. Unfortunately, there's no time to celebrate. Right after the game, Joe D., Bob Lemon, and I jump a cab for the airport and a long ride west. To Oakland.

It'd been a while since I'd been back to Oakland, and despite playing another Equitable Old-Timers Game on Sunday, it felt good to be heading home to the Bay Area. To the cool climate, the gentle night air. The weather was one of the main reasons the A's were so successful on the road. No matter how hot it got in Baltimore or Detroit or Texas, the Oakland air always picked us up, revived our bodies and minds, while other clubs withered in the hot summer sun.

On the plane I found my mind traveling too, back to the '70s to the special men who made the Oakland A's what they were—one of the best damn baseball *teams* ever assembled.

Other teams may have had better *players*, individual talent, but not a better *team*. Our team had grown up together, lived together for almost five years. You learn a lot about a man in five years. What he drinks. What he does in his spare time. If he hustles when he's not hitting. If he likes to pitch under pressure. Which way he runs in a fight. The Oakland A's of 1972–1974 certainly stirred up debate, endless questions about our attitude, dress, and desire. And you know what? In our own never-to-be-repeated way we answered every last one of them. Nobody did it better for three straight years in the early '70s, and frankly, I don't think we ever got the credit we deserved.

Game day. What a homecoming! It was great to see Rudi, Fosse, Billy North, Luke Appling, and Rollie. Fingers, who I think is working on his fourth wife, was hysterical as always, walking around with a portable phone so he wouldn't miss any calls. For dessert there's Reggie, back with the A's in the final season of his incomparable career, dressing at the same locker. First one to the right of the door.

"Well, Reg," I said, "still got the best seat. Ready for the writers?"

"Nah," said Reggie. "Now they pass me up to go see [Mark] McGwire."

After starting, and collecting the win, in the Old-Timers Game, I stayed around to watch six innings of the regular game, just long enough to see why Reggie's struggling. It's not the bat so much; it's the eyes. Reggie's just not picking up the ball as quickly these days. I flashed back on the home runs he clobbered to left, his towering drives into the bleachers in right. Reggie had always been able to do whatever he wanted. The harder he worked, the better he played. But now, he can work and work, and time won't let him triumph as often. But people still paid to see him try. And that, my friends, is one of the true gifts Reggie Jackson brought to this game.

Next day. I can't believe my eyes. An All Star workout and the place is packed. Where were all these people when we were playing? They must have headed on over to the park after that fireworks display last night. Word was that more than 250,000 people were downtown to see it. Me? Forget it. We (Helen and the kids were with me) stayed put at the Edgewater Hyatt, away from the All Star festivities taking place near Jack London Square.

I told her after the Equitable game, "Helen, they're expecting 250,000 people downtown for the fireworks tonight." I didn't have to ask if she wanted to go. After twenty-one years of marriage you get to read each other's minds pretty good.

"Think we'll stay right here," I said, "and watch the fireworks from the window."

On Monday, the day before the game, I threw fifteen minutes of batting practice, a wonderfully efficient way to check out strike zones, weigh the greatness of, say, a Mattingly versus a Boggs. As soon as I had finished, Duncan strolled up and started quizzing me about Boggs. "How would you get him out?" he asked.

I thought a second and said, "I don't know, pitch him up and away. He has more trouble with that pitch than any one."

"Yeah, I know," said Dunc. "Trouble is with the Wall you can't do that in Boston. Plus he looks for that pitch."

That's why Boggs and Mattingly were the best hitters I saw all day (Willie Randolph was a close third). They all followed the same set of rules: They hit the ball where it was pitched. They used the entire park. They rarely got fooled. They didn't chase pitches out of the strike zone—even an inch or two out.

The fifty-eighth annual Major League All Star Game was played in twilight at the Oakland-Alameda County Coliseum the next day. As the late-afternoon shadows worked their way across home plate, the scoreboard played clips of my career. Every guy went down swinging.

"I didn't know you threw hard enough to strike anybody out," said Guidry.

"Showing you everybody I ever got," I said. "That's my strikeout footage."

Once the game started I stayed glued to the front step of the dugout. It's always been the best place to watch a game. I can tell even without seeing the pitch whether it's going to be a ball or a strike. I focus in on the release point and to see if the arm is even with the shoulder. The best pitchers I saw all night were Bret Saberhagen of Kansas City and Seattle's Mark Langston.

As soon as the game ended, 2–0 in favor of the Nationals, I unwittingly became the subject of some questioning by the press. In thirteen innings the two teams had combined for only 14 hits and 17 strikeouts. The continuing debate, at least on this night, over "rabbit" balls and corked bats had ended. Now the press wanted to talk about twilight.

"Wasn't your perfect game pitched just about this time?"

"No," I said politely. "This game started at 5:30. My perfect game began at six."

I knew what they were sniffing for. Finally, somebody asked straight out: "Because it was so hard to see at night, is that why you pitched a perfect game?"

Remember now, we're talkin' almost twenty years ago, and while I've heard about "story angles," this belonged in left field. What did they think I was going to say? "Sure, guys, glad someone finally brought that up. I've been waiting to settle that issue for years. The only reason I pitched a perfect game was because it was twilight time. The hitters never saw anything."

But I wasn't ever going to say that. For one simple reason. It wasn't true. "Well, it might have been the case," I said, looking the writer dead in the eye. "But I got three hits that night, now didn't I? I guess I could see pretty good up there."

I left the next morning. Or should I say afternoon. The original flight was for 7 a.m., but right at the airport, after the 5:30 a.m. wakeup call, and a bus ride over, a skycap takes one look at our tickets and says, "Oh, that flight is canceled."

"Right," I said, "but there's another plane."

"No," says the skycap, "it's canceled."

Next flight: 2:30 p.m. It took Helen two hours to get the tickets changed and another forty-five minutes to check our luggage. When we finally got home at 11 p.m., the sound of the dogs barkin' and the smell of pine put baseball and All Star games in the far corner of my mind. But not for long. A day in Cooperstown, my day, was just around the corner.

17

STEPPIN' INTO THE FUTURE

The bellman outside the Otesaga Hotel in Cooperstown, New York, crinkled his nose and sniffed the air around him. All right, so I didn't exactly look or smell like some future Hall of Famer; a day at a dairy farm will do that to you. The kid took another whiff and then stared down the end of his nose at my dress shoes.

"Reservation, sir?" he asked.

I stepped right through the door and over to the front desk. Checking in. Last name Hunter.

That smell again. The desk clerk leaned over the counter and stared down at what by now was obviously the source of the odor. You could almost hear him thinking, *Geez, this guy's such a hick he didn't even bother to wipe the shit off his shoes. Probably got his tractor parked out front.*

Actually, it was cow manure and a rental car, in that order, and I can explain. Really. No way was I importing North Carolina cow dung. When I'd left home a few days earlier my hair was cut and combed, my shoes were shined, and a brand new suit I'd bought in Elizabeth City just for the occasion was packed in my travel bag. My shit-polished shine came along compliments of some family friends, Dr. Doug Hart, a veterinarian in Pine Plains, New York, and his wife, Rae. They live about an hour's drive from Cooperstown, so Rae invited the family to spend a few days before my induction into baseball's Hall of Fame on July 26, 1987. So that's just what we decided, arriving on Wednesday for the Sunday ceremonies. Doug and I hit it right off, talking about heart worm treatments for dogs, mechanical milkers for cows. We spent almost one whole day baling hay into Doug's barn; Todd loved that second load. Next day Todd and I accompanied the good doctor on his rounds of the neighboring dairy farms (getting the picture?).

As it turned out, we were at one farm from eight in the morning until late afternoon. Doug poked and prodded all around, one place more than most, saying things like: "Yeah, this one's two months pregnant." Or, "No, the ovary on this one . . ." Or, "You need to breed this one today."

After about the fourth hour of this Todd decided he'd seen enough examinations for one day. I found him with his head back, eyes closed, in the car, sucking in some fresh air. Or what passed for it on the farm. I couldn't resist.

"Why don't you come on out and watch?" I asked.

Todd shook his head. "I ain't watchin' someone stick their hand up a cow's ass all the time!"

Does that explain the smell? And, anyway, a little cow dung on my shoes never hurt nobody; I venture to guess a couple of those fellas in the Hall, guys like Cobb and Hornsby, played in their fair share of cow pastures. Their pictures are in the Hall along with the others voted in by the Baseball Writers Association of America. In among statues of Babe Ruth, Norman Rockwell paintings, pieces of Ebetts Field, baseball's first pro contract (dated 1879; the guy signed for $75 a month), and computer terminals. As both the caretaker and celebrator of great men and memorable moments in baseball history, induction day at Cooperstown is truly a once-in-a-lifetime experience.

My memories of that day began to build on Saturday with a leisurely game of golf and autograph sessions. However, I spent most of that time thinking about my speech—what to say, how to say it. You know I'd rather clean the dog kennels for a month than step before a microphone, so I did the next best thing. I shoved a piece of paper in Helen's hands. "I want you to write my speech," I told her.

"What do you mean speech?" she asked. "You don't ever write a speech."

"I know," I replied, "but I want to give you some words. You write them down." And she did. Finley was one word. Steinbrenner was another. Family. Friends. I was purposely steering clear of one subject, knowing full well that if I started talking about my parents, I'd break down like I did during my Catfish Hunter Day speech at the high school. They were both gone now, my mom having passed away a year and two days after my dad. Momma never complained none either, just loved people and kids like there was no tomorrow. In the end she faded away just like Daddy had. Same damn disease. Only Momma never smoked a day in her life. Strange, isn't it, how they were together even in death, fighting it every inch of the way—and then some. One time her doctor told me, "She's really gone, but her heart's still beating. She's just gonna lay there until it stops." No, some things are better left unsaid.

Sunday broke bright and clear, the temperature pushing its way toward a hundred as thousands of fans filled Cooper Park. Some spread picnic lunches on the grass. Others sat in folding chairs as, on stage, Billy Williams, former Negro League star, third baseman Ray Dandridge, sportswriter Jack Lang of the New York *Daily News,* and St. Louis broadcaster Jack Buck waited for our day in that sun. Helen, the kids, brothers, sisters, their children, Francis, Freddie, Bobby Carter, Mr. Cherry and his son Tom, and Joe Flythe. Mr. Steinbrenner made the trip, too, sitting right down the row from Mr. Finley.

OTHER VOICES—BASEBALL COMMISSIONER PETER UEBERROTH

"He was the heart of those great and flamboyant A's teams that dominated the American League in the early seventies. But Catfish was a winning pitcher in another way. He was such a great player that when he became a free agent following the 1974 season, teams lined up to bid for his services. The Yankees won, as you might recall, and in return Catfish earned the distinction of playing for both Charlie Finley and George Steinbrenner . . . which is enough in itself to put a player into the Hall of Fame.

"Ladies and gentlemen, this man was never a thrower. He was a pitcher in every sense of the word. A great pitcher. With great character. Please welcome into baseball's Hall of Fame . . ."

All I'm thinking now is how Jack Lang had lost it after bringing up his mom and dad. Don't cry. Do something. So I made a joke, talked about how Helen had helped me write my speech.

The crowd laughed and that relaxed me, as did seeing all those familiar faces sitting on the right side of the podium. I took another deep breath and started telling stories. About being scouted in high school. The nickname. I thanked Mr. Finley for being smart enough to give it to me. I thanked Mr. Steinbrenner for paying me all that free-agent money. Then I spoke my piece.

"Like I've said before, when I pitched in the big leagues with the Oakland A's and New York Yankees, there was no way I could pitch and win a ball game by myself. I had to have the defense, the offense; everybody had to play together. That's the only way I know how to win. To be together. To win together. Play together. To want to win. I think that's what made me win as many games as I did. Because the players were behind me, the coaches, the manager, the owners, were all getting the players to produce.

"A lot of times you see players who don't want to play baseball. I know today they're makin' a lot of money. A lot of 'em don't want to play. They get out there once in awhile and jake. We always loved to get on somebody that loafed. I want to tell them that if they don't want to play—go home. That's the way I always thought about playin' baseball. Any sport. Or any thing.

"The only thing you can do is give that 100 percent. To me there's no such thing as 105, 110 percent. If you don't give that 100 percent, you're not going to succeed at anything. And thanks to the Good Lord, I'm here today. And thanks to the fans that supported me, and my friends and neighbors who are here from North Carolina. It's the greatest honor that any guy could ever receive. Thank ya."

From there it was all downhill, topped off by a members-only Hall of Fame gathering on the hotel veranda. The sun was working its way down into the lake. A cocktail waitress took your drink orders (you never had to tell her twice) as guys like Ted Williams, Bobby Doerr, Willie Mays, and Bob Lemon sat around swapping stories. I mean *stories*.

I got into Lem's shit a bit, telling one about the time I went out to the mound to find it already occupied.

"Don't remember that one," said Lem.

"You have to remember."

"Nope."

"Well," I said, "we were in Texas one day losing 5–1 in the

fourth, fifth inning, and I go out to the mound and here's somebody else already out there picking up the ball. 'What the hell you doing?' I asked. 'I'm in the game,' the kid said. 'Mind giving me the ball for a minute?' The kid says, 'Sure, no problem.' I took the ball and march into the dugout and stand right in front of your face. 'See this ball,' I say. 'Well, stick it dead up your ass. I never want to pitch for you again.' After that, I waited underneath the runway hoping you'd come down so I could kick your butt.''

"Don't remember that one," said Lem.

"Well, then how come you told the trainer in the locker room afterward that if I was him, I'd have hit me too?"

"Still don't remember," said Lem. "But then again, George was calling me so much back then I didn't know what end was up half the time."

By Monday night, Catfish had again been put to rest, replaced, once more, by Jimmy. Might be interested to know, however, that Cat may be back. Remember that talk Reggie and I had during the All Star break in Oakland? Well, I didn't tell you *everything* we said. Like how I kidded him about being the richest ballplayer ever, thanks to his investments in real estate and antique cars. "You've probably saved enough money to buy the A's one day," I said.

Reggie chuckled a bit. Leaning over, he whispered, "I thought about it." He paused for a second or two before speaking again.

"Cat," said Reggie. "If I did buy the A's, or another team, would you come back and be the pitching coach?"

"In four years, I might," I said, "after Kim's out of high school."

So who knows? Maybe four years from now, Reggie will be campaigning to be the first black commissioner. LaRussa will be managing the A's. Dunc, Lache, and Rudi assisting him in the dugout. Maybe we could even talk Sal into coming back as general manager, and maybe, just maybe, we'd hire Charlie O. to handle promotions.

But right now I guess I like hunting and fishing and farming, simple pleasures that never grow old. Training a dog, coaching a team, walking the woods behind some hound. But wherever I walk, whatever I do, one fact will never change: Daddy will always be walkin' right there with me.

FROM HIGH FIVES TO LOW BLOWS — GET THE INSIDE PITCH FROM TODAY'S SPORTS LEGENDS!

___ **SNAKE**   0-441-77194-7/$3.95
Ken Stabler and **Berry Stainback**
The on-and-off-the-field exploits of football's wildest renegade.
"I loved it. A helluva read!" —Larry L. King

___ **THE MICK**   0-515-08599-5/$3.95
Mickey Mantle with **Herb Gluck**
The sensational *New York Times* bestseller *plus* a new section
of career stats and a scrapbook of memorable photos!

___ **ONE KNEE EQUALS TWO FEET**   0-515-09193-6/$3.95
**(And Everything Else You Need To Know About
Football)**   **John Madden** with **Dave Anderson**
The *New York Times* bestseller! Here's Madden at his
incomparable best!

___ **DISTANT REPLAY**   0-515-09015-8/$3.95
**The Stars of the Green Bay Packers Look Back
Jerry Kramer** with **Dick Schaap**
"Brilliantly recreates a team from two decades ago and
brings added life to the legend." —USA Today

___ **CATCHER IN THE WRY**   0-515-09029-8/$3.95
Bob Uecker and **Mickey Herskowitz**
By the man who made mediocrity famous, outrageous but true
stories of baseball. "A pure joy to read!" —Publishers Weekly

___ **I'D RATHER BE A YANKEE**   0-515-09073-5/$3.95
John Tulius
The men behind the legend tell the story of baseball's greatest
team in their own words. "All in all, a Yankee fan's dream!"
— Kirkus

Please send the titles I've checked above. Mail orders to:

BERKLEY PUBLISHING GROUP
390 Murray Hill Pkwy., Dept. B
East Rutherford, NJ 07073

NAME _____

ADDRESS _____

CITY _____

STATE _____ ZIP _____

Please allow 6 weeks for delivery.
Prices are subject to change without notice.

POSTAGE & HANDLING:
$1.00 for one book, $.25 for each
additional. Do not exceed $3.50.

BOOK TOTAL $_____

SHIPPING & HANDLING $_____

APPLICABLE SALES TAX $_____
(CA, NJ, NY, PA)

TOTAL AMOUNT DUE $_____
PAYABLE IN US FUNDS.
(No cash orders accepted.)

10

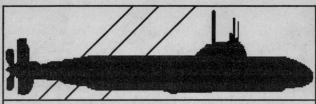